CENTRAL INDIA

DURING THE REBELLION OF 1857 AND 1858

A NARRATIVE OF OPERATIONS OF
THE BRITISH FORCES FROM THE SUPPRESSION OF
MUTINY IN AURUNGABAD TO THE CAPTURE OF GWALIOR UNDER

MAJOR-GENERAL SIR HUGH ROSE, G.C.B. &c.
AND
BRIGADIER SIR C. STUART, K.C.B.

BY

THOMAS LOWE
M.R.C.S.E. L.A.C.

Medical Officer to the Corps of Madras Sappers and Miners

LONDON
LONGMAN, GREEN, LONGMAN, AND ROBERTS
1860

TO

LIEUT.-GENERAL SIR H. ROSE, G.C.B. &c.

WHO

BY HIS INTREPIDITY, GALLANTRY, AND MILITARY SKILL

RESTORED CENTRAL INDIA TO BRITISH SUPREMACY, PEACE, AND ORDER,

SUPPORTED THE WEAK,

STRENGTHENED THE STRONG AND FAITHFUL,

AND

AVENGED THE MURDERS OF OUR COUNTRYMEN,

THIS NARRATIVE

OF OUR CAMPAIGNS IS, BY PERMISSION,

INSCRIBED

BY HIS VERY OBEDIENT AND FAITHFUL SERVANT,

THE AUTHOR

PREFACE.

In the following narrative of the operations of the British forces in Central India in 1857 and 1858, I have endeavoured to give as faithful an account of the trials, the dangers, the pleasures, and the hardships of a camp life as opportunity permitted.

In the Deccan and Malwa, Brigadier Sir C. Stuart's column accomplished much. The course of mutiny in the Deccan and Southern India was diverted, Mhow timely relieved, and our beleaguered countrymen in Neemuch set free by the glorious victory over the rebel forces under Heera Sing before the city of Mundasoore.

When Sir Hugh Rose assumed command of this column, and of the one then assembled at Sehore, the delirium of rebellion was at its height; mutiny had destroyed the whole of the Bengal army; numbers of native princes, with their hordes of armed plunderers, had joined in the common cause, and Central India, with its rivers and jungles, forts, and mountain passes, was their grand focus.

In this enormous territory, extending from the river Nerbudda south, to the waters of the Jumna north, there was every evil to contend against. How Sir Hugh Rose met and overcame all difficulties, how his gallant troops marched and fought and endured, until they had trampled rebellion under foot, I have endeavoured to chronicle.

At this rather remote period, since the thrilling interest felt in the course of the events has naturally died away in the self-satisfying knowledge of safety, since murder is no longer feared, and the voice of mourning hushed, the reader may, perhaps, wonder that our vengeance was so great. It was necessary. Nothing less could have answered the ends; and though a drum-head court-martial is a short affair, and soldiers long accustomed to scenes of blood sit in judgment, yet justice is done. The people were drunk with the blood of our countrymen, mad with excesses, blind to everything but fatalism, and desirous of nothing but rapine and political chaos, and for such a state of affairs an active and potent remedy was needed.

When we showed them mercy, they laughed us to scorn; to spare the rebel whose hands were raised in supplication, was to receive a bullet in the back, an instant after mercy had stayed the avenging arm.

Few people in England can appreciate the intensely acute sufferings their brethren then endured in India. To comprehend the character of the natives, one must see them, deal with them, suffer from their cunning, their hypocrisy, their bare-faced lying and deep-laid treachery, endure their habits of filth, tolerate their insolence of caste and bigotry, perhaps feel the sharpness of their tulwars, or know that a brother's, wife's, or children's blood has been spilt by domestics who had been the "best servants in the world;" then, perhaps, a just estimate of the "*mild Hindu*," and the way they should be dealt with will be formed. So much for our vengeance.

I am fully alive to the many short-comings, and the occasional *non-military* air of certain passages; for these I solicit the reader's indulgence. What I actually saw I have endeavoured to record and portray faithfully.

I must here remark that my journal would never

have been published, had not the earnest solicitation of friends prevailed, all of whom were desirous of reading a connected account of the long and harassing campaigns brought to so happy a termination under the able generalship of Sir H. Rose; and as no other account of the events has appeared in such a form, I hope that the following pages may impart to the reader a portion of the pleasure I have enjoyed in recounting them after having escaped so many perils in passing through them.

I am deeply indebted to Lieutenant-General Sir H. Rose, to whom this narrative was submitted, for his testimony to the truthfulness of the details sketched by my pen, and for the very valuable assistance he rendered in placing at my disposal official and other papers, which I trust will enhance the value of the work.

T. L.

CONTENTS.

CHAPTER I.

State of country on arrival in Bombay.—March to Arungabad.—An up-country railway hotel.—The mail.—The "Thul-Ghaut."—Temple Hill near Nasik.—Nasik and the Godavery.—*En route* to Toka.—Flying bridge over river Godavery.—First sight of mutinous sepoys at Deysgaum.—Arrival in camp.—Arungabad.—The mutiny going on.—The salvation of Asseerghur.—Conduct of mutineers in Arungabad.—Blowing away mutineer from a gun, and execution by musketry.—City of Arungabad.—The "Taj." —Dowlatabad.—March to the "relief of Mhow."—Chowker Pass.—Crossing the "Taptee."—Death of Major Follett, and conduct of 25th N. I. sepoys. — Asseerghur. — Execution of mutineers.—The river Nerbudda.—Simrole.— Mhow - - - - - - Page 1

CHAPTER II.

Mhow after the mutiny of Bengal troops.—Treasury looted.—Fall of Delhi, salute fired on 27th September, 1857. —Preparations for march upon Dhar.—Arrival of siege train at Dhar.—Camp.—Position established for siege on 25th October.—Firing village.—The siege.—Flag of truce. —Breach examined.—Storming breach.—Fort empty.— Fort, palace, treasury.—Hyderabad Contingents under Major Orr arrive.—They march for Mahidpore, 7th November.—Mutiny of Mahidpore Contingent.—Force marches from Dhar, 8th November, for Neemuch.—Dhar town, and visit to the Rajah - - - - - Page 54

CHAPTER III.

March to Oneil.—News of the battle of Rawul.—Defeat of mutineers.—Gallant conduct of Capt. Abbott and Lieut. Johnston.—The Rohillah.—Taul, Nawab of Jaôra.—Difficult position of native princes.—Crossing the river Chumbul.— Hernia, execution of mutineers.—Before Mundasoore, the affair of the 21st November.—Flank march past Mundasoore.—Battle of Mundasoore, and "relief of Neemuch."— March to Mundasoore, capture of rebels, execution of rebels, Mundasoore city.—March to Mahidpore.—Execution of rebels.—Oojein.—March to Indore, state of residency, durbar of Maharajah Holkar.—Departure of Col. Durand. —Remarks on Malwa.—Advent of Major-General Sir Hugh Rose, and Sir Robert Hamilton - - - 95

CHAPTER IV.

Major-General reviews troops and inspects hospitals.— Preparations for campaign in Central India.—General events.—Siege train marches to Sehore to join second brigade.—Arrival in Sehore.—Execution of mutineers.— March for Rhatghur.—Bhopal.—Siege of Rhatghur.— Escape of rebels.—Affair of Barodia.—Death of Capt. Neville.—Relief of Saugor.—March to Gurrakotta.—Capture of fort - - - - - - 152

CHAPTER V.

General prepares to march upon Jhansi.—Court-martial on Bombay sapper.—March of the force.—Affair at fort of Barodia.—Troops benighted.—Forcing Malthon and Mudanpore passes.—Defeat of the Rajah of Shahghur.—Fort and garden of Sorai.—Murrowra.—Annexation of territory of Shahghur.—Baunpore.—Destruction of palace.—Tal-Behut.—Capture of fort of Chandaree.—Investment of Jhansi. — The siege. — Arrival of Tantia Topee. — The "Battle of the Betwa."—The "storm."—The capture.—The palace.—Escape of the Ranee of Jhansi - Page 198

CHAPTER VI.

March to Calpee.—Poonch.—Capture of fort by Major Gall.—Koonch.—The battle of Koonch.—Defeat of rebels. —Dust storm.—Destruction of fort of Hurdooi.—Orai.— Effects of the sun upon the troops.—Camp, Calpee.—The Ravines.—Battle of Golowlee.—Capture of Calpee.—Calpee, town and fort.—General Rose's "order."—Rebels capture Gwalior.— Scindiah flies. — Sir Hugh Rose defeats the rebels, and reinstates the Maharajah Scindiah.—Remarks. —Journey from Calpee to Cawnpore and Calcutta.—Mutilation.—Allahabad.—Dâk to Calcutta -   -   - 270

CHAPTER VII.

Collateral Notes   -   -   -   -   - 318

DIRECTION TO BINDER.

Place Map opposite Page 1.

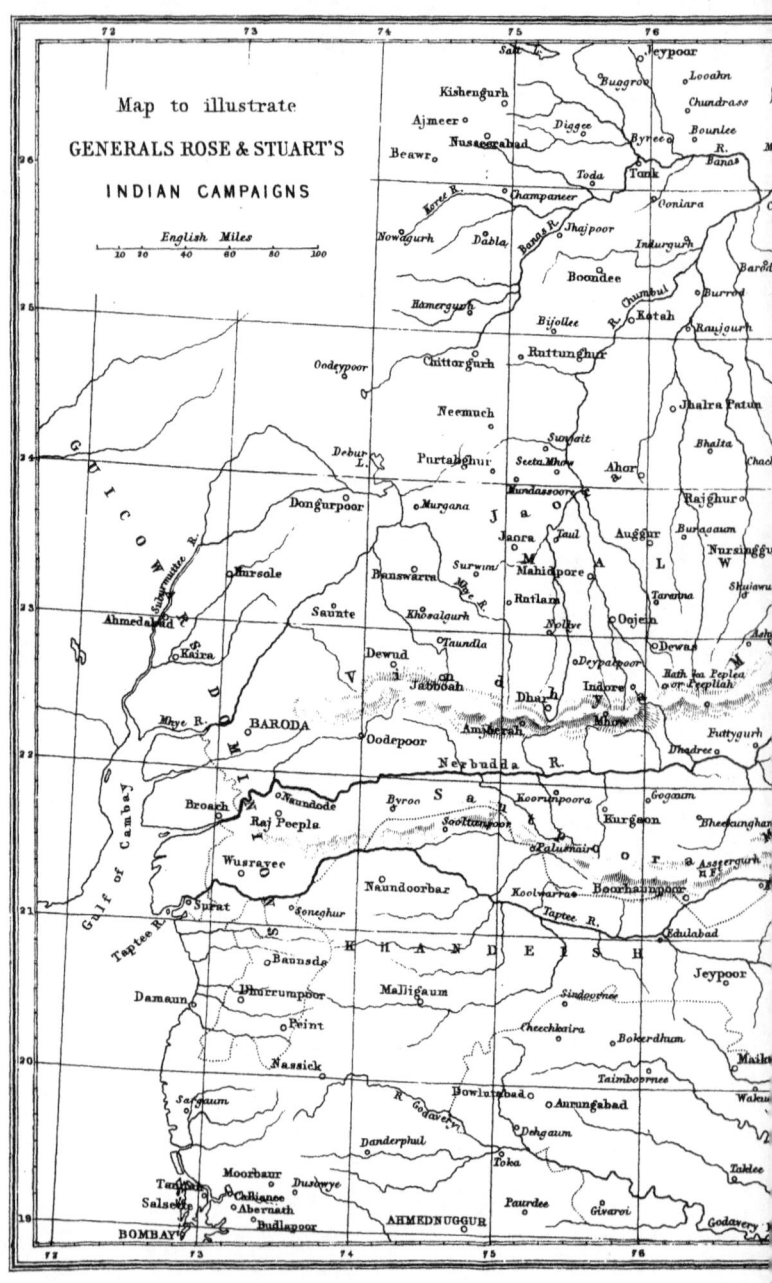

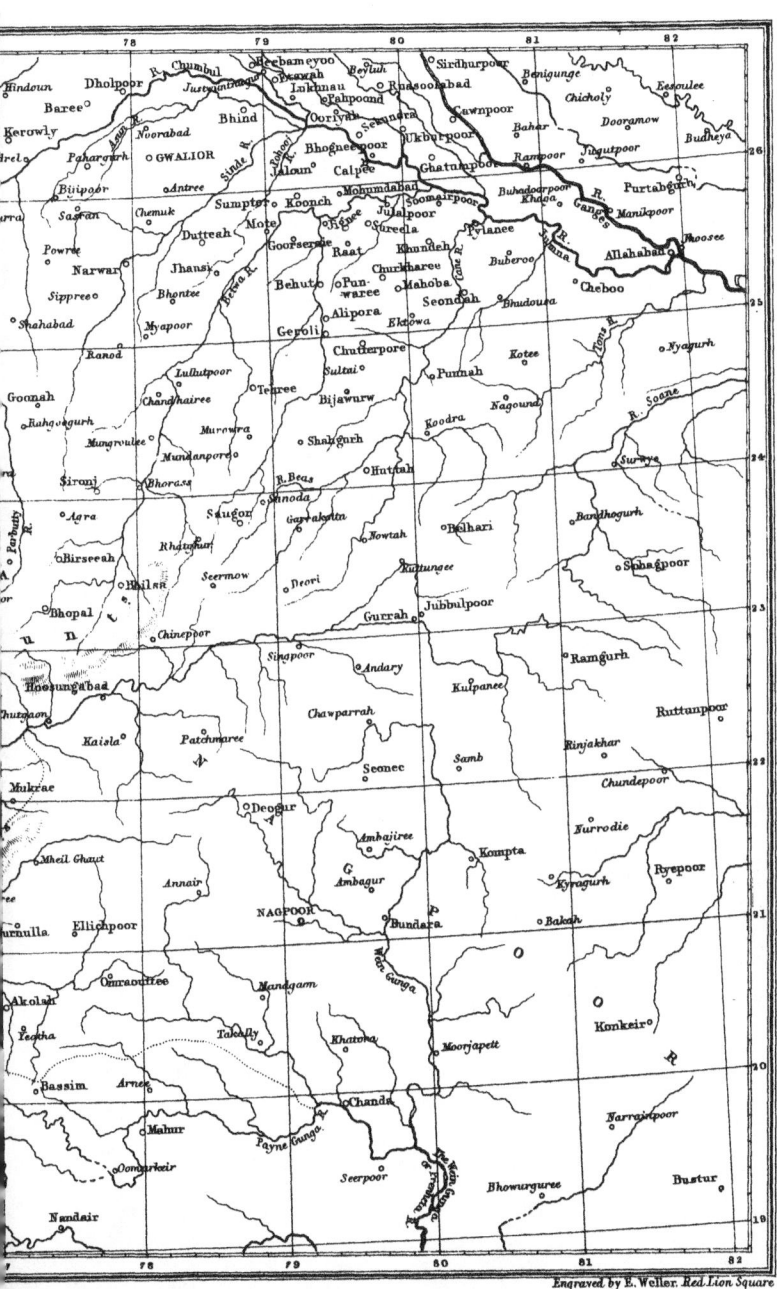

CENTRAL INDIA.

CHAPTER I.

" What stir is this ? what tumult's in the Heavens ?
Whence cometh this alarm, and the noise?"—Henry VI.

State of country on arrival in Bombay.—March to Arungabad.—An up-country railway hotel.—The mail.—The "Thul-Ghaut."—Temple Hill near Nasik.—Nasik and the Godavery.—*En route* to Toka.—Flying bridge over river Godavery.—First sight of mutinous sepoys at Deysgaum.—Arrival in camp.—Arungabad.—The mutiny going on.—The salvation of Asseerghur.—Conduct of mutineers in Arungabad.—Blowing away mutineer from a gun, and execution by musketry.—City of Arungabad.—The "Taj."—Dowlatabad.—March to the "relief of Mhow."—Chowker Pass.—Crossing the "Taptee."—Death of Major Follett, and conduct of 25th N.I. sepoys.—Asseerghur.—Execution of mutineers.—The river Nerbudda.—Simrole.—Mhow.

ON the 31st of May 1857, the transport ship "Hibernia" sailed into the harbour of Bombay with a detachment of troops from the seat of war on the shores of the Persian Gulf. This detachment was the B. company of the Madras sappers, who had orders to return to their own Presidency now that peace with Persia was declared. In the same vessel were several other officers returning to Bombay and Bengal. The whole of the time occupied in the passage from Mohurmah to Bombay had passed very pleasantly. The men were in high spirits, and delighted to think that they were so soon to be restored to their families ; but when the pilot came on board and related the news, astonishment, anxiety, and uncertainty took the place of the bright visions of home. The cities that had fallen from our power in the Bengal mutiny were named, the mutinous regiments numbered, the atrocities detailed, the movement of troops canvassed, and the untimely death of General Anson reported ; and, worst of all, that the rebellion was spreading with mercurial speed from city to city throughout the whole land. The word Delhi was in everybody's mouth. What will be the result of such an unexpected catastrophe ? and will it spread to the armies of the sister Presidencies ? Such, with a hundred similar ones, were our questions one to another. No one doubted the ultimate result, but in the meantime, long before relief could come from England—what might not occur ? What fearful tragedies might be committed ! The newspapers teemed with portentous articles ; extras and telegraphic messages flew about with wonderful publicity and speed ; the mercantile community were in a high state of trepidation ; the homeward bound ships soon filled with passengers ; the military, aroused to the high sense of the vital importance of the daily events in Bengal, were as energetic and determined to do their best as though the honour of the British realm depended upon individual talent, industry, perseverance, and courage. While military preparations were being made, and assistance in the field, already occupied by contending troops, accorded, the Government of Bombay, in its promptitude and wisdom, stretched out another mighty arm to the struggle. She despatched ships of her navy to the nearest British possessions for succour, and obtained it ; she transported troops, elsewhere destined, to the seat of war, and by her timely foresight stayed such as were far on the high seas for the conservation of these our long held possessions. All this time our position looked anything but favourable. Cloud upon cloud gathered darker and darker, day after day told fresh tales of mutiny, murder, and crime, and already the land was red with the blood of our brethren, and mourning sat in many a house.

Delhi was the goal—troops were reported to be gathering around its walls daily, and its fall into our hands was almost hourly expected. Indeed, one or two reports about the middle of June stated that it had already succumbed to our forces. These false statements, I need not say, had their corresponding effects upon the native minds, already too eager to hear of our overthrow. Delhi had not fallen, nor was this event destined to be the harbinger of the glorious past for many months afterwards. In the meantime, the troops at Neemuch and Nusserabad had fallen from their allegiance, and foul murder had marked their perfidious conduct in this as in almost every other instance. Central India tottered from Gwalior to the Nerbudda; the Deccan had symptoms of smouldering, and a fearful tempest seemed to be gathering over our devoted heads from every possible quarter. Whether this was to be averted, or who were to fall when it should burst, will be seen hereafter.

In this season of excitement, when the balance of power in Northern India seemed so much against us, it will, of course, occur to every mind that the services of every available man to be trusted were not only sought but eagerly accepted, when offered. It was under such circumstances that the Bombay Government were induced to accept the services of a single company of Madras sappers. This was done in a most graceful and flattering manner, and after the necessary preliminaries had been arranged, the company received orders to march to Arungabad, and there to join the moveable column of the Deccan, then under the command of Major-General Woodburn, C.B.

THE MARCH TO ARUNGABAD.

On the 16th June, the company marched into the railway station at Bombay for the train that was to convey them to Wassind, some 60 miles on the road. All being as it was desired, the "fire-carriage" screamed, then groaned, and at length got into its usual rapid Herculean pant. The train passed out of Bombay like a shot, as though it had been commissioned to transport us as quick as possible from everything humanizing to the scene of war. The company cheered on the road up over and over again, joked the people in Tamil, and the people stared at them as though they had been shot out from his Satanic Majesty's magazines. This pleased the fellows. They admired the bridges over which we passed, they shook their heads knowingly at a cutting here or a tunnelling there, and laughed and joked till we at length felt the train drawing in its speed; a shrill scream again, as at starting, only more prolonged, informed us that its period of exhaustion had arrived; slower and slower, and at length we were politely told to walk out. This we did, and found ourselves in a very pretty spot, with good encamping ground, plenty of bullock gharies awaiting us near the station, and an excellent well-supplied "Railway Hotel." What more could we want? There was the finger-post pointing to "The Hotel," and, some 100 yards off the station only, stood that most glorious of establishments, in all its purity and aërial beauty, and well stocked with all that could contribute to gladden the heart of man, improve his general state, and fit him for the march on the road which was indeed to come on the morrow.

Before the all-important hour of seven P.M. should arrive, we had all been attracted by a peculiarly beautiful peak in one of the neighbouring hills hard by. It was a most tempting afternoon, and as all had been done to make the men comfortable in the camp, two of us determined to have a walk as far as the curious peak on the hill. So we lighted our cheroots and started. By-and-bye we arrived at the margin of the wood, or, as in India, they call it, the jungle, and struck off into a path leading direct to the peak. On we wandered and talked, admiring the glorious foliage around us for some two hours, about which time the sun, that had been pencilling in rosy and golden tints every object around us, suddenly dipped behind the hills we were nearing. The wood dove coo'd in silver sweetness, the birds sang richly in the balmy air, the hare skipped before us, and everything seemed in peace. The

AN UP-COUNTRY HOTEL. 7

hills grew deeply blue, and the smoke of the cottages curled upward from the distant thickets as softly as though tempest never visited that spot. On and on we went till at length we came to an open, and found that the hill which seemed at first so near was still so far off that we must return without having accomplished our object. We turned back, but long before we could gain the open it was dark. The lightning flashed, the thunder roared, and large drops of rain told us what was in store. We hurried along and arrived at the hotel scarcely in time to avoid the storm. As we entered we heard the sound and rattle of dinner; we were not too late. A good board was spread, and just as we were entering feelingly into the merits of the same, Lieut. Gordon entered, rather the worse for the rain, with a stranger, who was introduced to us by him as Mr. ———ham. Now the stranger was a quiet, bland, smiling, gentlemanly man; never said a word about his existence, but enjoyed the dinner and the table-talk. As the sweet restorer of tired nature was evidently diffusing his balm around we parted for the night. Now it appears that Lieut. Gordon, while looking after his horse at the station house, met this stranger, who had just alighted from a train, upon which the gentleman said to him, "Where am I? I ought to be in Poona, or some such place." It was pitch dark.

His position was forlorn for the time, but the hotel and the table comforted him. Indeed, these were sad times to be taken so far into a country one might naturally wish to avoid, and he accordingly made as rapid a retreat the following morning as steam would enable him.

You will naturally wonder what kind of an establishment a railway hotel up country in India is. When I tell you what this was in 1857, you will be able to appreciate others. The magniloquent cognomen at once suggests to the mind comfort, luxury, brilliance, cool marbled-slab'd tables, soft inviting couches, bitter beer, sandwiches, and comely waiters! Do they get this kind of thing up country in India? Wait a while! For the East it ought necessarily to be something light, aërial, and cool. If you can conjure up the elegance of a Sydenham Palace design, wrought into the all-accommodating structure of an hotel, with cool and zephyry verandahs, easy chairs, and servants mute in snowy investment; if you can fancy this, and imagine yourself thus canopied and comforted doing a Turner with a Ruskin's egotism for your guide, or anything alike Epicurean in the declining rays of a gorgeous sun, then you will fall far short in your realization of what an up-country hotel really is. Yes, it *is* beautifully light and airy, much as Robinson Crusoe's house must have been, with bamboos for the walls, straw for the roof, straw for the windows at night, and plenty of man-eating tigers in the vicinity! But we must say thanks to the enterprising Parsee, for through him we get in almost every Hindu town something that reminds one of home, and in this miserable apology for an hotel we fared as well as any traveller could wish, enjoyed our bitter beer, and a good night's sleep. What more could one desire in such times? Originally it was intended that we should march from Wassind to Malligaum, there to join other forces, but on the march our route was changed for Arungabad, from whence news came to us that mutiny had broken out among the troops of the Hyderabad Contingent. In marching through this part of Western India from stage to stage we generally halted at the bungalows, so that our journey from Wassind as far as the famous old town of Nasik, was one of no great hardship, for in all of these way-side houses we found everything that could conduce to the comfort of a traveller, and to be obtained at a very reasonable rate. In this respect the system of bungalow management in the Bombay Presidency is far superior to that of Madras, as are also the bungalows themselves. In fact, the Government seem in every way to consider the comfort of travellers, not only in the arrangement of the houses, but in their management. In each there is a mess-man ever ready to supply the sojourners with excellent food, beer, and spirits, if needed, and who has every necessary article at hand for the comfort of the meals, so that a traveller in these parts need not encumber himself with food, or the necessary paraphernalia of the table. Each person pays one rupee per diem for the use of the bungalow, and a very moderate charge for his viands. This was a great comfort to us, for no sooner had we ended our day's march, and seen to the well-being of the men, than we were agreeably greeted on our return to the bungalow by a savoury meal. None, save those who have travelled in both Presidencies, can fully appreciate this superior system of the Bombay bungalows. Madras would confer a boon were she to adopt the same plan. Thus we fared on our march to the Arungabad force as far as Nasik. Little or nothing occurred of interest upon the road to excite one, save an occasional arrival of the mail-cart flying on its way burdened with news of fresh disasters. The mail's arrival was always an exciting moment, and as the sound of the post-horn echoed from hill to hill every one seemed moved by anxious expectation. The horses of the mail-carts or mounted carriers always came rattling along that splendid macadamized road at a gallop, the man simply blowing the post-horn to apprise us of his arrival, and throwing down the welcome letter-bag as he dashed past on his important duty. The mail thus carried thoroughly reminded one of the old coach and mail days of England just antecedent to the times of steam and the electric telegraph. The scenery all along this road as far as Nasik is most varied and beautiful. The beauty of the verdure and extent of the tropical forests, spreading here and there for miles on either side of the road, give a most gorgeous feature to the whole landscape. Vast plateaus, broken here and there by large boulders of granite or trap, and intersected by winding streams, are covered with acres of green vegetation, or undergoing renovation by the plough; the arid-looking palmyra seldom reared its sombre rigid head among other trees, but the stately tamarind, and peepul, and teak trees grace the roads and homestead, while the distant jungles shine in luxuriant richness and grace. Everywhere there are neat villages, small towns, carefully cultivated fields, and well-stocked gardens, yielding the plantain, the melon, the cucumber, and other succulents. This scene is occasionally diversified by an apparently pathless semi-barren ocean-like extent of land so unvarying in features that it seems bounded by an horizon from which the midday sun could be taken, and from which it rises and beneath which it dips in all the glorious majesty of heaven's brightest robes. I cannot help noticing in this place the superior piece of engineering on this road, called the Thul-Ghaut, not only as a work of art, but as a specimen of tropical scenery of the most superb kind. In all India I have seen nothing so rich in verdure as the hills and valleys through which this pass is cut.

For some twelve miles before arriving at the foot of the Ghaut, the road-side scenery gradually increases in richness and beauty. Higher and higher as the road ascends the vegetable world multiplies in variety, fantastic forms, and mellow tints. One feels that another climate is soon to be enjoyed, for everything looks cool, and nature everywhere seems rich and inviting. The pass commences at the foot of a high range of hills, and runs winding around the sides of the different peaks higher and higher till the table land beyond the summit of the highest points is gained, and the clouds are left under one's feet. The road itself is as perfect as a London street, and of so easy an ascent as not to tire the pedestrian, while a carriage can be driven up or down with ease and safety. This ghaut—some seven miles long—was engineered by Lieut. Chapman, who was afterwards drowned in the Indus. The hillside of the pass is nearly always perpendicular, that of the open guarded by a low wall, over which the valley scenery is seen. We entered the foot of the ghaut, about 3 A.M., when the fire-flies flitted about in thousands, and the stars above shone brilliantly. As we ascended morning broke over head, while it seemed night in the depths below us. Gradually nature seemed to awake from her sleep, and then all was emerald and velvety, and subdued in the distance like the softest misty pencillings of Turner's happiest pieces. The giant trees of the forest were clustered together in the valleys and on the hill's sides like tufts of embossed velvet, lightening and darkening with every gleam of coming day; here and there trees of varied blossom formed stalwart supports for fantastic creepers revelling in wild profusion, while on the decayed trunks of others gorgeous parasites had made their homes; yonder a tiny cataract poured its crystal drops to bound from rock to rock to the peaceful valley below; here was an embowered well for the thirsty traveller, shaded by mango trees drooping with golden fruit, near which the birds sang as sweetly as though they lived on honey-dew and breathed an air untainted by earth. The very grass seemed to live in luxury, and smile as aurora passed over, and as cloud after cloud dissolved, and the bright sun-beams stole over the hill's tops, the arborescent grasses and distant trees seemed burnished with silver and gold as they waved in the wind. As the sun warmed the valleys below, every object seemed to exist in sweetest harmony—so peaceful, pure, and happy. But what pen can portray nature? Here all was beauty, majesty, and peace: no cottage, no herd, no happy children, no woodman's distant-sounding axe, no village spire, no church bell to call to the altar of the Creator of all! no, nothing but silent grandeur— the everlasting hills mutely pointing heavenward!

Once over the Thul-Ghaut, we found ourselves on a fine open country everywhere bearing evidences of good cultivation and plenty. The houses on the road-side were well built and clean, and the larger houses of the land-owners in the distance bore strong resemblance to well-stocked farmhouses in England. There were large stacks of golden-coloured grass, numerous herds of well-fed cattle, excellent wells and tanks, fine timber trees giving ample shade from the mid-day sun, and the houses and out-buildings well built and *tiled.* The wheelwrights' shops of the villages showed signs of industry and work in every way, and stores of grain and fruit and other necessaries lay exposed for sale in the many little houses, giving a very pleasing feature to the scenes. The further we journeyed towards the seat of mutiny and war, the richer the country appeared, and the happier and more peaceful the inhabitants. At length, after passing six days upon the march up, we found ourselves within sight of the famous old Hindu town, Nasik—famous for its proximity to the source of the holy river Godavery, on whose banks it is built; famous for its numerous and beautiful Hindu temples; and for its being still a town of great sanctity and Hindu power. We halted for a while on the road between the holy hill of *Sanika* and the town which lay before us, surrounded by dense clusters of trees. This holy hill, rising to a considerable elevation from the road-side, is one of a number through which the road runs, and has been from time immemorial an object of adoration to the Hindus and of great interest to the European. It stands out from the plain between it and the city like a gigantic grotto. About midway from its base a road has been cut around it, and from this cutting numbers of doorways and windows open into the numerous temples and caves cut out of the solid rock. From the hill above these beautifully carved entrances, thousands of fantastic creepers droop, clothing the time-worn pillars and their ancient sculptured gods and goddesses with a gorgeous robe of evergreens. There is something very beautiful in the idea of man building his temple to the Creator in the immoveable eternal hills. Races and dynasties may pass away, and cities lie crumbled in the dust—everything that marked his proud path and cunning hand may be swept into oblivion, but the mountains remain, and on the fretted pillars of their temples man may read—perhaps thousands of years afterwards—how the knee was bowed in mute adoration at the altar to the wisdom, power, and goodness of God, while gratitude of the creature to the Creator, finite reliance upon infinite omnipotence, and the incomprehensibility of the great mystery of the Godhead, are as plainly written on the stones of these simple fanes as in a book, and there show us by these acknowledgments that man has for ever worshipped, and in all ages builded a temple consecrated to the King of kings! And to have thus made their holy places afar from the scenes of busy strife and unholy minglings, where man might in death-like peace commune with his God, is to me very beautiful!

We marched into the bungalow compound at Nasik at 7·30 A.M. on the 22nd June. Bad news was in everybody's mouth, and although at that time nothing had occurred to endanger the peace of the place, there was a haughty bearing and an insolence of manners very apparent in the people, which plainly showed us that they cared not to evince their hatred and disgust of our supremacy. Whatever Nasik might have been in the days of the Peishwah, it exhibits little of interest or importance now. Its streets are narrow, dirty, and winding; its bazaars are large and well-stocked, and here, as in most other towns of the Bombay Presidency, we found the all-obliging, speculative Parsee with a shop full of English goods. The houses, like most Hindu houses, look like dirty barns; that which was once the palace of the Peishwah is going to ruin. Part of it is now occupied by the assistant magistrate, for whom an European suite of apartments has been built on the top of the old palatial ones. I need only mention one thing to show the mutability of all human affairs. On and between the beautiful and elegantly-carved pillars of what was once a fine open corridor the wild bees have built their hives in numbers, thus converting a palace into an apiary as they would the remotest wilds of a forest. So changes grandeur and human greatness with "cormorant devouring time." The Hindu temples built on either side of the Godavery are fine old picturesque specimens of architecture. Some are most elaborately carved, and many are in excellent preservation. From the bases of these temples the steps run down to large slabs of granite lower and lower to the river running at their feet. These granite slabs are so built into each other and descend so deep into the water that the river at this spot appears like a congeries of open baths with rapid, clear streams running from bath to bath with pathways between. Add to the interesting nature of these buildings a constant swarm of natives bathing, washing in the holy water, and reclining on the stone-works and river's sides in their light and gay-coloured dresses, tents and horses, sheep and buffaloes, and a body of troops with glistening arms crossing over the river, and you will have a picture at once pleasing and novel. Such a scene, notwithstanding its intensely interesting nature at first glance, however, can only be viewed by an European as a gaudy *picture*, for the pleasure soon vanishes when the semi-animated objects forming its most striking features are analyzed. Instead of seeing the jocund-faced youth with light heart, and the man of honest purpose, or the stalwart busy artizan, the eye rests upon the cunning youth, the debased and premature in age, and the lethargic, attenuated workman, whose tools hang down from hands of delicate form, or who sits lazily smoking his pipe, always intending to complete to-morrow what should be done to-day, while the whole atmosphere around them seems filled with knavery, treachery, and petty sedition,— sunshiny and laden with the most fetid exhalations! On the evening of the second day we marched out of Nasik for Arungabad, and here we left the made road for a cross country, one little better in most respects than a mere bullock-track. As we wended our way on over miles and miles of cotton soil, with scarcely a tree or shrub to break the monotony of the landscape, we found that we had at length arrived at a period of trial. The villages we passed appeared only poor mud-built heaps of hovels, the bullocks half-starved, and the people as amazed at our presence as savages. There were no more bungalows, so we pitched tents after each day's journey. As we marched along we were frequently met by armed sowars, looking as fierce as tigers; we were also constantly overtaken by these same vigilant gentlemen bearing letters or useful information for us. These fine, courteous, soldierly men were "Tap's horse," and exercising a careful watch on the boundary of the Nizam's territory, nearer which we were approaching daily. Of course we were all on the *qui vive*, and looking out for runaway mutineers. The further we went the less inclined people seemed to render us any assistance; but as the time had come for action, we never waited twice for an acquiescence to any reasonable demand. I remember in one of our marches towards Toka we saw something very like a *bear* on the side of a hill, then it moved like a man, and it was voted a *sepoy*, and then a *bear*, and if a bear, why not have a shot? This however was stopped by the object rising erect in the shape of a villager. From Nasik to Toka there was little to see. No traveller met us, and the only break in the unvarying scene was an occasional team of bullocks drawing a plough which seemed merely to scratch the surface of the earth.

Cotton soil, barren, ugly belts of hills, and barren plains broken by heaved-up masses of trap, and the whole surface covered with innumerable specimens of quartz in all varieties of crystallization and colour, were the physical features of this district. *Toka* is the poverty-stricken, ruined remains of what was once a fine town situated at the confluence of the Godavery and Pera, on the high road from Ahmednugger to Arungabad.

Extensive works of stone masonry of a very elaborate kind still remain untouched by time along the bank of the holy river on the side of the town. They were evidently erected to protect Toka from inundation at the great freshets, and also to serve as bathing and washing places for its inhabitants. They are beautifully designed and highly finished, and from the northern bank of the river lend a charm to the desolation and ruin above and behind them. For miles around Toka there is scarcely a blade of vegetation save a long avenue of fine old mango trees in which we pitched our camp. A little below the town on the other side of a large tributary stream, the Pera, is the Dâk bungalow, and the *flying-bridge* across the Godavery. This flying-bridge is one of the simplest and most efficient means of crossing Indian rivers I have ever seen. From a strong pier on either bank runs an iron chain across the river, and from this chain a second hangs vertically from a ring, and is fastened to a large raft-like boat below. As soon as the raft is laden and loosed from either bank, off it runs to the other in some three minutes, guided by a helm, and kept to the line of road by the vertical chain which runs along the one suspended from pier to pier. This kind of bridge is eminently useful, easily repaired if necessary, and necessitates but little outlay. All the kit and engineering implements were passed over the river above Toka by pontoons. To get the bullocks and horses across was the most laughable and tiresome business. Six or eight biles would go into the river, swim half way across, or even further than that, then turn round just as their owners had consoled themselves that that was all right—and swim back, to their mortification and disgust. The horses plunged and kicked and screamed, lay down in the water and rolled, then swam out twenty or thirty yards, evidently enjoying the bath, and then back to the side again, where they lay down in the water like immoveable hippopotami. This game could not be endured longer; swimmers were sent up from the town to swim the beasts across. Some dozen men came up as nearly naked as possible, with huge necklaces of dried gourds to act as buoys while they stemmed the current and conducted their unwilling charges across. No sooner were horses and bullocks driven into the water than in they plunged and buffeted and capered about the snorting brutes like river gods until they urged them to the opposite shore. The fellows could have done their work on *terra firma* no better; and their reward was a few pice! All being ready on the north side of the river for the onward move, we resolved to march from Toka on the evening of 3rd July, and after having received kindness at the hands of two officers of the 24th Bombay N.I., who lived at the Dâk bungalow for the time being, we bade farewell, crossed the rivers, and started on our way for Deysgaum about 9·30 P.M. It was a delicious night, cool, and almost as bright as day. We were again upon the high road, and only two marches from Arungabad. We were in good spirits, the men walked at a fine rate, and sang their songs and joked all the way. One of our party dashed ahead of us at a sharp canter, and we concluded that he would be at Deysgaum bungalow in no time. Some three-quarters of an hour after this we thought we saw something in the gutter on the road-side. We went towards it, lo! it was human! The moon has great influences at these times of the year. Off he went again, if possible, faster. This time he is for the bungalow doubtless. On we went, and halted to drink at a stream. As we ascended the bank on the other side of the river, we saw something huge

ARRIVAL AT DEYSGAUM.

and white in the middle of the road. It was a crowd of natives huddled together, and a little a head of this ghostly gathering was our friend, this time snoring away on a cot. This night's air, like that of Mont Blanc, was too soporific, *nolens volens* he must sleep, and so seized upon the cot, while the shivering natives said, "Sahib take to sleep, what can I do?" A bed on the high road was too good a thing to resign; the next couch might be a stone, so we left him to draw upon Morpheus *ad libitum.* In about half an hour a horseman passed us like a shot, 'twas our friend of the cot, who had awoke to a sense of his loneliness in the wide-wide-world, and was now intent upon the bungalow bed : we saw him no more that night. We arrived at Deysgaum about 2 A.M., and once again rejoiced in bungalow comforts. Here it was we first saw anything of the mutineers. A number of them were prisoners under a guard of the 24th Bombay N. I., and on their way towards Ahmednugger. A mild form of cholera now appeared among the men in our little camp. They had undergone great fatigue, and the water here was very bad, in fact, too foul for use. No death occurred. The next day, July 5th, we marched into the standing camp at Arungabad, and at length formed a part of the Deccan field force, then under the command of Major-General Woodburn, C.B.

The *coup d'œil* of the camp at Arungabad, although a small one, with the cantonment and town, and the surrounding hills, and the strong fortress of Dowlatabad in the distance, was one of the most picturesque sights I ever witnessed. Although the column was small, the tents of the force covered a large area, and gave quite an imposing feature to the landscape. We marched into the camp at an early hour on Sunday morning. We found them all in a state of quiet excitement. The mutiny, partial as it was, of the 1st Cavalry of the Hyderabad Contingent, on June 13th, had given a very serious air to the affairs of Central India. The musselman population was evidently strongly influenced against the British Raj. The fearful convulsions that had affected the North-Western Provinces, Oude, Bengal, and the lower states, began to manifest themselves among the people of the central territories. The circle of the moral cyclone was rapidly widening and destroying such as were weak enough to be attracted by its force. The whirlwind of disaffection passed over Agra, Gwalior, Indore, Mhow, Nagpore, and Hyderabad in the Deccan. The strongest and oldest pillars of our empire were shaken. The same day that witnessed mutiny at Arungabad saw also the discovery of a plot for the murder of all Europeans in Nagpore. This originated in the irregular cavalry of that station. Prompt measures and the fidelity of the Madras sepoys prevented bloodshed and pillage in Nagpore. The treacherous troops were disarmed, and three of the leaders hanged. News had arrived in the camp of the horrid massacre of our people in Jhansi, second only in magnitude to that of Cawnpore, and the mutiny of the right wing of the 12th B. N. I., the Irregular Cavalry and Artillery, at Nowgong on 14th June, while two companies of the 56th N. I., with followers of the Nawab of Banda, seized our treasury there. About this same time revolt and bloodshed seem to have been well nigh universal. We were, indeed, literally surrounded by villains thirsting for our blood. Almost the whole of that once splendid and powerful contingent, the Gwalior, had broken from their allegiance and stained their hands with the blood of the Feringhees, while they carried away with them unopposed treasure amounting to several lacs, thousands of rounds of ammunition, a park of artillery, and other munitions of war, that made their revolt sound like a mighty tocsin to our ears. On 14th June fires broke out in the officers' quarters in Gwalior, and mutiny declared itself. Those who could escape, fled—some to the protection of the Maharajah, others to Agra. Many died of *coup de soleil*, and many were killed; and the rebels were reported to have taken up a strong position at

Calpee, on the banks of the Jumna, and but a few miles from Cawnpore. Scindiah all this time behaved with marked loyalty and wisdom. The mania spread further south, and the blasting contagion at length broke forth among the troops of the Maharajah Holkar, in the city of Indore. On July 1st a couple of Holkar's regiments commenced an attack upon the Residency at Indore, then occupied by the Governor-General's acting agent, Colonel Durand. Guns were planted by the rebels in the Residency grounds, and they fired upon the house and commenced the work of murder in the various bungalows. Col. Durand despatched orders for Hungerford's battery, at Mhow, twelve miles off. Before the guns could arrive, all who had escaped falling into the hands of the rebels fled as best they could, and the battery, then on the road, returned to Mhow. The ladies, Col. Durand, and officers escaped to Sehore, thence to Hoosingabad, where the presence and fidelity of the Madras sepoys *again* insured security to the unhappy refugees who had only escaped with their lives. Thirty-four men, women, and children had perished; their houses were plundered, and then burned. A Parsee tradesman was blown away from a gun, for his knowledge and intercourse with Europeans, I presume. On the evening of the same day troopers rode from Indore into Mhow, frantic with having tasted blood, and at once incited the men of the 1st Cavalry (right wing, the left having already mutinied at Neemuch), and the 23rd Regt. N. I. to rise against their officers and murder them. They did so *en masse,* and in their coolest blood they slew their commanding officers, Col. Platt, of the 23rd N. I., and Major Harris, commandant of the 1st Light Cavalry, and Adjutant Fagan, of the 23rd. The other officers, ladies, and children, and European soldiers, their wives and children, and Parsee merchants and families escaped to the fort, there to defy the cowardly villains, and to await a timely succour. Still further south was the famous old stronghold Asseerghur, and this, it was feared, would also fall into the hands of the rebels, as it was garrisoned by a wing of the 6th Gwalior Contingent. This fort was saved to us by a clever stroke of policy of the commandant, Col. Le Messurier. He had felt that there was a spirit of disaffection among the troops forming the garrison, who were indeed openly boastful in the bazaar of the Pettah of what they intended to do ere long, and therefore wished to get them out of the fort before they could know of the Indore and Mhow disasters. He embodied a few faithful men from the town and district, and then ordered the sepoys to encamp outside the fort, that they might join the field force then coming up from Arungabad. The same night the detachment of this regiment stationed at the large town of Boorampore openly mutinied and started off for Asseerghur, a distance of only 12 miles. A loyal havildar with two sepoys were sent off by the commandant from the fort to meet these rebels, and endeavour to pursuade them to return. He was successful. The next morn the remaining sepoys marched out of the fort, and the new levies marched in without their knowledge. The company at Boorampore was disarmed by a corps of the Bheels, and those who had marched out of the fort were, to their amazement, surrounded by a body of the 3rd Cavalry, Hyderabad Contingent, commanded by Lieut. Clark, and forthwith disarmed also; thus was Asseerghur, one of the strongest fortresses in India, saved. But disaffection was spreading fast. The Bheel corps at Bhopawar, under the command of Col. Stockley and Capt. Waterman, rose and joined in the rebellion. In this station plunder and fire did their devastating work, while the officers, ladies, and children had to fly, as best they could, and endure privations and trials of no ordinary kind.

This, then, was the general state of the country through which our force was about to march on its way north. The relief of Mhow was the first and great object, and to get there before the rains set in was a matter of the highest import. How this was accomplished we shall see by-and-bye; in the meantime I must return to Arungabad, and the events that transpired there prior to our departure. Every day of our sojourn in the camp at this station there was some little excitement afoot. Courts-martial were daily sitting in the mess-house upon such prisoners as were known to have been concerned in the mutiny of the 13th June. Major-Gen. Woodburn had now reported sick, and was about to leave the force for safer and quieter quarters. The command of the force devolved, *pro tempore*, upon Major Follett, then commanding the 25th Bombay N. I. On the memorable day of the 13th of June, the 1st Cavalry, Hyderabad Contingent, refused to march or fight against men of their own religious persuasion. Capt. Abbott remonstrated with them, and as the terrible events of the northern stations were not to be unheeded, the ladies of the cantonment were at once sent away, and the mess-house barricaded. Here the officers took up their quarters. The force under Gen. Woodburn marched into Arungabad on 23rd June. The general, at the suggestion of Captain Abbott, proceeded to the cavalry lines to disarm the men. His force then consisted of two squadrons H. M. 14th Dragoons, Woolcomb's battery, the 25th Bombay N. I., and a detachment of Bombay sappers. The cavalry bugles sounded the assembly, and the men fell in from their lines on foot. The native officers only were mounted. Captain Abbott then rode past, ordering the faithful men to fall out, thus the mutineers remained alone in their front. Woolcomb's battery was only some thirty yards off, each gun loaded with canister. The general and his staff, with Capt. Abbott, then rode up to the men, the latter officer addressing them on their allegiance and religion. At this instant, a jemadar, who was one of the chief rebels, said " This is not good, it's a lie!" Here Capt. Abbott properly drew his pistol to shoot the scoundrel down, but the general turned round to him and said, he desired Capt. Abbott would "not fire on his own men." Again Capt. Abbott addressed them, and a second time the jemadar told him *he was a liar*, and ordered his men to " prime and fire!" In an instant, with a rattle, every pistol was in each man's hand, and the timid general and his mortified staff not half a dozen yards from them! Instead of firing, they turned and fled, and the general then rode behind the guns, where Capt. Woolcomb stood pointing one at them. There was the port-fire ready, one word! and they would have been blown into eternity; but the general said, " No! there are good men among them." They had now gained their horses, and were impudently mounting them only some 250 yards off. Woolcomb now went to another gun and pointed it, but he was not ordered to fire, even

MUTINY AT ARUNGABAD.

though the general was being thus bearded ; at last he cried out, "May I fire, sir?" Again no order came. In another moment they were all mounted and away like the winds ! By-and-bye came a feeble order that Capt. Woolcomb might fire ; but they were off, and of some thirty rounds fired, only a few donkeys, horses, and a poor ghorawalla were killed ! They had cleared the lines, and then drew up upon the maidan, out of range of the shot. The 14th Dragoons were then ordered to charge, but before the 14th could close with them, they turned and were off east, west, and south. The dragoons cut up some dozen only. Capt. Abbott was with the dragoons, and as he had not marched 40 miles that day like them, he overtook a native officer and would have sabred him, but the fellow prayed for quarter with his sword in his mouth. Abbott, like a Christian and a good soldier, stayed his hand, and spared his life, but as he passed the fiend drew his pistol, and discharged it at Abbott's head. The ball flew past, and the rebel escaped for the time. He was caught towards evening, and paid the penalty of his treachery the next day. The remainder of the corps was then paraded and disarmed, and the bad characters imprisoned for trial. The audacious jemadar escaped *in toto*, with some sixty others. Now, it is quite clear that had the general acted in a decisive, bold manner, as his position and the exigencies of the case warranted, he would have quelled the spirit of turbulence at once and in a never-to-be-forgotten manner, but his indecision marred the whole transaction. It became a subject of no light remark. The courts-martial ceased, and on the morning of the 7th July, at 5·30 A.M., there was a parade of the whole troops. We all marched on to the ground in silent expectation of something awful. We formed three sides of a square, thus: the Hyderabad Infantry and Cavalry on one side; the 14th Dragoons and the 25th Bombay N. I. the side opposite the open; the Artillery and Sappers formed the third side, facing the Hyderabad Contingent; the fourth was open and occupied only by a solitary gun, with the port-fire burning beneath. Three prisoners were then marched into the square by some twelve sowars. Their names were then read out, their offences, and the sentence of the court. Two were to be shot by musketry and one blown away from a gun.

Up to this moment they were ignorant of their fate. The two were speedily blindfolded and placed in a kneeling position, when twelve dragoons dismounted and marched towards them. There was a sharp rattle of musketry, and they fell down like logs of wood. The third was then tied to the muzzle of the gun blindfolded. Fire! and in an instant he was blown to atoms. His head flew up into the air some thirty or forty feet—an arm yonder, another yonder, while the gory, reeking trunk fell in a heap beneath the gun. Scarcely had the head and arms fallen to the ground before the carrion birds were glutting themselves upon the warm and mangled flesh, and the whole air was tainted with a most sickening effluvium. Such was the fate of those who sought to welter in the blood of the unoffending! Such a lesson ought to have wrung their comrades' hearts—perhaps it did, but nothing less than such a fearful example could then be thought of. It was woeful to witness for the first time, but in such times and in such scenes justice, indeed, should be blindfold; and we should thank God that war with all its horrors only lasts for a time, otherwise the better feelings of our nature might become almost extinguished.

After the terrible scene of the morning parade, I strolled into the town of Arungabad, and afterwards paid a visit to the very beautiful Taj in its vicinity. The city, once extensive and beautiful, and still renowned, presents a truly marked picture of desolation, poverty, and fallen greatness. Like most large Hindu towns, little remains now to interest the sight-seer, while there is much to disgust and hasten his departure. Squalid poverty sits squatted in rags beneath many a time-worn, elaborately-carved portico, through which the proud and gaudy Musselman once strode; houses, once inhabited by the wealthy Mahrattahs, are now fallen to ruin, their ornamental carvings alone remaining to show where opulence once dwelt; mounds of ashes and filth lie in every street; children scream at your presence, and astonished adults peer out of their miserable abodes upon you with lustreless eyes, while the Pariah dogs start from heaps of ashes, howling as they disappear among the gullies and huts of their owners. And this is the city that once boasted of a college, that once gloried in a palace of immense size and of a monarch's presence, that once was surrounded by walls some seven miles in circumference, with its many gates! Little remains now of the ruined wall and its gateways, still less of the palace of the great Aurungzebe. The Pariah dog now barks in the sun by day, and the jackal prowls by night upon the very spot where this monarch's throne once stood. But there still remains in melancholy sadness a beautiful memorial of this ruler's splendour and taste—the Taj, or shrine built to the memory of Aurungzebe's daughter. This stately tomb, like all other beautiful works of ancient grandeur, is fast falling to decay. The massive gate, inlaid with brass-work chastely devised, though time-worn and covered with dirt, still shows traces of what it was in its grandeur. The white marble dome of the mausoleum and the four minarets, whose spires still glisten with tarnished gold, give a most attractive feature to the spot. The tomb stands enclosed in the centre of what was once an extensive garden of roses and other beautiful flowers, but now little better than a garden of weeds and jungle plants. In the porch inside this fine old gateway sat an old woman in rags, close beside an equally wretched cow; to her I gave some copper coins, for which she returned a profusion of blessings. Immediately beyond the porch is a small tank filled with clear water, in the centre of which are the remains of a tiny fountain; beyond this, for some thirty or forty yards, are other shallow basins of clear running water, in the centre of each a fountain, and around each stone-work and flower-beds filled only with weeds, but even these looked beautiful as they drooped over and were reflected in the running streams beneath. There were crimson velvety dragon-flies, too, flitting from shallow to shallow, that seemed to sport as they would had Aurungzebe been there, and to mock at the decay and neglect. Beyond these stands the still beautiful tomb of white Malwa marble in which the body of the princess lies. Another exquisitely carved door inlaid with brass opens into it. Its shape is octagonal, and the inside is lined with spotless white marble, carved so delicately as to appear like network. In the centre is the sarcophagus, covered over with dingy time-worn cloth, and surrounded by a marble rail-work some eight feet high. A marble wicket-gate opens to devotees who kneel at the shrine as they smear their faces with ashes from a little broken earthen pot within. An equally beautiful gallery of marble runs round this tomb, from which you may gaze upon the grave below. There are four marble windows, all of the most tasteful, delicate fret-work carving ; each looks like a curtain of lace. Many sepoys visited this sepulchre while I stood within. Some threw down their mite, smeared their faces with ashes, and seemed to kneel devoutly before the grave ; others seemed to do so merely because their companions had knelt before them. My orderly, who stood by my side mumbling sugar-cane, sacrilegiously observed, smiling, " What good all that Tamashah, Sahib ? " As usual in such places, scores of names were scribbled in pencil on the spotless marble of this shrine. Here was the autograph of my lord, there one of a baronet, some in Hindustani, some in Mahratti, and there ones of the ubiquitous Jones, Smith, and Robinson. Wherever you go, Jones is certain to have been before you, and to leave a reminder, too, that he *has* been. In all four quarters of the globe, and in every most unexpected corner, whether upon a tree, a rock, a door-post, or on the unspotted marble of a royal mausoleum, people will scribble their names.

THE "TAJ." 37

Why they do it has always been a puzzle to me. Do they add to the antiquity, the grandeur, the beauty, or solemnity by their unknown scribble. What does my lord or Brown's name add to the Taj? Do people go there to read their names? Then why deface its beauty?

Around this octagonal building are fine verandahs, and from the top of the minarets one may have an extensive view of the city and country. The verandahs are beautifully chunamed, as are also the pillars, and beneath their shade one may ensure a delicious hour's enjoyment, if there be pleasure in sitting in a cool breeze and contemplating such a scene. The gardens, the walks, the water, the stone-works, and the extensive wall surrounding all afar off, all in reckless beauty and decay, impress one with no mean ideas of the wealth, the exquisite taste, and the largeness of mind that once belonged to the ancestors of this wretched people. A short distance off is a triangle of jungle-clad hills, rosy and purple, and from their heights flows the stream that yet supplies the basins and fountains of the Taj with water, bubbling as it runs in mockery through the silent ruins. Though this beautiful memorial of love, a fitting monument of Aurungzebe's greatness and splendour, has outlasted his palace and kingdom, it is fast crumbling away beneath the feet of time. We go to Nineveh for their hideous stone bulls, and to Greece for their marble gods, and we build a palace to exalt them—is it not almost to worship!—yet do we allow the *bijoux* of our own empire to pass into oblivion and dust! As I sat there pondering over such thoughts, an old Musselman came into the verandah, spread his mat, and commenced smoking his hookah as calmly and abstractedly as though no other person was near him. He puffed away for some time without once noticing me, then quietly putting his pipe on one side, asked me if I had seen the Taj. I had, and I spoke of it in great praise. He simply bowed his head and stroked his beard. He then said, "God is good," and recommenced smoking more vehemently. Having calmed himself again, he said, " Look ! Kings die, dynasties change, the poor cry, the dead are disturbed, and their tombs tumble upon them ! Allah is great and Mahomet is his prophet ! These are sad days ! " At this instant the sound of the bugle from camp broke upon the stillness. He looked up in a most imploring way, again stroked his beard, and consoled himself with his pipe. I offered him a rupee, but he said, " No ; I am an old man, I don't want money, I want only to die in peace. The air of this place is very pure, and I come every day to smoke and pray." Having stayed long enough to satisfy my curiosity, I returned to camp to find that we had to march on the morrow to repair a road over some hills about fourteen miles from Arungabad. There was no doubt now about our movements. Brigadier Stuart, of the Bombay army, joined and assumed command, and everything was life and expectation. Paper after paper came into camp burdened with accounts of the fearful political condition of our Northern territories : to balance this was the good news of what our few Europeans were doing and could do. Neil and Havelock, and Barnard at Delhi, seemed working miracles against the overwhelming odds, and at such a season of the year, too! There was everything to stimulate us to a great and glorious work. The task was one of fearful magnitude, and I am sure each man felt a personal responsibility urging him to perform his best for the general weal of our empire. What will not British soldiery endure! What will they not achieve when necessity requires! There is no obstacle they will not overcome, no trial they will not cheerfully face and brave to obtain their end. The wonder is that they should have achieved so much in such a climate under such unavoidable disadvantages, and in so short a period, as they did. In a short time we were all excitement about the march up to the pass of Chowker, and this particularly as we were to go in advance of the main body of the column. On the evening of the 8th we left Arungabad, and having made the pass fit for artillery, we returned on the 10th, rather an unnecessary step, as we all marched off from that city on the 12th instant. During our temporary stay at Chowker we kept a sharp look out to the north, shot hares and peacock in the jungle for the evening's dinner, and otherwise took it very easy, considering the times.

During our second stay at Arungabad I had an opportunity of tasting the grapes grown at Dowletabad. They were very fine, and quite a delicious treat. How the poor people can bring them so far and sell them so cheap I can't imagine—only an anna per pound!

I am unable to speak of this remarkable fortress of Dowletabad, as I had no opportunity of visiting it, although it stands but a few miles from Arungabad. What I saw of it in the distance looked like an enormous block of dark rock rising abruptly from the plain to a great height. Those who rode over to inspect this fort declared it impregnable. The only way into it, I was informed, was through a narrow passage excavated through the solid rock, at the top of which an iron grating for fire would preclude any enemy's further progress, supposing he ever got that far. In the fort is an enormous gun, about which curious stories are told. This fort belongs to the Nizam of Hyderabad. On the morning of 12th July the column left Arungabad at an early hour. It was a remarkably fine sight to witness the ascent of the troops over the rough pass of Chowker, which had been repaired a day or two before by the sappers. We had a bullock battery of the Hyderabad Contingent with us, and what through stupidity of drivers and unwillingness of bullocks, it was not surprising to see gun, tumbrel, ammunition-waggon, and bullocks too, go headlong over the side of the road into a deep gully beneath. The biles backed, and snorted, and looked wild, when they ought to have done the reverse; and at this moment their drivers, who sit upon the yokes, jumped off and ran away, while the biles turned round, got their heads out of the yokes and their legs into them, and otherwise tied themselves into most perplexing knots, and down went the whole, gun and bullocks together. Then followed the unyoking, the unchaining, the patting, and coaxing, and gentling, and re-yoking—a pitiable business, and enough to tire and disgust the most patient Job. This kind of thing generally occurs in most unwished-for places. Fancy our artillery being left to the mercy of such beasts as a team of bullocks in these days of progress, whose intelligence is about their least point of recommendation! On the evening of the 15th July we arrived at Adjuntah, famous for its ancient caves, and encamped on the south side of the town. Around this fine old town is the very beau-ideal of an Indian fortified wall, with fine imposing bastions and magnificent old gateways.

19th July, we reached Edulabad in the evening, where Captain Keatinge kindly entertained us. On the other—the northern—bank of the river Poorna he had pitched tents for us, and had a bazaar in readiness.

On the 20th we encamped at Anthoolee on the south bank of the river Taptee. Cholera broke out in the camp at this place, and in a few hours many men, Europeans and natives, died. Major Follett, commanding the 25th Regiment Bombay N. I., died here about 9 P.M. He was a fine man, and much beloved by his regiment. About 1 A.M. the column marched for Boorampore; we had to cross the Taptee. When we arrived at its banks we found it little above knee-deep, and the whole troops and baggage soon crossed. The natives remarked that " God was evidently fighting for the Sircar, for " everywhere the roads were good and the rivers " almost dry, although the season for the rains was " far advanced." I know no sight more pleasing to the eye than that of a force crossing these Indian rivers in the cool of the morning. Horsemen in advance soon cross and appear on the opposite banks among the brushwood and trees, while the column moves slowly on, filing down the narrow road that leads to the ford. Once upon the shingle at the water's edge, the infantry commence taking off shoes and stockings to cross, some mount upon each other's backs like school-boys, having tossed up for the ride over. Then there's the joke; hundreds stay to drink of the clear cold water, native and European mingling together, then quietly wade across and form up upon the opposite bank; then down comes the artillery, gun after gun, dashing the stream about in a thousand rainbows as they pass through; there are the dragoons and gaudily-dressed irregulars in groups quietly watering their horses; there dhooly-bearers carrying the sick men across, sprinkling their heads and dhoolies with the precious water as they go; yonder is a long line of camels jingling with bells, stalking over; and there is the great unwieldy elephant sucking up gallons of water for his capacious stomach (with a huge bunch of leaves tucked up between his trunk and tusk), or blowing it over his heated body and limbs. When he has quenched his thirst, he takes down his leaves and fans the flies away as he carefully moves off. Both banks are lined with men, horses, and followers, and droves of sheep, goats, and bullocks; all, and every animal, seem delighted with the river. I wonder not that natives worship rivers in this country, for no one can too highly estimate the value of clear, cool, running water, wherein all may wash and be clean, quench their burning thirst, and cool their heated, weary frames after a march over an arid country and through clouds of choking dust. The very dogs seem to luxuriate in anticipation as they bound down the banks, with hanging tongues, to rush into it to bathe and drink; and the sick man thanks God for the refreshing, clean, cold draught he then can enjoy, as he lies in the cool shade with the dancing, rippling river before him. High banks, covered with foliage and soldiery, and the clear blue sky, with the morning cloud above him, all lie down there reflected in the river in a hundred pleasing moving pictures. We passed through the town of Boorampore and encamped on the north side. Here the body of Major Follett was buried; and as a proof of the love his men bore for him, they carried his body, dug his grave, and heaped up a rude mound of stones over the spot when the ceremony was ended; and these were *high caste* men, too! But that this regiment should do such an act seems only natural, they are such fine soldiers, and commanded by such superior officers.

22nd July. We encamped about seven this morning on the north of the Fort of Asseerghur, in a little plateau surrounded by dense jungle.

Towards evening Mrs. Durand, Mrs. Keatinge, and Col. Durand, who had found their way thus far south, came into camp from the fort.

23rd July. Parade of the troops at 6 A.M., for the execution of three mutineers of the 6th Infantry, Gwalior Contingent. They were tried by drumhead court-martial the evening before, and sentenced to be shot by musketry. They were a havildar, a private, and a bheestie. A similar disposition of troops to the Arungabad execution; the criminals were placed near a hill, twelve dragoons dismounted, and blindfolded them, and in another instant they rolled to the earth to be buried where they fell. The rattle of the carbines had scarcely died away when screams were heard outside the square. They came from a poor woman, who was running through the camp to the scene of death. She was the wife of the havildar, and evidently had never dreamt that she was thus to be robbed of her husband, so soon, too, and for ever. When she heard that he was dead, she appeared wild with grief, poor devoted dependant!

24th July. We marched for the Berwai ferry on the river Nerbudda. In this march to the Nerbudda we passed through a considerable amount of jungle. The land on either side of the road was but little cultivated, although light and loamy, and capable of producing everything useful to man and beast. During the march up thus far I had taken the precaution to administer every evening small doses of quinine. True, every encamping ground was tolerably well-cleared of brushwood, but I am inclined to believe that this precaution kept us free from fever, while it sustained the nervous power, and thereby rendered us less likely to suffer from the effects of over-fatigue and malaria, of which there is no lack all over the district between the Taptee and Nerbudda. All along this line of march the woods abound with game, large and small. Antelope and peacock and hare supplied the place of butcher's meat and fowls, and these we obtained in such abundance that one may say we feasted every day in a princely style. On the evening of the 28th the whole of 3rd Hyderabad Cavalry, under the command of Capt. S. Orr, joined us. We were now upon the south bank of the Nerbudda at the Berwai ferry. The river was rising very fast—indeed in a few hours it rose several feet. High and large boulders rapidly disappeared; the current increased in rapidity, while huge trunks of trees, bushes, and logs of wood came floating down. All this was a sufficient warning to us. The sooner the force crossed the river the better, for rains had certainly fallen, and heavily too, in the hills, and we might expect them ere long. Large boats of a rude description were ready, and upon these our troops, artillery, and baggage crossed over. Here, also, several fugitives came into camp—the worse for flight, and painful apprehensions. A little fellow of the telegraph department had been beaten about the head sorely; and those who had escaped unhurt looked very woe-begone and anxious. In the bungalow on the north bank of the Nerbudda were Capt. Waterman of the Bheel corps, and Mr. Theobalds of the Geological Survey Department. These gentlemen had had a long run for their lives, and scarcely boasted of an article other than what they stood in. They accompanied us to Mhow.

1st August. We marched to Simrole through the exceedingly picturesque ghaut of that name. The bed of the valley torrent was then dry, but I can fancy how beautiful it would be when filled with water. The scenery all through this pass is very charming. It also abounds in game of every description. Very heavy rain fell all night.

2nd August. The morning was fine and cool, and we now commenced our last march to the relief of Mhow. We had pitched our camp in and about nice smooth-looking fields of fine black loamy cotton soil. In the morning, after the intensely heavy rain all night, the whole camp was a mighty sheet of soft mud. It was difficult to march through, more particularly for the guns. The elephants sank knee-deep into the mire, but this was nothing to them.

It continued fine, and the column went along quietly. At length we sighted the cantonment and town of Mhow, and as we neared it, fresh horses came out to assist the artillery along the still heavy roads. As we drew nearer there was the sound of a heavy gun, another, and another, until twenty and one were counted. "What could this be for? Has Delhi fallen? It must be so!" But no! though perhaps it was an equally important thing to the people here; the salute was fired from the fort, for the "relief of Mhow." This timely succour was, indeed, equivalent to a victory in this part of India, for all around were enemies—every hand was against us from Neemuch to Saugor, from Gwalior to Mhow. Indore, only twelve miles off, was full of sedition—of evil people only biding their time for our destruction. The rains had held back for us, and we attained our object, and by this we established a centre of effective operations of an offensive kind; re-opened communication with distant parts that had long been closed to us; re-established the electric telegraph, the wires of which had been cut and stolen; and now showed a menacing face to the boastful cowards who had long defied the pent-up Europeans of the station. Not only had they need to rejoice at the presence of a relieving force which dissipated their fears, but they were now able to escape from the millions of fleas and other vermin, which formed no very agreeable society to them while shut up in the fort, and to re-occupy the bungalows, the barracks, and other buildings, which had escaped the incendiary, in safety. So they fired the salute, and rushed out of the fort, like prisoners whose chains had been loosed, and we marched into Mhow, the 25th band playing rejoicingly, and severally took up our quarters in such bungalows as were not burned, glad that a period of rest had at length arrived. It was indeed a sabbath, a harbinger of long repose to both man and beast, during which the energies of all were husbanded for the long and daily trials soon to be encountered upon the battle-field.

Having now detailed so many of our movements to the establishment of our force in the cantonment of Mhow, I ought not to forget to mention the many striking physical features of the country through which our troops had marched, as this may prove of interest to those who have an eye for the beauties and peculiarities of nature as well as for the doings of an army constantly on the move.

Almost all the enormous tracts of country between the great rivers—the Godavery, the Taptee, and Nerbudda as far north as Mhow—consists of deep , loamy deposits of black, alluvial clay, densely wooded with jungle in some parts, in others open and cultivated for the growth of cotton, hence its name "cotton-soil." These open flats of cotton-soil are very extensive, and so uniformly uninterrupted by rock or tree, that they give one an idea of an immense motionless sea, and this is very marked, indeed, about mid-day, when the dancing, glaring mirage flickers over its whole surface to its horizon, making every object appear giant-like, and as though it moved along upon the face of rippling water high above the earth.

In the neighbourhood of the various belts of hills there are vast boulders of trap, which appear on the surface of the soil as though they had been hurled down by volcanic convulsion. In other places are thousands of loose masses of trap which have undergone changes in both texture and colour, irregular lumps of quartz in all possible varieties of colour and crystallization, and upon and near the banks of nullahs specimens of mica-schist and silex. In other localities are vast masses of sandstone, of which some of the small forts and musjids are built. The old fortified wall of Adjuntah is built of this sandstone.

On approaching the Nerbudda we observe traces of basalt, and in that river there is a considerable amount. From the alluvial banks of this river the natives obtain common salt, and an impure carbonate of soda effloresces and is also collected. I saw several specimens of greenstone slate brought from the neighbourhood of Mundlasier. Laterite and iron ore of a rich quality abound, but I imagine are scarcely worked except by the rude Bheels in their primitive fashion.

All the hills in this district are very peculiar, having generally flat tops and sloping amygdaloid extremities. They mostly consist of strata of granite, basalt, and trap, and though occasionally separated from each other by considerable breaks of flat cultivated tracts, they bear such a similarity as to impress one with the belief that they once formed one continuous belt. At the basis of these hills beautiful specimens of various coloured quartz are obtained—nodular, mammillary, acicular, and stalactitic—and some in such masses of microscopic crystals that they glisten like diamond dust. In the Simrole-ghaut there is a curious columnar feature of the rock, which appears as though it had been hewn from the solid in prismatic pillars of great height and size. This columnar arrangement, so striking in appearance, is evidently basaltic, and is alternated with enormous layers of trap. In the dry bed of the valley torrent there were great quantities of crystallized silicious minerals, most of them bearing evidences of having been long washed by water containing an abundant amount of lime. Carbonate of lime, in the form of beautiful white marble, is found in Malwa. All through these districts, particularly in the valley of the Nerbudda, every species of game abounds. The tiger, the cheeta, the bison, antelope, and bear, and wild hog are in great quantities, as well as every other kind of small game. The peacock is very common, and fine for table. The land, on the whole, is eminently fertile, with almost boundless plains of deep, rich, alluvial soil, large rivers, winding streams, and peaceful valleys, clothed with all kinds of exuberant vegetation; trees, yielding timber; shrubs, spices and brilliant dyes; and plants, medicines and odorous perfumes; while the whole is interspersed with villages surrounded by fruit-bearing trees and gardens filled with luxuriant cool succulents.

The health of the troops during this march was altogether good. We had an accession of cholera after passing through the town of Boda. The water at this place was very bad, and in the town it was said there was nearly always more or less cholera. The water in many of the wells we drank from was nearly milk-white in colour, loaded with myriads of microscopic animals, and of most unpleasant flavour; but there was no other water for us in such places: the rains were very late this season. After crossing the great rivers, and a fall of rain, cholera left us. Save this slight scourge, we had little to complain of. Fever, so much dreaded north of Asseerghur, scarcely appeared among us, and as we continued to ascend to the high table-land of Central India, we enjoyed cooler weather. The bright starry nights were almost cold, and the early morning marches were quite invigorating as we passed through clouds of rising dew. The vicinity of the hills was always cool. Cold currents of air seemed to blow down their declivities all day ; the vital activity of extensive jungle foliage, not only precluding terrestrial insolation, but producing great evaporation and a large surface for radiation, also assists to cool the air ; while from the surfaces of the great rivers a copious evaporation takes place which is deposited as dew, or collected into mountainous heaps of clouds to break the intensity of the solar rays, and by-and-bye to return to the earth again as rain. All these—jungles, rivers, and extensive ranges of high hills—conduce to effect a most beneficial change of climate, which becomes remarkably evinced on gaining the high plateau of Malwa, in the happy results it seems to bring about in the constitutions of both natives and Europeans. The men seemed to regain an elasticity of step and a joyous freshness of countenance that were quite pleasing to witness.

CHAP. II.

Mhow after the mutiny of Bengal troops.—Treasury looted.—Fall of Delhi.—Salute fired on 27th September 1857.—Preparations for march upon Dhar.—Arrival of siege train at Dhar.—Camp.—Position established for siege on 25th October.—Firing village.—The siege.—Flag of truce. — Breach examined. — Storming breach. — Fort empty.—Fort, palace, treasury.—Hyderabad Contingents under Major Orr arrive.—They march for Mahidpore 7th November.—Mutiny of Mahidpore Contingents.—Force marches from Dhar, 8th November, for Neemuch.—Dhar Town, and visit to the Rajah.

In my last chapter I detailed the few interesting events which broke upon the general monotony of our daily march from Arungabad to Mhow. We effected a timely relief of that important post, and at once commenced a series of labours necessary to the well-being of the place and the operations we were about to undertake in the field against the enemy, who were only a few miles from us and openly defying our power while they spread a terror of no light nature over the whole state of Malwa. Mhow was for the time being a strong basis of our military operations, but to denude it of the troops and leave it in a position similar to that in which we found it would have been impolitic in the extreme. To obviate this, and to give it an air of real military strength, the wretched thing that had gloried for years in the name of "The Fort" had to undergo extensive alterations. An earth-work was thrown up all round it, deep and wide ditches were dug, and batteries established in an admirable style. A strong battery faced the gateway, looking towards the cantonment to the north; others of equal strength looked south and west; a covered way was run out from the fort wall, south, to a well, there being no water in the fort; the angular corners of the old tumble-down walls, forming the quadrangle of the so-called fort, were built against from without and within, and large guns mounted thereon, pointing over cantonment, town, and country; the four walls were heightened and loop-holed all round for musketry; and at length this badly placed stronghold—for it is commanded on three sides—assumed a really imposing feature, and looked as though people could confide in its strength if necessity should compel. During the whole of our sojourn in Mhow, from the day of our arrival in the beginning of August to the middle of October, every preparation was being made for the coming struggle to be commenced as soon as the rains permitted the movement of troops, with all their unwieldy paraphernalia. Very heavy rains fell almost incessantly up to the week before we marched to take the field;

many of the cattle of the force drooped, emaciated, and died; but the men generally seemed to pick up an almost robust state of health. Fortunately for our force the rebellious regiments had only destroyed some eight or nine bungalows on the night of their mutiny; they were too anxious to get away with their blood-stained plunder, and Hungerford's guns were too quick and terrible to tempt them to complete the horrid work of destruction they had commenced, so that our troops were well housed in good buildings, the native lines being all tiled—(a plan far superior to thatch or palmyra leaves); our sick were placed in admirably built bombproof hospitals; and the artillery lines and barracks of the Bengal cavalry remained as before the outbreak. The library, with its well-stocked shelves of goodly tomes and maps, and the prettily built church, escaped the firebrand, while the chaplain's house hard by, with all his worldly goods, was burnt to the ground; where the mess-house once stood was a heap of ashes, with a tumbling pillar here and there; further on, on either side of the road, the blackened walls and fallen pillars of destroyed bungalows showed the march of the mutineers, as they fled from the cantonment they had plundered and partially destroyed to join the other reckless masses all pouring upon Delhi. It was a sorry spectacle to look at; and when one gazed upon the graves of

Platt, Harris, and Fagan, who lay buried in a remote corner of the fort, and remembered that even a service of nearly forty years with a regiment was requited by foul murder, it cannot be wondered at if unrelenting revenge filled the bosom! Years of kindness and paternal consideration, of companionship in the battle-field and sports, acts of forbearance and deeds of bravery, and every manly virtue—dignity of office and respect of years, all were forgotten in one wild moment, and the hand that was raised in salutation in the morning was imbrued in the life's blood by sun-set. All had disappeared to a man; even the native servants had leagued with the murderers of their masters, and hurried away with the destroying stream.

I am about to relate a curious and shameful occurrence which happened on the night of 6th August; whether this had anything to do with the difference of discipline observed in the Bengal army or not it is for others to judge. The treasury, which had been removed to the fort for safety, and was guarded by men of the 2-6 battery, Bengal artillery, was robbed to the extent of some thousands of rupees. A case of wine was also abstracted the same night. Now, it fell out that the men of this battery had been permitted to levy a toll upon all goods, beers, wines, &c. consumed by their officers and their families while they were all locked up in this fort; and that sundry articles had been appropriated by the men. This had positively been permitted to go on unchecked until Mhow was relieved by our force; then followed the looting of the treasury. A court of inquiry sat, and the money was hunted for. Some Rs. 3,000 were found in bags in a nullah close behind the fort. The European guard was placed in confinement, but no punishment of any serious nature was awarded to the guilty persons. Other moneys were found, but the major portion of the treasure was never recovered. Such an instance of depravity was most humiliating at this season, and in the eyes of the natives must have been looked upon most unfavourably. Mutinous regiments had done no more in several stations! Shameless recklessness and an utter want of principle and good discipline can alone be accorded to such an act. A guard of H. M. 86th Regiment supplanted them in the office for which they had proved themselves totally unworthy. The Moharam passed off very quietly. Strong guards were posted about the bazaar, and the pickets on the Indore road were strengthened, lest any rising might be attempted. Nothing, however, occurred to break the peace, and the weather was most unpropitious for any inflammatory demonstration, for the rain poured down in torrents almost the whole time.

On the night of 4th September a troop of the 3rd

Cavalry H. C. came into cantonment, unchallenged by a soul, and picketed their horses. An enemy might have done the same. After this a little more vigilance was observed. All this time most distressing reports came into our camp from north and south, east and west. Mutiny among Bombay troops, sedition and conspiracy in Poona, rebels increasing in force in Malwa, Holkar's remaining troops—some 10,000—more than distrusted, and here were we, immoveable on account of the rains, while Pandy was getting more powerful and mutiny more universal. An anxious eye was cast towards Madras and the Nizam's people, but no great manifestation of sympathy or sedition was apparent. Everywhere terror had stricken our homes, and I doubt not more safety and strength was felt in the camp than in the city; in either case one's position was not an enviable one; real security and life were upon mere lease. To live in India now was like standing on the verge of a volcanic crater, the sides of which were fast crumbling away from our feet, while the boiling lava was ready to erupt and consume us!

On the evening of the 19th considerable excitement was occasioned in Mhow by the sound of artillery firing at Indore. After the first few sounds, the dragoons had saddled their horses, and the Bombay artillery, under Capt. Woolcomb, were all in readiness for action. Boom after boom came over the distant hills, one after the other, like the commencement of an action, and then they died away. It was the salute of the Maharajah's people on the beginning of the Dusserah, and so our excitement quietly subsided.

On the morning of 27th September, just as service at the church was over, a salute from the heavy guns of the fort was fired in honour of the capture of Delhi! This famous stronghold was again in our keeping. It had fallen by assault some thirteen days before. This news was known in the native bazaar two or three days prior to the official announcement, when twenty-and-one guns poured forth their loud voices on the still air of a bright sabbath morn proclaiming the glorious achievement of General Wilson's army. I hesitate not to say that every soul felt grateful for what this noble army had endured and effected. A burden seemed at once to be lifted from the heavily oppressed hearts of the British, and now they could breathe more freely and again exult, as of old, in their prowess.

From May 11th, when mutiny broke out in this old sink of Mogul iniquity, up to Sept. 14th, rebellious sepoys had flocked from all quarters of India to immolate themselves to the mock royalty and chaotic government they had set up. They trooped in thousands to do homage to an enfeebled debauchee and puppet, and then insulted him—their proclaimed king—and threatened him with death when money was not forthcoming. They had selected a grand centre of operations, well stored with every munition of war a first-class arsenal should contain ; a city well fortified, rich in native wealth and splendour, containing one of the largest treasuries of the British, and a powder magazine of enormous magnitude, numerous field-pieces of various calibre, and two complete siege trains, thousands of muskets, and all the vast and goodly etceteras belonging to these engines of war. With the time-honoured representative of the Mogul empire, a Mahomedan population inimical in every feeling to the British, a city as holy and eternal in their eyes as Rome or Jerusalem are to other nations, and containing within its fortified walls everything needed for the assumption of power, and, as they imagined, the ejectment of Europeans from the land, it was not to be wondered at if they hurried from their allegiance to strangers of other colour, creed, and country, to rush to this centre of all their vain hopes, there to bask, as they believed, in an elysium, and behind its strong towers to defy the wrecked remains of that power they had so openly and vilely trodden under foot.

For many long weeks they poured in streams

into this city with blood-stained hands, unopposed and grand in their respective infamy; but far off on the horizon was a little cloud at first dimly seen and unheeded by them, and this waxed greater, and darker, and more angry every day, fresh winds wafted other cloudlets to it, and at length the dark storm approached nearer and nearer this doomed Gomorrah of our own day, overshadowed the heavens, and burst upon the infatuated spillers of innocent blood in a whirlwind of fire and death-dealing bolts that ceased not till it had purged the place by its never-to-be-forgotten and terrible blasts. The spirits of the departed followed their slayers, and the angel of death was there to revenge them! It was nobly done, but how many brave souls perished in its accomplishment!

From June 8th up to the memorable day of assault and capture of Delhi our little army had done nothing but conquer. They were assailed from the city in their front, and from fresh arrivals of the enemy in their rear; daily attacks were made by vast masses, but our brave band stood each and all unvanquished; many, of course, perished in these affairs, but how so many escaped is the wonder, for not only had they to combat an ever vigilant enemy by night and day, but there were the sun, the terrific falls of rain, fever, anxiety, isolation, privation, and cholera—a legion of evils—

GALLANTRY OF TROOPS.

besetting both body and mind ! For nearly fifteen weeks our troops endured what were almost fabulous to relate ; deeds of gallantry worthy the Curtii were performed. Never, perhaps, did an army achieve so much or display such brilliance of conduct individually and as a body as that brave band commanded by General Wilson in the capture of this enormous city against such overwhelming odds. The brilliance of their deeds was untarnished by any single act of cruelty, though they stood upon the very ground where violation and inhuman butchery had been suffered by their countrymen, women, and children.

When we read the published list of casualties we felt how great had been the struggle, and how dear the honour and prestige of our country to them. To root out the vast hordes of fiends we had once nurtured and pampered as spoiled children cost us no less a loss than 61 officers and 1,178 rank and file killed and wounded ! But they had sounded their own tocsin, and in their cry for our blood they sang the dirge of their own dynasty.

The news of the fall of Delhi gave a fresh impetus to our forces, and we heard the hundred and one guns fired at Indore, when their festivities ended, without alarm.

Everything was now progressing fast with us for a move against the rebels in the neighbourhood of

Dhar. The hammer and the forge were going night and day in the fort, gear for elephants and siege-guns was making, untrained bullocks were being taught the draught of guns, and commissariat stores were being prepared.

October 12th news came into Mhow that a body of rohillas was about to move on Mundlaisir to plunder the treasury there. The 3rd and 4th Troops of the 3rd Cavalry, Hyderabad Contingent, under Lieut. Clark, were ordered off forthwith to the village of Goojeeree to intercept this project of the enemy. They had been burning and pillaging several places in our neighbourhood, and only ten miles off had destroyed the Dâk bungalow at Mânpore. Another detachment of the 3rd Cavalry was sent off to Mundlaisir to Capt. Keatinge, the political agent there.

About 1·30 A.M. on the 14th instant an order suddenly came from the Brigadier directing three companies of the 25th Bombay N. I., three guns, and fifty dragoons of H. M. 14th L. D. to proceed without delay to the support of Lieut. Clark, of the Hyderabad Cavalry, at Goojeeree and Mânpoor. The 25th went off with their excellent commanding officer, Major Robertson, and now to us, who remained behind in Mhow, there was only the excitement of a speedy movement in the same direction to comfort us.

October 16th more ammunition was sent out to the force under Major Robertson; and on the 19th orders were issued for the force to march, and all Europeans left behind to go into the fort. The cantonment was to remain in charge of a detachment of H. M. 86th, a portion of the 25th N. I., and the detachment of the Bombay sappers under Lieut. Dick, Bombay Engineers. On 20th half the B. Company, Madras sappers, with the 86th, under Major Keane, Woolcomb's battery and the remaining troopers of the 3rd Cavalry H. C., and a squadron of dragoons marched out for Dhar.

Early the same morning two companies of the 2nd Infantry H. C., a squadron of the 1st Cavalry H. C., and three guns of the H. C., under the command of Captain Speed, arrived from Simrole.

The remaining portion of the Madras sappers waited till the morning of the 21st to conduct the siege train from Mhow to Dhar. We were up about 2 A.M., and started about 6·30, A.M., and arrived at Juswunth-nugger about 7 P.M., a distance of only ten miles having been accomplished. But this was not to be wondered at considering the bad state of the roads, the stubbornness of the bullocks, and the fragility of the tackle. Almost every fifty yards the bullocks refused to go; pricking, and twisting of tails, and yelling, availed not; and not until the willing elephant came to the tug could we extricate the guns from the many holes and heaps of mud they got into. This occurred more or less every mile of the country we had to travel over, until we sighted the fort of Dhar. The coercion we were obliged to use to induce the bullocks to move was most cruel, and yet what could be done? The heavy guns were wanted at Dhar and must be conveyed there, by hook or by crook, by these untutored, unwilling brutes. The labour was most trying to the officers and men, as well as to the animals; and when we arrived at Dhar our faces and hands were blistered by the heat of the sun. Lieut. Christie of the Bombay artillery, who was in charge of the siege train from Mhow to Dhar, was most unremitting in his exertions and labours to expedite the transit of these unwieldy machines across this broken, muddy country. The Rohillas had all retired from their predatory pursuits on the approach of our force into the fort of Dhar. On October 22nd our forces had arrived there. The enemy left the fort and came out to attack us. They had planted three brass guns on a hill south of the fort, and from this battery they extended in force along the east face, skirmishing in splendid style.

In this instance the 25th Regiment behaved admirably. The guns were charged and captured, and the 25th speedily turned them round and fired upon the enemy. The 86th Regiment, with the sappers, were in the centre with Woolcomb's and Hungerford's batteries, the dragoons on our right, and the native cavalry on our left. The enemy made a move to get round to our baggage, but were frustrated. They soon retired to the fort, leaving some forty of their brethren upon the plain. We had three dragoons wounded by sabre cuts, one jemadar and one sowar of the 3rd Cavalry H. C. killed, and two wounded.

The siege train arrived at Dhar on the evening of the 24th. As we passed down into the valley wherein our camp was pitched, the enemy opened fire from the fort upon a picket. We continued to move onward, and by-and-bye were greeted with vociferous cheers from the Europeans, who longed for the arrival of the "big guns," that they might breach the fort walls and drive the villains to the winds.

Dhar.

The camp at Dhar was pitched about one mile and a half from the fort, on the south side, in an enormous ravine surrounded on all sides by heights broken by gigantic fissures. From the neck of this ravine was a gorge, through which ran a road towards a beautiful large tank surrounded by stately trees, and onward to the town of Dhar.

This road was quite hidden from the enemy by hills, and then led into a broken circuitous lane skirting the filthy suburbs of the city. As the camp lay thus snugly protected, it presented a very happy, busy scene. There was little to be feared from the enemy ; they were too safe behind the solid stone walls of that admirably built fort, and the lesson they had just learned taught them better than to venture into the open again. A randomly-aimed shot occasionally flew over our camp, and a few came bouncing into our midst, but nothing was feared. On a hill some two thousand yards south of the fort we had thrown up a sand-bag battery, from whence we constantly threw shell into it. On the east and on the north faces we had thrown out strong cavalry pickets of dragoons and irregulars, and also of infantry of the 25th N. I. and H. M. 86th. To the west was another tank, or rather lake. It thus appeared, from the disposition of our forces, and the solitary position of the enemy in the fort, supposed to number about 4,000, that we had arranged a trap from which there was no escape for them. As our reconnoitring parties went out, the enemy always opened fire upon them from the guns on the bastions. It was quite evident the walls of this place must be breached, and to establish a breaching battery a position must be taken up as near as practicable. This was effected on

Sunday morning, 25th Oct., in the following manner. The 86th and Madras sappers marched off about 5 A.M. through the gorge from the camp leading towards Dhar. They turned along the circuitous broken lane skirting the suburbs, and soon found that they could advance almost totally under the cover of natural parallels, huts, and mud walls to within some 500 yards of the fort. A few trees were cut down, miry nullahs filled up, and walls knocked down for the field batteries and heavy guns to advance and take up their position. As our troops neared the fort, a very smart fire of musketry, gingalls, and round shot was kept up by the enemy. The artillery dashed along in splendid style, and speedily opened fire upon the bastions, while the 86th with their rifles subdued the heat of their fire from the matchlock men. Shells from the mortar battery continually poured into the fort, but with little apparent effect. A house upon one of their bastions at the south corner, commanding the road into Dhar from the fort, was a good deal damaged, as were also some of the parapets to the south ; but below these, and the creneletions of the curtains, the walls remained as perfect as adamant. An artilleryman was shot through the chest from this corner bastion. Another line of attack was taken up all along a high mound of earth, extending from this corner road the whole length of the west face, terminating at the large lake. All along this line were houses, protected from the fort by the mound behind them, which rose above them three times their height, and formed excellent cover and accommodation for our troops. At the extreme left of this line was a large open square and a capacious building, and numerous other houses and shops. This position formed the head-quarters of the 25th Regiment N. I., and was in every way suited for the occasion, as the men lining this long parallel were easily relieved and comfortably housed. Facing this natural parallel for offensive operations was the west face of the fort, with the palace at the extreme left, towering high ; the intricate, almost impregnable gateway in the middle, flanked by strong bastions on either side, mounted with guns, and a thick zig-zag loop-holed wall running upwards from the lower gate to the curtain, and again, beyond this, another loop-holed curtain, another strong bastion, and another similar curtain running to the large corner bastion commanding the road and maidan to the south. The fort is built of fine-grained sandstone, and everywhere was in almost perfect repair. The south, east, and north faces were quite inapproachable from the maidan, upon which there was little or no cover, and the approaches on all these sides were almost perpendicular, while the walls and bastions were equally strong, and considerably higher, on account of the fall of the hill on these sides. It was therefore determined to erect a breaching battery upon this long mound facing the west, only some three or four hundred yards distant, and a spot opposite the corner curtain was fixed upon. All this time, from about 6 A.M. till 12 o'clock, everything was dash, bustle, and clamour. Horsemen rushed backwards and forwards, the field guns were blazing away, while the infantry established themselves in the houses and along the mound, from whence they kept up a continuous rattle of musketry. The inhabitants of this part of the town deserted it almost to a man; one or two decrepit old men and women alone showed themselves at the doors of their miserable hovels. There was a vile effluvium of decomposed skins and putrescent tan liquor in the part occupied by the chucklers; loose goats and sheep were bleating and rushing about between the legs of men and horses; camp followers, in a hundred varied dresses, were looting chickens, pigeons, and the wretched rags they found in these huts; rows of dhoolies and their miserable bearers, half frightened out of their lives, were being urged on to the front; red-turbaned sowars and very hairy dragoons came jingling, all heat and excitement, among the stream; quartermasters and adjutants rushed backwards and forwards, threading their way at a walk or dashing onward like messengers of death; obedient, bulky, indispensable elephants, with the needed engines of fort destruction, moving slowly and ponderously along; crowds of Europeans and natives, sappers and artillerymen, the 25th and 86th, all hauling together, hooting and laughing, all very hot, and all aiding the transit of the siege guns to the front. Such a scene, such a din, such semi-serious excitement! It appeared wonderful that men should have built such a splendid fort, and have left an enemy such extraordinary facilities of capturing it; for nearly the whole way from our camp to the large mound so near to it, and, as it were, placed purposely for the erection of engines for its destruction, our approach was almost a covered way. About mid-day some of the enemy, who had concealed themselves in the houses of this part, fired upon Woolcomb's battery. The 86th men, with the Madras sappers, soon despatched these rebels. In some of the houses where they had secreted themselves we found cartouche boxes full of ammunition, caps, cartridges, and other articles of plunder, and muskets with the bayonets fixed. The site for the battery was selected by Major Boileu of the Madras engineers. The battery was thrown up during the night; the next day it was improved, and the embrasures blinded. The enemy were not idle; we

INCIDENTS OF SIEGE.

could see them throwing up a battery on our left flank near the palace. This was rendered too hot for them by the excellent practice of Woolcomb's guns on our left, while a mortar battery erected still further to our left, and closer to the gate and palace, sent its deadly missiles among them every quarter of an hour. The effect of this shelling on the palace was terrific, as proved afterwards.

Our heavy guns opened fire upon the curtain of the fort as soon as the battery was ready. For a long time little or no effect was produced, but by-and-bye shattered fragments of stone began to crumble away. The thundering weight of metal continuously battering at one spot had its inevitable result. Little by little the stone-work crumbled as the eighteen-pounders continued to pour their contents upon it. The fearful din of the rapid bang-bang in the battery was followed by a sound equally loud when the balls reached the fort wall. Every time we fired, a shower of bullets and gingall balls replied to us; while here and there, along the whole curtain, might be seen at uncertain intervals a puff of smoke, and then a firing over head, followed by a sound like "dead," as the ball of the enemy struck a house or a wall hard by. It was great fun to see the bobbing and peeping going on by all in the batteries. If a blue puff was seen to come out from a loop-hole, down went the best and oldest soldier's head while the ball flew past; and there was invariably plenty of time to do so, for the matchlock is not like the rifle, nor does native powder combust so rapidly as ours, consequently the flight of the bullet is slower, although sometimes fatally true, and then, alas! too quick. On the evening of the 26th, about 9 P.M., the village at the foot of the fort was fired by a party of our force. It was but a partial burning, and the next morning the place looked none the worse for the fire-brand. To proceed upon this work of destruction our men had to descend the front part of the mound we occupied, cross over a portion of the lake running between it and the fort and village, and expose themselves, then and there, to the whole enemy in the fort, as well as any who may be in the village. It was no laughable duty, but they effected their purpose, and returned in safety.

A spy of the enemy's was taken by one of our pickets dressed up as a fakeer. He told us some hundred of the enemy were killed and wounded on the day of the action before the fort, and about twenty horses wounded and killed. On the night of the 27th Oct. a second firing party volunteered to enter the town again between us and the fort, and to attempt a more effectual destruction than followed the first trial. The volunteers were Major Woolcomb, Lieuts. Strutt and Christie, and some men of the Bombay artillery, Lieut. Fenwick and a company of the 25th Regiment N. I. This party was accompanied by a native guide, who trembled like a leaf with fear, although a large reward was to be paid him when the business was over. They went in silence about 9·30 P.M. It was a bright moonlight night, and we feared lest the enemy should take cognizance of this small body. They crept down from the front of our battery, crossed over the valley below, skirted the water's edge, and were then lost to us among the trees and cottages. A blaze soon sprang up from one spot, then another, and another, and we could see the burning port-fire flung through the air to other houses. The conflagration spread faster and faster, and the whole town was enveloped in flames flickering high and broad; then arose a din of voices, amid volleys of musketry, rattling, and screams, and howlings of dogs. Roof after roof tumbled in, and soon the village was one huge burning pile, overshadowed by curling clouds of smoke dancing high above the flames, and darkening the bright starry sky. It was a gorgeous sight, and if beauty could accompany such a picture, it was there, as every flame, and cloud, and burning timber lay reflected, bright and changing, on the still bosom of the lake below. They all returned from this errand in safety, after having despatched some of the enemy, and run the gauntlet back to our battery through the scorching flaming streets.

The timid guide having lost his way and presence of mind totally, our people had to return almost the same way as they went. Lieut. Christie missed his path across the lake, and, while floundering and swimming about to get to the shore, was greeted by a shower of grape from one of his own guns as he rose up all dripping from the water, crying out, "Don't shoot me!" This probably saved his life, as another charge was ready for him.

Our eighteen-pounders and twenty-four pound howitzer had made a considerable hole in the curtain by the morning of the 29th. Enormous masses of stone rolled down after each weighty succussion from our metal. Still the enemy were just as vigilant and annoying to us. Rifle-shooting against such walls availed but little, even from the most patient and practised shot. The sharp report of the rifle was generally followed by a second sound of the lead flattening itself against the walls, while the enemy could walk leisurely along the ramparts inside, take their aim and discharge their pieces in perfect safety. By the time our riflemen saw the puff, and could take their aim, they had sauntered away to some other part; and so twenty men behind walls could thus easily engage the attention and harass hundreds outside. Two men were wounded this day in the battery, one shot in the head the other in the hip. The breach was widening rapidly, and now we could see the thickness of the walls, which was astonishing. This evening the brigadier received a letter from the fort requesting to know upon what terms a surrender would be granted. An unconditional one was the reply, to which they said, "Very good, we don't care; you are only destroying the Rajah of Dhar's property, not ours; we have only lost a few men, but our cattle are being killed by the shells." So we went on with the siege.

The enemy now commenced to escape from the north and east faces of the fort in the night-time by means of a rope and basket. We captured almost all of them, most being disguised in some way or other, some as fakeers, others in women's clothes. On the morning of the 30th the enemy hoisted the white flag—wily dogs!

For some time there was considerable altercation in our heavy-gun battery about noticing the flag of truce. All the while this fierce war of words, and senior-officership, and commands, &c. was being carried on by the various officers who poured into the battery, the gunners continued to load and fire sharper than ever. The white flag popped up over the parapet, and whiz went the rifle at it, but the fellow was too knowing to expose himself; up and down it went, and at length the order to "cease firing" was given; the eighteen-pounders were loaded and must be discharged, and bang, bang they went; then all was quiet. The staff then came up, and a vakeel was sent up to the fort gate to hear what they had to say. During the conference of the vakeel with the enemy at the gate our men swarmed outside the batteries and along the whole face of this mound; the enemy boldly paraded upon the bastions and parapets of the fort, each with his shield, matchlock, and tulwar, walking up and down or quietly sitting to gaze at us; grey-bearded, gaudily-dressed fellows came up to the breach, carefully examined it, and then walked away, and scores of others, all well armed, followed them; they looked down at the rubble and heap of stone-works outside, and then, having thoroughly examined the breach, walked away. By-and-bye the vakeel returned, saying that they requested to know who sent him, when he replied that he was sent by the brigadier; they coolly told him that "they had nothing to do with the sircar, nor could they understand why the sircar was fighting against them, and that had one of the Rajah of Dhar's officers been sent, they would have conferred with him," and then they drove the vakeel away. Of course this was a ruse on their part to gain an opportunity of examining the breach.

They did this thoroughly, and acted accordingly on the following day. The breaching and the shelling from the mortar batteries was resumed with twofold vigour after this instance of impudence. Shell dropped in every part of the fort. The dust caused by one smashing in the roof of the palace had scarcely settled, when another and another followed in its destroying wake, booming loud and terrible when they burst within its rooms. To-day Lieut. Christie, Bombay artillery, was shot through the left chest while pointing a gun. The ball entered about an inch below the heart, and was cut out from the back.

On the 31st the firing was kept up unremittingly from all the batteries, but the enemy grew less annoying; most of them, doubtless, had other business on hand. Two corporals of the Madras sappers volunteered to examine the breach for the storming party, who were now ordered to be in readiness for the night. The men forming the storming party were thirty of the 86th under Lieut. Henry, and sixty of the 25th under Capt. Little, and fifty men of the Madras sappers under Capt. Brown. Corporals Hoskins and Clarke, of the sappers, went off to the breach about ten o'clock; when they arrived at the fort two blank charges were fired from the siege-guns, and they went to the top, made their examination, and returned. The breach was easily ascended. Immediately after this firing was heard and seen on the maidan to the north-west beyond the lake. Dragoons and irregulars were instantly despatched. The storming party were ordered to enter, which they did, unopposed by a soul. The fort was deserted!

That the enemy had fled was soon known, and dragoons and irregulars were sent in pursuit after them. The remainder of the 25th Regiment, with their band, now entered through its many gates, officers who could get there did, and dhooly-bearers; too, with their dhoolies. All crowded into the fort, glad that an end had come to the siege. By-and-bye the brigadier and staff were there; everybody seemed pleased with the success, and the band of the 25th accordingly struck up "God save the Queen!" The night was like day, the music charming, and lacs of treasure and jewels were in the palaces! Officers patted each other on the back in a highly paternal-like, congratulatory manner; our good brigadier was very proper; "he did not care for the money, but was delighted the work was done;" and officers went suooching about through the pestiferous atmosphere and darkened rooms with lightened cheroots, and, of course, set fire to heaps of loose gunpowder and blew themselves up! perhaps because the enemy had not done so. In this way Dr. Butler, Bombay artillery,

Lieut. Thane, Commissary, and Lieut. Giles, 14th Dragoons well nigh ended their brief sojourn in this wicked world. An enormous heap of gunpowder lay in a room, and was exploded forthwith by this trio. Lieut. Thane was in flames in an instant, jumping in the open air like a wild man, and crying out, "Oh, put me out! put me out!" There lay Dr. Butler blown down, horridly burnt, listening to this cry of "Put me out," while other grains of gunpowder were quietly fizzing close to him and running away in tiny combustion in various directions,—may be, to another heap, which would assuredly bring the building about his inquisitive head. Lieut. Giles was more singed than burnt. These gentlemen soon found dhoolies in waiting, and were carried out, in a manner they never dreamt of when they entered it, to their beds that night. The 25th Regiment guarded the palace and the gate and breach, and at some time about the small hours of the morning we retired to our undisturbed beds, the first time for ten days, to dream of the glorious plethoric bags of prize-money promised to the force on the capture of the fort of Dhar, then lying snugly locked up in the huge chests of the treasury of its palace.

That the enemy should have escaped from the fort after what had been said, viz., that "a mouse could not get away unobserved," was indeed a marvel to all. The firing seen by us on the maidan to the north-west, at the moment the breach was entered, was only a skirmish with the tail-end of the enemy and the out-lying picket of 3rd Cavalry, Hyderabad Contingent. The main body had passed by them and the dragoons wholly unobserved, and were well away before the alarm could be of any avail. The pursuers, after a hard ride of some twelve miles, only came up with a few wretched stragglers, some of them were slain, others made prisoners and brought into camp. Those who escaped made the best of their way towards Mundasoor, plundering and destroying various places as they fled. The jemadar commanding the irregular picket was placed in arrest, but it would appear, from the evidence adduced on inquiry, that he was not much to blame. The trooper sent by him to warn the picket of dragoons, after it was known that the enemy were off, fell with his horse on the way and was at once disabled; at the same time the European picket, which had been there for some days, and knew the whole locality well, happened to have been changed the very day of the escape. There was a good deal of noise and animadversion upon this ill-luck in various quarters at the time, and, I fancy, the merit of Brigadier Stuart's siege was robbed of much *éclat* by the censorious inactive world, who fancied they could have done the thing in a way so far better while they sat at home at ease augustly solving the problems of war. But the future has proved how hard a thing it is to manacle your prey, although you may have entrapped him. The slippery foe did not escape from Lucknow, where an overwhelming European force was awfully arrayed against them; they did not escape from Calpee, Jhansi, Gurrakotta, Chandaree, Rhatghur, or from any other of the numberless places and forts wherein they have been caged by us in our superior tactics ! yet I am not aware that the heroes of these said expulsions and captures met with the kindly approbation the world, for the time being, lavished upon the captor of Dhar. Perhaps then more was expected of commanders than the future proved they could accomplish, and this was excusable, in a measure, when we remember that every pulse and passion was swollen into just, burning indignation and unrelenting revenge by the awful deeds of a Nana and his villainous compeers.

To have slain every man of the enemy, I dare say, would have given universal satisfaction. I believe we did fulfil our part in this respect, so far as lay in our power, as will be seen hereafter, in other localities; but I am inclined to the opinion that this kind of warfare has had few ensamples since the time of Joshua.

At Dhar there was much to favour the escape of an enemy who chose to apply the adage,—

> "He who fights and runs away
> May live to fight another day."

Our force was, in reality, very small to effect the reduction of such a stronghold; we were lamentably short of cavalry, as has been the case in almost every instance of the late innumerable actions fought in this rebellion. We had no horse-artillery, and immediately around the fort of Dhar, to the north were extensive plantations of high-grown sugar-cane and jewaree some eight or ten feet high, and darkly-shaded groves of mango and tamarind trees. Now, nothing in the world gives such cover for escape as plateaus of sugar-cane and these gigantic cereals; a foe cannot be seen in them a couple of yards from their edges, and, I would ask, who knows how to turn them to his advantage better than a wily Rohillah or a houseless Pandy? Through these mazes the enemy fled from Dhar, after they had made themselves acquainted with our intentions by carefully inspecting the highway we had forced through its enormously thick walls, and through which the bayonet would, ere long, have been their portion. So they ran the gauntlet to put off the evil day yet a little longer, and left to our keeping the goodly fort with its treasures, and, to our disgust, an air piquant with putrescent carcasses.

In the fort we found a good number of brass guns—about thirty—of various sizes, most of them wretched pieces, rudely mounted, and so honeycombed and ragged at the muzzles that the wonder is they dared fire them at all. Upon the various bastions were heaps of loose gunpowder and rudely hammered balls of all sizes lying about, here and there a cot, a broken sponge, ragged clothes, cooking-pots, and a dead man. All four walls were particularly strong, varying in thickness from twenty to forty feet. The thinnest part, curious to say, was the spot through which we had effected our breach, and this was upwards of eighteen feet! All around the fort in the thickest portions of the walls were dwelling-houses and extensive chambers for stores. On the north side was a long casemated building for troops and horses, sundry sheds, detached buildings, and a gaudy place of worship.

In all of these the enemy had left something or other behind them. Little heaps of grain, powder flasks, belts, shoes, hats, and dirty linen, all lay together in confused heaps; in some rooms there were the tawdry tinsel, hand-punkahs, bits of silk, and broken bangles of their women; the temple they defiled by cooking in and storing their rubbish. In every spot there were evidences of a precipitate flight and the terrible effects of our shells. Copper pots, drums, spears, matchlocks, muskets, bayonets, tulwars, bows and arrows, carpets, tents, wounded horses and bullocks—dying and dead ones—and their own groaning wounded men, conspired to make up a picture of the horrors of war by no means attractive. The palace was literally torn to rags by Woolcomb's admirable mortar practice. It is scarcely possible to credit the wreck and ruin brought about by a few hours' constant shelling upon one spot. The massive pillars and beams of the building were almost torn into shreds by our shell ; and I am inclined to believe that this alone kept the enemy from the treasure known to be there. In the centre of the fort was a large water-tank containing filthy water. This tank was searched, but nothing was found in it. In the inner chambers of the palace was the treasure, and, as reported, the jewels too. A prize-committee had been elected, and were soon busily engaged in counting out the gold and silver. It was a most gratifying spectacle to behold bag after bag disgorging their shining contents of silver and gold ! Each bag of silver contained about 2,500 rupees, the bags of gold mohurs—large and small—varied in value : I believe there were some £15,000 in gold. An enormous chest was opened. First there came out some dingy, fusty cloth ; then some more, and then a huge piece of faded purple velvet, ornamented with a silver border and silver bells (the remains of an elephant's trappings), then beneath this was a chaos of huge silver basins, dishes, plates, cups, lamps, and vases ; and beneath these were several great bags of silver lying at the bottom of the chest side by side, with tightly constricted necks, in solemn repose ; they were unceremoniously hauled out to the companionship of their brethren, and at once counted. Each bag contained its 2,500 rupees. All the time this tedious, yet pleasant business of taking accounts was proceeding, the pick-axe and shovel of the sapper were going deep into hollow-sounding floors and walls. In one dark dusty room we found a large four-post silver bedstead with all its trappings in silver. The posts lay against the mouldy walls in filthy bags, the silver rails, and steps, and bells belonging to the bed, were all lying in a heap upon the floor. The sappers dug and picked about in various places, but no jewels were discovered. They probably lay deeper down in the palatial recesses, or had been carried away by others ; we did not find them, although this treasury was said to be rich in jewels, and the amount captured by our force, including elephants, camels, &c., was something less than nine lacs ; this was sent under an European guard to the fort of Mhow. The bastions and curtains of the fort were partially destroyed by the sappers. Our force was now strengthened by the arrival of Major Orr's column of the Hyderabad Contingent. They marched into Dhar on the evening of 4th November, and again moved out on the 7th for Mahidpore, at which station we now learnt that the enemy from Dhar had been joined by the Mahidpore Contingent, and unitedly seized the guns, destroyed the Europeans, and looted and burnt down the cantonment. This was sad news. Orders were now out for our force to march towards Mundasore, and we started from our encamping ground at Dhar on Sunday the 8th November, at 5 A.M., and by-and-bye entered the territories of Scindiah. As we marched from Dhar we left that once stately fort behind us a heap of ruins, the palace and gates burning piles. The flames shot up from the crackling masses beneath them in wild luridity, and glimmered upon the departing masses in ghastly beams, as they threaded along in silent tramp beneath the shadows of its dismantled bastions and walls. It was a cold morning, and our men gazed upon it for the last time with a savage, unrelenting satisfaction. Prior to our departure from Dhar I took a peep at the town and the palace of the Rajah. I must now tell you what I saw of these places and their infant ruler.

The town is of considerable size, and surrounded by extensive gardens and groves of shadowy fruit-bearing trees, and still further off by tracts of land covered with sugar-cane and gigantic cereals, and is well supplied with water from the two large tanks before mentioned. There are several fine old temples about it. Through the heart of the town runs one main street, which is paved, and from this numerous others diverge in various directions. The houses are generally well built, mostly double-storied, and many of them are embellished with elaborate carvings in wood-work.

Considering the times, it displayed a considerable amount of busy life in various parts. Those localities nearest to the position taken up by us for the breaching batteries had been almost entirely deserted, and for a very good reason, too, as almost all the shot fired by the enemy at us from the fort went into the houses in these parts. I cannot say much for the shops and bazaars I saw open, or praise the articles exposed for sale. Most of the wealthy merchants had absconded, and their dwellings were closed. In the upper stories of many houses one might see the inquisitive eyes of the ladies, old and young, peering down upon you; while below, in the shadow of their porticoes, sat some miserable hanger-on in front of the door locked and bolted behind him. The sight of an European face was not a premium; on the other hand, the inhabitants appeared either too careless or too frightened to court a gaze. The native troops of the Rajah were dressed in a similar garb to our own, and presented arms as one passed by them, though in a slovenly way. I paid a visit to the Rajah, then living in his palace in the town, and a strange place it was for the habitation of Royalty.

After riding through the open gateway of the palace I found myself in the midst of hundreds of idle pompous retainers, lolling and squatting about in various groups. My presence being announced, I alighted, and was ushered up a dark dirty stone staircase into a kind of lobby, from whence I was conducted by several servants through a pillared ante-room, in which sat numerous sage-looking turbanded scribes, all busily engaged, as I imagined, with the affairs of state, if I could judge from the amount of paper, pens, and ink lying about them. Behind these officials numbers of other servants lazily sauntered, all armed with the tulwar, dagger, or matchlock; on one side of this room the windows opened into the square beneath; on the other they were glazed and curtained; and within these the voices of females and children sounded loud enough. Having passed through this apartment I was bowed into another, and politely handed to a dusty seat.

Long before the Rajah made his appearance the Dewan (Chancellor of the Exchequer) came in. He was a middle-aged man, and dressed from head to foot in spotless white cloth. His head was well formed, he had lost the sight of one eye by cataract, his features were of a heavy Mahrattah stamp, and he wore silver spectacles. He appeared to me to be a compound of Hindu profundity and cunning. He was very quiet in manner and polite, and seemed in a very nervous state. He talked a good deal about political matters, seemed very anxious to entertain me in every possible way, expatiated on the long continued friendly relations of the State with the Government, and on the fine character of the late Rajah, whose likeness, admirably executed by Carpenter, he took out of a case to show me. He dusted the glass very carefully, and then contemplated the picture in a profound meditation. A tear stole into his eye and over his cheek as he gazed upon it. The days had indeed changed! The departed Rajah had built the room we then sat in, and evidently had done much to confer an air of elegance and grace upon it, though now it was in a sad condition.

If I say it was filthy I should convey but a faint idea of its state, for it seemed not only so, but in beggarly negligence, too. English couches, and Parisian time-pieces, and tarnished mirrors, and elegantly-made chairs, and bureaus, and tables, and handsome carpets, huddled together in heaps, all covered with dust, lay here and there in sublime disorder and incipient ruin. One or two gaudy coloured prints hung in frames from the walls, and over them the spider had spun his web. Not a clock told the hour of day, for they were all neglected and placed out of the perpendicular, and the glass shades covering them had acquired quite a hoary cap of dust.

By-and-bye there was a murmur from without, the glazed doors opened, and the child Rajah, attended by his uncle and other magnates, all armed, entered into this dingy saloon. I rose up and met his advance, as he waddled along like a little showboy, in a crescent of attendants. He was a mere child, of about ten or eleven years old, of very dark complexion, had a very heavy, unintelligent countenance, and a badly-developed head. He was in mourning for a relative, and, consequently, dressed in a very quiet style. He wore some valuable jewels, and a jeweled-handled dagger in his little waistband. His uncle was also dressed in very sober apparel, of a brick-dust hue, and wore a golden-handled tulwar in a crimson velvet scabbard. He was a quick, shrewd, wiry, little man, had very finely-chiseled features, and looked a soldier in every gesture.

The little Rajah scarcely spoke, the Dewan and uncle did all the talking while the child bowed his sleepy-looking head, very like an automaton, as he sat perched up on his large chair. Perhaps he was frightened out of his wits by what we had been doing about his city and fort; by-and-bye, however, he mustered up courage to speak, and then said, in a little soprano voice, that "the English had always been the friends of Dhar, and that he should make haste to learn their language." The poor boy, I fear, had not much chance of attaining the requisites for this education or wisdom among such people. Sir J. Malcolm's work on India lay upon one of the tables. The Dewan, and one or two others, who knew English well, seemed to prize it very much, and spoke of Malcolm Sahib in very eulogistic terms! Every one of them appeared in a highly nervous state of mind as to the probable results of their present unfortunate political position, and anxious to glean from any one a hope that Dhar would not meet with the fate of so many other vaster states in India—annexation.

Having concluded my visit, I took my departure. I was shown out by the uncle of the Rajah, who took me by the arm, and behaved in a most courteous manner, bidding me adieu as warmly as he might have done by an old friend.

I have nothing to say upon the political merits or demerits of their case. It would appear that they had acted in some very unwise manner, if we are to judge by the bearing of the Governor-General's political agent towards them, for in a day or two after my visit the old Dewan was sent a prisoner into Mhow.

CHAP. III.

March to Oneil.—News of the battle of Rawul, defeat of mutineers.—Gallant conduct of Capt. Abbott and Lieut. Johnson.—The Rohillah.—Taul; Nawab of Jaôra.—Difficult position of native princes.—Crossing the river Chumbul.—Hernia, execution of mutineers.—Before Mundasoore, the affair of the 21st November.—Flank march past Mundasoore.—Battle of Mundasoore, and "relief of Neemuch."—March to Mundasoore, capture of rebels, execution of rebels, Mundasoore city.—March to Mahidpore. Execution of rebels.—Oojein.—March to Indore, state of residency, Durbar of Maharajah Holkar.—Departure of Col. Durand.—Remarks on Malwa.—Advent of Major-General Sir Hugh Rose, and Sir Robert Hamilton.

WE continued our march through Western Malwa towards Mundasoore in pursuit of the enemy. At every place we encamped we heard of the doings of the rebels who had preceded us. In several of Scindiah's villages and towns they had plundered the inhabitants, beaten them, and carried away their women. On our arrival at Oneil, on the 14th November, a despatch came into camp from Major Orr, who had overtaken the enemy and the mutinous contingent of Mahidpore near the village of Rawul. The news was as startling as it was gratifying.

Major Orr with his force had followed upon their heels so quickly that they were taken by surprise in their fancied security near the village of Rawul. He instantly engaged them. They had placed the Mahidpore guns into position loaded with grape. These guns were charged by Captain Abbott, Lieutenant Johnstone, and their sowars. As they rode up to them the enemy fired, and the grape passed over their heads, with a rushing noise like a covey of birds. In another instant they were upon the guns, sabreing the enemy. The rout then became general, and the fighting continued until the sun went down. Lieuts. Clark and Murray's horses were shot under them; Lieut. Samwell was dangerously wounded in the abdomen by a ball, and nearly 100 were killed and wounded on our side !

The guns were retaken with all their ammunition, quantities of loot, carts, bullocks, tattoos, &c., some 150 of the enemy were slain, and between 70 and 80 taken prisoners. The remainder fled to Mundasoore. In this instance, again, the escape of the rebels was favoured by the luxuriant crops of sugar-cane and jewaree, through which it is next to impossible to follow them.

In chronicling the events of war it is scarcely just to recount the deeds of bravery performed by the conquering host alone. However vile our enemy may be, or however just the plea of warfare carried on to extermination against them, one ought not to shrink from paying tribute to the brave, though they be our foe. In the Rohillah one encounters an implacable antagonist. His life, his position, his faith, lead him to look upon death with cold and dignified indifference. He is a fatalist, and thus life or death are to him as one. If fate wills that he dies in the heat of battle, death has but unloaded him of his burden at the journey's end, that he may enjoy the best of rest—eternal luxury and sleepy beatitude.

To relate one little incident will suffice to show how these men face death and die upon the battle field.

In this encounter with the enemy and the Mahidpore Contingent, Doctor Orr of the Hyderabad Contingent came up with one of the Rohillahs who was dressed in a very superior manner. He was a fine fellow, and perhaps a leader. He was requested to surrender, this he refused to do ; he was then told that unless he did so, death would assuredly be his portion. At this he scoffed and boldly defied the officer to combat. Then ensued the struggle for life in deadly conflict, which he manfully maintained upon foot till the cold sharp spear of his antagonist pierced his breast ; he then fell upon the field, cast an agonised withering look of a still unvanquished spirit at his foe, threw his arm across his eyes, and died without a groan! The Rohillah affects to despise death,—his faith teaches him that to die thus is to enter at once into the elysium of the blest, where every sensual pleasure will be meted out to him in undying sunny ripeness. Cradled in war, nurtured in arms, imbued with a pompous sense of their all-saving faith for time and eternity, proud by nature, and daring by habit, it is no wonder he forms a figure of no mean type in our pictures of the battle-field, or a foe by no means despicable in single combat.

I have seen him rush into the jaws of death as boldly as though the shackles of "age, ache, penury, and imprisonment" had just been loosed, and a career as free and boundless as the wild horse's were before him. Nor can we wonder at this, for Mahomet tells them in his Koràn, "the sword is the key of heaven and hell. A drop of blood shed in the cause of God, or one night spent in arms, is of more avail than two months in fasting and prayer. Whosoever falls in battle, his sins are forgiven; at the day of judgment his wounds shall be resplendent as vermilion, and odorous as musk; and the loss of his limbs shall be replaced by the wings of angels and cherubim!"

In our pursuit of the enemy we passed through the town of Taul in the little state of the Nawab of Jaôra. Here we learnt that they had departed

THE ROHILLAH:—TAUL, NAWAB OF JAÔRA.

some hours prior to our approach, after having frightened the good folk there out of their senses.

The town was saved from loot or ransom by the enemy by a curious incident. They had determined to plunder the town or have 30 lacs of rupees paid to them, as ransom. A debate ensued among them as to whether they should accept 25 lacs—the sum offered by the people—or 30, the amount they demanded. The folk could or would only muster 25, the enemy had set their hearts upon 30, so they conferred, and quibbled, and argued until sunset, when the sound of a bugle was reported to the counsellors; this put a period to their deliberations, they struck their camp and fled, *minus* the ransom offered by the inhabitants, or the loot they intended to appropriate in its stead.

As we marched into Taul, the Nawab of Jaôra was there with an anxious retinue to welcome our presence. He was a fine young man in every sense of the word, very enlightened, and desirous to continue a friendship with us which had already lasted for years. He was well known to many of our force who had joined in the chase, the race, and festivities with him in former times. His liberality was as large as his purse, and every mile of his territory bore evidences of the wisdom of his rule. His villages were clean, well-built, and inhabited by people who furthered our progress with a willing, unsparing hand. The difficulties these princes had to contend against were exceedingly trying at this season. The struggle between affection and duty; the babble of deluded masses of dependants whose spirits were swollen and flushed by cunning and weaning promises of riches and power; the importunities of unwise officials, and the dread of being alone and pennyless, if perchance their British allies should be driven into the seas, were incentives strong enough to draw these lords of little principalities from the attraction of an apparently waning star into the fast increasing circle of satellites, then moving in erratic turbulence around the blazing meteor of rebellion.

Nor was it to be expected that these men *could* know how soon the orb then dazzling the moral heavens would sink dark and deep below the bloodstained horizon, and in its awful fall drag the lesser lights in its train down to worse than perdition.

To have placed implicit reliance upon our word *then* must have been a hard and trying exercise of faith, and, indeed, all who did so deserve no small encomium. If the British nation *can* accept a compliment, I think the adherence of these princes in such a season, surrounded as they were by sedition and conspiracy, was one of no mean character.

Only a few days prior to our entry into Jaôra, the fever of rebellion had struck the Court of the

Nawab, and carried away his *brother* and some thousands of armed followers. Hardly, indeed, must his trust in our truth and power have been tried; it was a fiery furnace through which they had to walk, and those who lacked faith were irreclaimably lost.

We were on the move again and fast nearing the city of Mundasoore, and on 19th November we pitched our camp at Hernia on the banks of "the Chumbul." We were now only some 20 miles from a large force, as spies gave out, consisting of Mekranies, Rohillahs, Villayates, and mutinous sepoys, altogether about 5,000. They were reported to have got guns into position, and to be making 400 pounds of gunpowder daily, and best of all that they had determined to give us battle upon the open field. How they had come to this determination I cannot say. Another spy also informed us that they had given it out in Mundasoore that they had defeated us at Dhar, and that they were now going to destroy utterly the few remaining of the "Feringhees" who had the temerity to follow them so far. And so I presume they paraded and stalked about the city and did as they generally do until they are ousted by an irresistible pressure from without. When we arrived at the beautiful river Chumbul, we expected a resistance from the opposite banks ; but, no, there was this admirable barrier to the progress of a force left entirely to us, and we forthwith commenced crossing.

It was a business of no light nature, for the banks were rugged and almost perpendicular, the river very rapid and deep, and its bed broken by enormous boulders of basalt. The crossing of the force, ammunition, and baggage occupied us nearly two whole days. The sappers had to cut a road down the bank for the artillery and carriage, and again up the opposite bank, for the late rains had quite obliterated any former road.

I never saw a more animated and beautiful picture in my life than when our brigade crossed this river. The steep, verdant, shrubby banks covered with our varied forces, elephants, camels, horses, and bullocks ; the deep flowing clear river reaching on and on to the far east to the soft deep-blue tufted horizon ; the babble and yelling of men, the lowing of the cattle, the grunting screams of the camels, and the trumpeting of the wary heavily-laden elephant ; the rattle of our artillery down the bank, through the river, and up the opposite side ; the splashing and plunging of our cavalry through the stream—neighing and eager for the green encamping ground before them ; and everybody so busy and jovial, streaming up from the deep water to their respective grounds; and all this in the face, almost, of an enemy, formed a *tableau vivant* never to be forgotten!

We halted a day after having crossed the river, and during this day the prisoners taken at Rawul were tried, sentenced, and executed. I remember at this time, so great was the indignation felt by us, that the question often asked was " why take any prisoners ?" They should all be slain in the heat of the fray, for Englishmen are prone to leniency in their calmer moments, and even a drum-head court-martial is not so awful a thing as it sounds.

To hamper a force with a large body of prisoners is doubtless a troublesome thing, and perhaps appears foolish, but we must remember that flesh and blood—even the hardy Anglo-Saxon's—cannot go on slaying from sunrise to sunset. However willing the spirit may be, physical force cannot endure it. Soldiery tire in the limb after great exertion as well as other good people, and thus it happens after a battle, when the animal spirit is exhausted by heat and long-continued excitement, that many prisoners must be made.

Among the batch of prisoners now in camp was one who murdered the serjeant-major and his family at Mahidpore, and who boasted of it, too; a boy of about fifteen, who endeavoured to betray Mrs. Timmins, the commandant's wife; and an *armless* man, on whose person letters were found. This cripple from his mother's womb was their spy—a most unsuspicious character to look at, of course, but a better for a spy could not have been found. The child murderer was told he would be shot or hanged, to which he replied "*very* good, I don't care!" and was "sorry he could not kill more!"

A parade of the troops was ordered at 5 P.M. The prisoners—some 76—were brought up, ranged in one long line and blindfolded, then advanced dragoons upon foot, men of the 86th, and the ragged few of the Mahidpore Contingent who remained staunch, to within a couple of yards of them. Their sentence and the reasons thereof were then read aloud by Captain Coley, brigade-major. Then there was a wail and groaning from some, while others cried out to the last " deen, deen !" But their *deening* soon ended, as the brigade-major rode past and said, " fire at the sound of the bugle !"

The bugle sounded! and a long rattle of musketry swept this fleshy wall of miscreants from their earthly existences. In one short moment they were no more than the clod they fell upon, and were covered by! The pale moon rose in silent beauty, and shone on our Sappers in coldly beams as they dug the mighty grave for their gory carcasses. The earth soon covered them, and our camp appeared as though no scene of blood had marked it; in a few more hours the bugle and drum called us away to other scenes of danger and death. This was a terrible ensample, few soldiers had ever witnessed such a scene, still fewer, perhaps, will see its like again.

On the morning of the 21st November, we arrived at our encamping ground before Mundasoore. Immediately in our front was high rising ground, and in front to the left of this a little village and gardens, beyond this several large topes, cultivated ground, and another village surrounded by gardens and trees; on our right were hills and villages, and between these and the hill in our front was an extensive plateau covered here and there with acres of uncut grain, and beyond this the city of Mundasoore. A reconnaissance was made while the camp was being pitched, and the men breakfasted. Our pickets occupied advanced positions in our front, and the village on our left. We could see the enemy mustering in force below the town, and their yellow and green flags waving about.

Affair before Mundasoore.

There now appeared some chance of a little excitement and open fieldwork. About 1 P.M., just as we were all enjoying our breakfast, and speculating upon the probabilities of an engagement, the bugles sounded! Breakfast and all the good things were soon left to the care of servants, and every man buckled on his sword and pistol, as the various officers were calling out to their men to " fall in — fall in."

The jingling of the dragoons as they galloped past to the front, the dashing rumble of the artillery, the clinking of steel as the bright bayonets were fixed, the straggling sowars swiftly threading their way, spear in hand, to the front, and the dashing right and left, backwards and forwards, of the staff, gave an air of glancing brilliance most attractive to witness. Most of our force were the heroes of other battle-fields, and they emerged out of the apparent confusion of the camp in an order of battle array as pleasing as a picture.

The enemy had advanced in force upon our left, and occupied the village in which we had placed a small picket, who retired. They also formed up into two considerable masses upon the maidan, their left resting upon Mundasoore. The Bengal battery, under Captain Hungerford, the Bombay battery, under Captain Woolcomb, were on our right centre, and the bullock battery of the H. C. on the left; the dragoons to our extreme right, the Hyderabad cavalry to our extreme left; the 86th and 25th regiments were in our centre ; the Madras sappers and Hyderabad infantry, under Capt. Sinclair, were on the left of the Hyderabad guns, and opposite to the village occupied by the enemy. The artillery worked away in a most animating style for some three quarters of an hour. Lieut. Strutt's shooting was very true. All the while this firing was going on at the village, a fine fellow, dressed in white, with a green flag, coolly walked out from the cover, and sauntered leisurely along the whole line of our guns, while round shot and shell were whizzing about him in awful proximity. He occasionally stooped down, but never attempted to run; he then quietly retraced his steps, when a shot from Lieut. Strutt struck him just before he regained the village. Such a feat is almost incredible. What his object could have been I know not, except that it might have been a daring show of bravery to his fellows. Just now, the enemy in the maidan began to waver; the order was given for the sappers and Hyderabad infantry to occupy the village, which was speedily done, for as they advanced the enemy evacuated it, and fled. The cavalry pursued and cut up a good number of them; the main body then fled into Mundasoore. By 5 o'clock the field was ours. The Hyderabad infantry occupied the village in strength after the sappers had loopholed several walls; and the force returned to camp.

Lieut. Prendergast, Madras Engineers, was shot through the chest when charging with the cavalry. This day the enemy were considerably cut up, for no prisoners were taken. We made a flank movement on the morrow from our last encamping ground, crossed the river " Soor " or " Sonor," and thus got upon the high road to Neemuch, about a couple of miles from Mundasoore. This movement was executed in a most masterly manner. All the baggage, commissariat, &c. passed over in safety, and we were now able to threaten the rebel force around Neemuch, or the enemy in Mundasoore, from an easy position of attack, if needed. As we neared the town in front, still moving on our left flank away from it, the enemy opened fire upon us from a heavy gun, without, however, doing any harm to us. It was amusing to see how we deceived them, as they crowded upon the bastions and walls of the old town to resist our entrance, and had placed guns to command the road to it.

The reason why we moved past Mundasoore and left the enemy in our rear was paramount. All the Europeans in Neemuch had shut themselves up in the fort, and were surrounded by some ten or twelve thousand of the enemy. They had nobly resisted two desperate attacks made by the enemy upon them, but provisions, and ammunition, and strength of body were beginning to fail them. They had sent word to us that they could not hold out many days longer; not that their hearts failed them for a moment, but that the means wherewith to oppose such an overwhelming force were becoming hourly more and more exhausted. To accomplish the relief of this brave little band was our object ; the only fear we entertained was that we might be too late.

Battle of Mundasoore, and Relief of Neemuch.

On the morning of the 23rd November we struck camp, and commenced our march for Neemuch. There was another small stream to cross, and before all the baggage could get over, the enemy came out from Mundasoore to fall upon the rear. The dragoons and two guns soon drove them back. We continued our march now in comfort. The rear guard was formed by a squadron of dragoons, under Lieut. Leith, and two companies of the 25th B. N. I., under Lieut. Fenwick. The column marched slowly, in order to keep the baggage close and compact on our left ; our right was carefully watched by our cavalry. We had marched about five miles upon the road when a halt was sounded. Immediately ahead of the column was a hill with a little house on the top of it. While the halt was going on down the line, we, who had gained the hill, saw something in front of us very like moving masses and flags waving above the high crops of jewaree. They became more and more distinct, and presently we could see a large body of horsemen and two bodies of infantry. It was, indeed, the enemy from Neemuch in force! They had selected a very strong position upon the road, their right resting on the village of Goorariah, their centre on a long hill, and their left well covered by fields of uncut grain, with broken ground, and nullahs in their front full of water and mud. As soon as it was well made out who our friends in front were, the order to send all baggage to the rear in left was given. The enemy were not a mile from us! It was wonderful to see the hulky elephant come trumpeting and trotting to the rear, with his driver almost green with fright, and the unwitting dhooly-bearers, who had strayed, in defiance of all orders, too far ahead with their sick charges, jolting the little life they had in them to pieces as they ran back, and perverse ghorawallas tumbling with fright as they made their retreat into the crowd of baggage, fast collecting in a jumbled mass. The artillery then rattled to the front like a railway train, with terrific impetuosity, the men waving their caps and cheering as they flew past to open fire!

The 86th marched down, forming into double line on the right of the guns; the 25th coolly fixed bayonets, unfurled their standard, and with the

BATTLE OF MUNDASOORE. 111

Madras sappers, *en echelon*, on their left, moved up in double line as beautifully as on a parade ground to the enemy's centre, from whence their guns now opened a sharp and heavy fire; left of these was the Hyderabad infantry; the Hyderabad Contingent battery opened from our left centre, and on either flanks were the dragoons and irregular cavalry.

Just as we were all hurrying down towards the enemy, I saw a string of *nineteen* other prisoners in charge of a guard of Hyderabad infantry, also marching down to the front. As it was evident every available man would be required for the battle, which had now commenced in earnest, this guard was relieved of their present duty by the instant despatch of these rebels.

We pounded away, and the enemy answered us with alacrity. As our infantry advanced they were met by an advance from the infantry of the enemy, and then commenced the rattle and din of musketry. They came down from their heights, with scores of banners and flags of all colours flying, with considerable spirit to within a few yards of our infantry. Major Robertson with his regiment charged them, and drove them back. Great numbers of them got into a deep nullah, and here we lost many valuable fellows. Lieut. Martin, of the late 3rd Bengal Cavalry, with some score of dragoons charged the enemy's guns and cut down the gunners; by some accident or other he was not supported, and so had to retire, having received a bullet wound in the knee. They were again charged and captured. The enemy continued to fight hard every inch of the ground, falling back upon the village on their right. Those who had not the chance of doing so fled along the Neemuch road, and in other directions through fields. The cavalry cut up great numbers in these fields. The infantry then moved upon the village, passing over nullahs filled with the enemy, and in these nullahs we lost a good many men. Numbers had taken to the trees, and hidden themselves in stacks of grass, and as our men passed them they fired upon them, and were then slain in return. Those in the trees dropped down like birds, and those who would not come out of the hay-stacks were burnt to death in them! One fellow actually remained in a stack of grass until his head was on fire, and then rushed out, the very picture of a hell-fire demon, yelling and mad! The enemy now opened a very sharp fire of musketry from this village. One fellow, more daring than the rest, or infuriated by liquor, rushed out of the village towards our infantry, fired his matchlock, then threw it away, and came running and capering down the hill, brandishing his sword a thousand ways, and jumping round and round like a maniac, untouched, though scores of

BATTLE OF MUNDASOORE.

bullets were fired at him; he even passed through the skirmishers of the 25th, and continued his antics, but a private with fixed bayonet advanced from the line to the front and awaited his approach, and, when within reach, struck him to the earth. To say that he did not seek this death would be absurd; he might have avoided it as others did, but he chose to run his race in his own particular way. He might have been insane—perhaps he was.

Another fellow essayed to follow his example, but when he saw his friend fall he thought better of it, and turned tail like a shot. We had now surrounded the village with infantry, cavalry, and our artillery, but the enemy kept up such a constant heavy fire that we could only advance to within a few yards of it. To have wasted more life in a forcible expulsion by our infantry would have been absurd, as the after events proved. It was, therefore, surrounded, and our infantry was drawn off for the night. About mid-day, when the battle was raging hot in our front, the rear-guard was attacked by a strong body from the city of Mundasoore. They were fiercely engaged by the dragoons, while the guns threw into their midst shell and shot. The 24-pound howitzer was served with great precision by a havildar of the Madras sappers, and soon discomfited them. In the charge of the dragoons, in this sharp encounter, Lieut. Redmayn was shot.

The enemy had gained a piece of ground in their retreat broken by deep pits, like rifle-pits, over which cavalry could make no way with certainty. Lieut. Redmayn's horse had carried him too far ahead of his men, so not only was he shot by the enemy, but robbed, and literally hacked to pieces. When his body was brought in, no feature could be distinguished. His horse, sword, pistol, and watch had been looted by these quick-fingered butchers, ere the dragoons could regain the body, and then, oh! what a mangled corpse! Wild beasts could scarcely have done more. No wonder we spared them not after such instances of tiger-like conduct. They are not content with the death of their enemy, but in all cases they hack them to pieces after death, and often decapitate them, and desecrate their narrow graves! But then, this is no new feature of Hindu manners and customs; from time immemorial their warfare has been stamped by the vilest excesses.

Night drew on apace, and the enemy in the village continued to show their determination not to succumb, although, by this time, it was one huge blazing fire all around them; death staring them in the face on every side. Our camp was pitched; the killed and wounded on our side was great; we had upwards of sixty officers and men killed and *hors-de-combat* by this action. It was a wearying day for most of us, and our beds were sought with not small anticipation of enjoying a well-earned repose. We were, however, doomed to be disappointed, for about midnight the alarm sounded, and the whole force was under arms again, weary, shivering, and wondering what was afoot. We were agreeably surprised to find that the alarm was caused only by our pickets firing upon the enemy endeavouring to escape from the village, so we turned in again, not a little rejoiced to think that we might yet comfort ourselves in the warm arms of Morpheus.

About 10 A.M. the next morning, the 18-pounders and 24-pound howitzer were brought up to within two hundred and fifty yards of the village, to destroy by shell and shot all who doggedly remained and continued to fire upon us. We shelled and tumbled the place into atoms about their heads; all that could burn had been consumed; the place was a mere burnt shell, yet they held out like fiends to the last. About mid-day some two hundred and twenty came out and surrendered, and at 4 P.M. the 86th regiment, the 25th Bombay N. I., and Madras sappers stormed the place, and thus ended the four days' fighting. The Rohillahs fought to the last. There was a good deal of slaying in the houses, and great difficulty experienced by our men in getting about the place, *for there was no street in it, and the houses led from each other into little yards and gullies like a rabbit-warren.* A stronger place could not well be imagined.

It grew dark and we retired again to our camp for the night. We had not been in bed more than three hours when the alarm again sounded and the whole force turned out, by-and-bye to retire again as before. This turn out was not without its good effects, as we learnt on the morrow when we marched back upon Mundasoore, for the five or six hundred rebels *then* in this city believed we were bent upon entrapping them, and consequently absconded without waiting for further proofs of our intentions!

The Field after the Battle.

A battle-field immediately after an action is no very inviting scene. More than one sense is sickened by the objects around; the air is tainted, and death stares you in the face in most hideous forms; swollen and bloated carcasses covered with vultures or being torn to pieces by the pariah dogs; corpses lying drawn up in a heap burnt to a cinder; some without a vestige of clothing, others lying peacefully as they fell; the village was almost too foul to pass through, almost every house had its inmates of dead in some ghastly form or other—what the sword had commenced fire had ended.

THE FIELD AFTER THE BATTLE. 117

Death and black ruin lay everywhere together. Spite all this, one old woman, who seemed nearly eighty years of age, had remained there a witness of the fearful consummation. Perhaps she was too feeble to fly, or held the little life then flowing in her veins as too worthless to prolong. She appeared starving as she sat on a stone feebly sighing and drinking water from a little earthen vessel. There was no one to comfort her, and the soldiery passed her by as they would a dog!

Down a well not far from the village we found a man hiding in a recess of the earth. How long he had been there no one knew, but he was too feeble to ascend by a rope which was thrown down to him. However, we helped him up, and when he gained the top he was too weak to stand. Some brandy-and-water and native bread was offered to him by Major Boileau, but this he refused as he might have done poison, although he appeared dying from starvation! another was discovered in a tree, where he must have been for three days. He refused at first to come down, a musket was pointed at him which had the desired effect; down he came, matchlock, tulwar, and powder-horn, too. In his belt we found eighty-eight rupees. This the men divided, and the bird was made a prisoner and sent into camp. In one of the fields an old woman was found with her right leg shattered by a shell;

in another *a little girl, of about nine,* with her left leg shattered! She had come with her father, who had been a sowar of the Nawab of Jaôra. All over the maidan were scattered English books, papers, envelopes, ladies' silk-dresses covered with blood, bonnets, parasols, elegant drawing-room chairs, and other things the rebels had plundered from Neemuch and other stations. The village still smouldered; the high crops were all beaten down; the earth torn up; nullahs filled with broken furniture, dead cattle and men; black heaps of ashes lay here and there, with charred corpses in their centres; the air was laden with sickening gases, in which vultures, kites, and crows circled and screamed, and circled over the horrid carcasses below; wretched camp-followers were prowling among the corpses and ruins—women, laughing and trampling through the broken corn,—men, turning about mangled bodies, diving into wells and tanks, climbing trees, and breaking down grain stacks—all searching for plunder like cowardly assassins, and revelling in the horrors of death like fiends!

Thus it fell out that Neemuch was relieved, and the rebel force which had fallen upon Mundasoore was dispersed and destroyed. Either their Mundasoore friends had wofully deceived them, or they had miserably miscalculated upon British prowess. The one thing is quite evident, they would never have left Neemuch to have coped with us in the field had they known of our movement the day before. Had we been a day later they would have united their forces in Mundasoore and necessarily have given us fourfold trouble. The result would, doubtless, have been the same, though considerably protracted by the cover and resources a fine large city would have given to them. As it was, we found no little difficulty in ousting them out of the village of Goorariah. What would it have been had they occupied the fort and extensive city of Mundasoore? They would probably have served us the same trick they did at Dhar, and have made for *that* fort again or *Indore*, while we should have had a work of no slight magnitude to have watched their movements and reduced the city and fort. The results testify fully to the importance of these battles, as will be seen hereafter.

I cannot pass away from the late scenes of excitement and death without paying a tribute to the exalted tone of the sepoys of the 25th regiment, and this becomes more prominent, considering the troublous times in which we were playing the grand game of hold-fast against such hordes of enemies. During the heat of the battle of the 23rd the sepoys of the 25th regiment suffered considerably; they came into the field hospital suffering from every description of wounds—arms and legs shattered by round shot, limbs and body perforated by musket-bullets and flesh wounds of no slight nature. To see these men as they sat or lay down in the burning sun enduring all the excruciating agonies their wounds had caused them, while the surgeons were busy with others who had preceded them, was truly noble. The general observation made by them was "Ah ! well, never mind, we have eaten the Sircar's salt for many years ; this has been good work, and the Sircar will be good and take care of us, or our families if we die." One poor fellow, whose blood was welling away profusely from a wound near the shoulder-joint, was offered a little brandy-and-water as a stimulant, when he nobly said "Give it to my brother first," who sat next to him groaning in agony; he then drank and said he "did not mind his wound, for he knew Government would not forget him!" Not a man refused to take what was offered to him as drink— even then, all-shunned wine was willingly accepted by them ; and when an amputation was performed, they bore it with heroic fortitude, for although chloroform was not administered, scarcely a groan escaped while the dreadful knife was severing the member from its body. In action they were cool, gallant, and intrepid ; under the painful ordeal of the surgical operation they displayed patience, cheerfulness, and fortitude.

CAMP AT MUNDASOORE.

As we marched back to pitch our camp under the walls of Mundasoore we were met by scores of the inhabitants tomtoming and salaăming. Some were crying out that they had been awfully looted by the rebels—particularly the sowcars—which I believe to be a lie; others bowing and cringing in all the dirty obsequiousness of a native who knows that the weaker has "gone to the wall;" and then there were children skipping and trotting along as naked as they were born, evidently enjoying the arrival of our host as they would have done any other army; and women, old and young, sauntering in groups, and tattered beggars, lame and blind, with their empty polished shells before them, and dogs looking heavenward and howling out our advent as we swept along, an august, conquering cavalcade!

After having pitched our camp several of us strolled into the town and up to the fort. The bazaar was open in the main street leading towards the fort, and a fine one it was. The houses were rather imposing, compared with those of other native towns, and all of them appeared occupied. The towns-people were evidently mortally afraid of our presence, for they flitted about from house to house like shadows, closing their doors behind them with a slam as we passed along. The fort, which once ranked as a first-class one, was fast tumbling to decay. It was occupied by a few of

Scindiah's sowars, who lolled about apathetically, watching our movements like cats. There were a few play-things in the shape of ordnance loaded to their muzzles with rudely hammered grape-shot, a few broken gun-carriages, some of which had recently been repaired by the enemy, and a hundred worthless pieces of rebel camp lumber lying in different directions.

I asked one of these fine gentlemen how it was that they had allowed the enemy to enter their master's fort, when he replied in a tone and accent that might have come from the lips of a London fop, "You see, when a large army comes to a place like this, and there are but few of us inside, we must doubtless run away—*buss*, enough!"

I did, indeed, think such an explanation from the bloated, emasculated fop, *enough!* These are the specimens of officers Scindiah then rejoiced in—no wonder they played their own lord and master false in the hereafter. The sun shines—it is *buss;* storm comes and drives them about like the seared leaves of the forest, and it is *buss* still; they gorge and sleep upon the very mine that is to explode and blow them to atoms, and that, too, is *buss*. Stolid indifference to anything in this world, save their own extensible paunches and purses, forms the main trait of their characters, and when they have filled them, they complacently stroke their moustaches and sigh out *buss,* as they take their pipes, indifferent of time, the world, or eternity! The crack of doom might sound, and I verily believe they would call for their pipes, and console themselves with *buss!*

Having satisfied ourselves of the feasibility of breaching this said fort—supposing it had required that terrific way of announcing our wish to come in—we strolled back again, taking another street for inspection. We made many inquiries of the inhabitants as to whether any of the enemy remained concealed in the town. At first they feared to confide in us, although they had salaămed and welcomed our arrival the hour previous. By-and-bye, however, one came forward and volunteered to show us several large houses in which the rebels had concealed themselves. While pointing out these dens the fellow trembled, and paled like ashes. We made up to one, burst open the doors, and there we found them engaged in the preparation of a meal. In this house there were seven men, two or three women, and their children. Tattoos and oxen stood in the yard. In the house we found the caps, boots, bayonets, and belts of the Mahidpore mutineers, tulwars, spears, matchlocks, and ammunition. Among other things was the beautiful sword of the late Capt. Tucker of Neemuch, who had fallen in one of the encounters with the enemy outside the fort, *and whose grave they had opened, severed the head from the body, and carried it away upon a pole and exposed it outside this city gate for several days!* They all pleaded not guilty, of course, although these evidences were before their eyes. One fellow was dressed up as a wild, savage-looking fakeer, and swore he was only a poor mendicant; this, however, was speedily disproved by a Madras sapper, who pulled off the matted-hair wig of the fakeer, and there and then displayed the close-cut crop of the sepoy: they were all made prisoners. In another house pointed out, a *burra sahib* was said to have closeted himself. We had great difficulty in forcing an entrance through the door, which he had barricaded within with a ladder resting against the opposite wall. At last we rushed in and there were three tattoos, saddled and ready for a trot, and a couple of spears, but no *burra sahib*. In the three rooms there was a large quantity of European loot, Commissioner's papers, and wax seals, looking-glasses, and the Korân; two large camel-trunks padlocked—full of European rubbish; but the man was gone although all had been fastened from within and escape seemed impossible. There was an upstair room also, shut up, this we examined, and were just leaving it when a cot in a corner was seen to move. "Here he is!" was the exclamation, and sure enough there was the great rebel Mikrani in his hiding-place. The *burra harámzáda*, as the towns-folk called him, was caught ; and now, they seemed more inclined to point out others.

In another part of the town a dragoon was strolling in undress, when a great fellow rushed out of a house with a terrific looking knife and commenced an attack upon him ! The dragoon sustained some severe cuts, for he had no arms, but got the fellow down, wrested his knife from him, and slew him. This villain was the kotwal of the enemy, and a good riddance. Others were found with recently blood-stained garments upon them and wounded, and almost every hour of the day prisoners were being brought into camp from the neighbouring villages. One fellow—a Rohillah—was asked who he was and where he came from? He refused to tell his name, and said in a scornful voice, " He had no country, knew no time, no master,—the *world* was *his* home ! "

We had now upwards of two hundred prisoners, and the drum-head court was sitting all day.

Prisoners were brought in also *from the villages with their noses cut off*—thus the strong Hindus do by their weak and fugitive brothers. Had we been worsted they would have done the same by us ; this is their way of showing allegiance to the conquering power !

A rebel jemadar—Cassim Khan—was hiding in

a village some miles off. A body of Hyderabad irregular cavalry under Lieut. Johnston went out to bring him in, dead or alive. He was caught, and while they were preparing the rope to bind him, he slipped under a horse's belly and was off. He was pursued and killed, and his head brought into camp. This head and that of the kotwal were then hoisted upon poles in front of the city gate, and the people beat them with their shoes—the cringing hypocrites! They had done the same to the head of Capt. Tucker, who had been slain by the rebels at Neemuch a short time before.

On the 30th of November a general parade of troops was ordered for the evening. The troops assembled and formed three sides of a square, three guns occupying the fourth. By-and-bye twenty-six prisoners were brought up, three of whom were the subadar major, the subadar, and jemadar of the Mahidpore artillery; these three were tied to the guns and blown into atoms. The twenty and three others were then blindfolded and shot by musketry! So ended the lives of these murderers. The head of Capt. Tucker was discovered buried in a basket beneath a grove of trees near our camp. It was sent back to Neemuch, to be again interred with the mangled trunk the rebels had left there.

Several of the officers from Neemuch came into our camp and told us how desperate an attack the force we had defeated had made upon the fort there on the night of the 21st. They had constructed a huge kind of covered ladder upon wheels, which they rolled along under its shelter close to the walls, but they were met by such a murderous fire that they retired, after three attempts at escalade, with howlings and wailings. On the morrow they were gone, and in due season received from our hands the chastisement I have detailed.

A considerable breach was effected in one of the walls of the fort of Mundasoore by the Madras sappers, so as to render the place untenable by a foe, should another spring up in this part of the world. Capt. Keatinge was installed, *pro tempore*, in the political charge of this city, and the force prepared to march back upon Indore *viâ* Mahidpore. Major Orr was to remain behind with his force of Hyderabad troops.

It can scarcely be doubted that the whole country would have been against us to a man had we not have achieved these victories over the rebel forces. The aspect of events had materially changed, and they now bowed down to us in abject lowliness and disgusting servility. One could scarcely look upon these people in any other light than as cowed traitors, liars, and knaves. Mundasoore is a complete sink of vice, *a modern Sodom under our own eyes*, in which the face of every European is hated.

To sympathize with such a debased race is impossible; fire and brimstone alone would purge them of their iniquity. They hate our justice, they despise our clemency, they only pray for our annihilation ; they will greedily snatch at our pecuniary alms, but fly, though starving, from our bread, as though we were lepers and pollutors of such superior souls ; they will bow down to the dust and kiss our feet, and turn away cursing and invoking a hundred plagues upon our heads ; they are unscrupulous liars, cunning as serpents, and as untrustworthy as the bloodloving tiger !

At length, having struck a quietening blow at the rebellion in Malwa, we turned our faces towards Indore, passing through Seeta-Mhow, the river Seepra, Mahidpore, Oojein, and other places lately looted by the rebels, in our route.

Mahidpore, once so beautiful a cantonment, presented the general melancholy features of rebellion and destruction. Every house was burnt down, and among their ruins were the shattered remains of carriages, palkies, chairs, boxes, and other furniture. Empty ammunition boxes lay here and there about the place, and beneath a fine grove of trees were several large guns spiked by the officers on the day of the mutiny ; beneath these trees, too, were about thirty fresh-dug graves ; here the enemy had buried their dead. In a nullah, on one side of the

MAHIDPORE. 129

parade ground, were several human skulls, most of them bore marks of sabre cuts. On the bank of the river was another gun, its carriage and limber destroyed. Separated from the cantonment by a small stream, a tributary of the Seepra, is the town of Mahidpore, a dirty, deserted, ill-built place. On the arrival of our force the inhabitants continued to desert the town in great numbers, and there was some little difficulty in obtaining supplies for our troops.

The house lately occupied by the commandant, Major Timmins, had been a very beautiful place. He had expended considerable sums of money upon it, and beautified the grounds around it in a most superior *home*-like style. He had stabling extensive enough for twenty horses, and every other arrangement equally good. Beyond his lovely garden was a paddock, surrounded on three sides by a fine-grown, well-trimmed hedge, fir and cypress trees, and separated from the garden by white posts and chains, and a wicket gate. Exquisite taste was displayed everywhere around the heap of ruins where his house once stood.

The hospital, the best built I have seen in India, was not much damaged. Its windows and doors were torn down, and the contents of the surgery broken and scattered wantonly about. Every other bungalow was a ruin.

K

The lines were untouched, and certainly they presented the prettiest, cleanest, best appearance I have ever seen. Each street was paved, and on each side was a gutter and well-grown trees. Before each house was a little plot of land full of flowers, vegetables, and shrubs, then a wicket gate opening into the street. The houses were all tiled and in good repair. Altogether it looked the very pink of cleanliness and the model of a first-rate cantonment. On the morning of the dreadful outbreak of the Contingent, there was little hope of life save in flight. Capt. Mills was slain, Dr. Carey wounded, and butchered as he was being carried away on a cot; the Serjeant-Major and family were slain, and the Major with a few faithful sowars escaped by flight. Lieutenant Dysart, of the late Bengal 23rd, which mutinied in Mhow, was acting Adjutant, and a second time escaped death with the faithful remnant of the Contingent. Mrs. Timmins escaped, and was concealed by her dursi. She was afterwards rescued by Major Orr.

The evening before our departure from Mahidpore two men were hanged upon trees above the new-made graves of their brethren. Thus we left behind us in every place of mutiny a wholesome reminder to those who had panted for our blood and danced at our travail.

We marched through the town of Oojein, a very

extensive famous old place, very filthy, and crowded with inhabitants. Some time after we had encamped, a salute of seventeen guns was fired from the tumble-down fort in honour of our arrival. A few more prisoners were brought into camp here.

This extensive town is walled in all round, and a little distance from this wall is a fine palatial house surrounded by gardens and timber-trees belonging to the Biza-Baiee.

After a day's halt we resumed our march and again crossed the Seepra. The noble bridge spanning it had been destroyed by the late rains, so that the troops had to cross over the river below it, at the old ford, and we encamped for the night only a few miles from the city of Indore, with a high belt of hills between us and that city. At an early hour on the morning of 15th December we struck camp and marched upon Indore, fully prepared for an encounter with the Maharajah's troops if they attempted any resistance to our entry into that city. It was necessary that the troops of Holkar should be disarmed, this he promised to effect if he could prior to our entrance. In case they resisted his behest we should encounter them, otherwise we were to march into the grounds of the residency. He could not disarm them until they saw our advance guard, then they tardily succumbed, and we marched through the suburbs and into the grounds of the resident, where we pitched our camp, heartily rejoiced in the prospect of a rest, and rather disappointed in not having had the opportunity of meetly revenging the deeds of infamy done by the Indore troops a few months ago.

Not a little amazement and chagrin were displayed by these said troopers and the disaffected of the people at our undreamed-of advent.

Little did they imagine, when they beheld the blood of the victims and the flight of all who could escape, and the flames ascending from the bungalows, the church, and the residency a few months before, that the British would be back in such force so soon.

The hour of retribution had at length arrived, and it was now our time to astonish and awe them beneath the very walls of their ruler's palace. Our force was numerically very small, but the campaign we had just concluded and the good tidings from the far distant north made us equal to anything.

They all thought the Feringhees were no more when they butchered the powerless few about them. Even Holkar himself is reported to have consulted the court astrologer as to the part he was to play in the grand tragedy. But this wiseacre had enough good sense in him to say that "though every European save one were slain, that one would remain to fight and reconquer." Few could have given a better estimate of the British character, for it is true to the letter.

Our onward determination astonishes and paralyses the native. He always calculates upon running away, such a thought never enters our brains. One day we are quiet in camp ruminating over the next upshot, another day we are fighting and blowing away from guns, and hanging, and imprisoning, as though the world's weal depended upon individual exertion; and this has been the character of all our late successes against the rebel armies.

The ruin here, as far as European dwellings were concerned, was complete. The residency was a chaos of disorder, its walls stood, for they were too well built to fall, but the doors, windows, and all the furniture had gone to ruin. Huge sooty copper pots lying upon drawing-room sofas, broken chairs and picture frames, smashed palkies and chandeliers, bedsteads, umbrellas, bonnets, yards of tattered silk, old shoes, prayer-books, Bibles, and newspapers, all lay together in pitiable confusion. And this was the state of the goodly house the resident of Central India had left behind him a few weeks before, and these were the remains of the property rescued by Holkar from the hands of the rebels! What a welcome home!

A short distance from the residency is the church,

a pretty little village-like sanctuary; this the rebels had gutted and defiled. Hospital, and other buildings of a less substantial kind were complete wrecks, nothing remained but blackened tumble-down walls. And this was the state of the Indore cantonment; the populous city on one side, the deep blue jungle-clad hills on the other, and naked desolation in the centre!

Our camp was pitched in the front of the residency.

About mid-day an invitation came from the Maharajah's court to all officers of the force to attend an open durbar at 5 o'clock, P.M.

By half-past four we formed a large and brilliant cavalcade, and rode to the palace of Holkar, some two miles off, anticipating a grand affair. We were all well armed, and preceded and followed by dragoons and irregular cavalry. For the first five hundred yards it was all very agreeable and pleasing, but we had not yet got into the enjoyable part of our ride to royalty. By-and-bye the earth answered to our tramp in clouds ascending, and every man's beard and moustache looked as though he had dipt his head into a flour sack, every blue coat was white, every red one grey or rusty, our unmentionables looked like the order of things pertaining to stonemasons; choking was no word for the pneumatic occlusion. In this pickle or powder we arrived at the palace gate of H. H. Maharajah Holkar about 5 P.M., and what a great, dark, frowning, stone gateway it is! In a square before this Holkar's sowars and infantry were drawn up, behind these were some thousands of the city folk looking on. The instant we turned into the square something began to blow, groan, and squeal an attempt at "God save the Queen." It is well for Her Majesty that she does not hear how all bands "Save her," or I fear she would be inclined to change the air: however, the motive was *laudable;* they wished to do us an honour, but I suppose Orpheus either would not or could not soar in Attic strains that evening, probably dust was in *his* throat too. I imagine a Mendelssohn would not elicit much out of key-bugle and a tom-tom, and these were the instruments upon which they essayed to honour our arrival at the palace.

We passed beneath the beautiful stately portal into the palace yard. Here again were troops, and two huge elephants, drawn up to look at us. Above, below, and around, in scores of windows and balconies, were the grinning mouths and glistening eyes of the gaudy-dressed heads of hundreds of Holkar's palatial hangers-on. It was motley. Here we dismounted, then ascended a few steps, and strode through an aisle of Mahrattahs beneath a beautifully carved balcony. We then ascended a dark, wide staircase; at the top were other big-wigs, with naked legs, mumbling betelnut and swelling about like divinities. We then passed through an upper open court, through a door, along a carpeted passage, and came to a stand. We were now entering the room in which sat H. H. the Maharajah. Long before we could get in we heard voices strike up the babel strains of nautch songs—the wondrous fiddle was very potent. We went in and seated ourselves, as best we could, upon tiny pillows on the floor; each pillow was just large enough for the knees—no more; this was very objectionable, but we sat down. At the top of the room, some 20 feet long by 12 wide, sat Holkar, cross-legged upon sundry large pillows, and leaning back upon others as though he had just swooned. Behind him was a crowd of tinselled Asiatics, on his left a man in green and gold, on his right Col. Durand, the Political Agent, and before him an attendant with a huge flaccid fan wafting about the close mephitic air. By-and-bye it became warm, and sundry other fanners posted themselves about the room and did likewise. The ventilation was Asiatic!

At the other end of the room stood his seraphic quire—a great, obese woman, covered with jewels and bursting herself in nautch soprano, was the middle cherub, on either hand two lesser beings vieing with the plethoric centre; behind these goddesses were three men blowing and grinding away at something made of wood and string. Of course this concert was very edifying and charming, and it went on without cessation the whole time.

In the process of time a large dish covered with sweetmeats came round. A handful upon a green leaf was given to each and all of us, but, oh! what should have been raisins was *betel-nut*—what sugar-plums, cardamoms—what currants, cloves! Here was a compliment! Then came bowls of silver. Now the treat *is* coming—punch or cool nectar, of course! It came round, but instead of sparkling nectar, we got an *eye-full* of rose-water from a silver squib! This was overpowering. To squib water into the eyes and over the red coats of British officers could scarcely be endured. What duels have been fought for less! but there we sat like patriotic martyrs. The next thing to be expected might be a scimitar, sharp as lightning, to cut one's head off, and a silver salver to bear it away, but this time there came a wreath of flowers, of Asiatic odour, and then another big-wig came round and took up your hand most confidingly. I thought he was a seer—a Joe Anderson—but, no! I was deceived again, for he quietly rubbed his greasy, slimy fingers along my palm, and, like a musk rat, left a piquant odour behind him; this was terrible. All this time it was getting closer and darker, and the discord swelled unintermittingly in prolonged, cracked *ha! ha! ha's!* and quavers that would have sent Handel to the seventh inferno. Behind us were three windows, and through these trembled the spasmodic music of a brazen band from below. This was very grand—it came from H. H. the Maharajah's band! Six red-coated men stood round a square table, bending their necks and wagging their heads over some paper they pretended was music. They played a sort of *post*-horn gallop-march-polka, for nobody could make out what it was. What with music below, music above, a fiendish atmosphere, blinded eyes, and throats full of dust, it was a very difficult thing to feel entertained.

It was getting very dark. Suddenly a man marched up to the warblers and seemed to administer *coup-de-bouche,* for they instantly put up their pipes. Simultaneously with this musical stop Holkar rose up, and holding Colonel Durand by the *little finger* led him out of the room like a babe with tata and bye, bye! Then he took the hand of the brigadier and nearly shook it off; he seemed pained, and perhaps this was a sneaking way of punishing him for his bravery and gallantry. Holkar said he "was very glad to see him and his victorious army." He then called Capt. S. Orr back and shook him very warmly by the hand. Then we went out, ran down stairs, rushed to our horses, and back for another dose of dust. Then commenced such a tom-toming, striking of gongs, firing of guns, blowing of asthmatic bassoons, hooting and shouting, plunging and kicking of our frightened horses as one seldom sees or hears in this world. The horses evidently considered this behaviour highly improper, as they did all they could to kill Holkar's people for it. By-and-bye we were in something worse than any London fog, but it must be endured, and so we rode on into camp choked, smothered, and dying for beer. How cool, and sweet the camp was! who would live in a palace?

Thus ended the Malwa campaign! Col. Durand left us that night; on the morrow Sir H. Rose, K.C.B., and Sir R. Hamilton, arrived in Indore, and the force then assumed the name of the Central India Field-Force.

In our march through Malwa we had ample opportunity of observing the peculiarities of the country we passed over, the villages, towns, and people. As our campaign in this part lasted from about the middle of October to the end of December, we probably had an opportunity of seeing the country in its most attractive and cheerful dress; certainly the season was the one most suited to

Europeans either for fighting or sight-seeing. The sun was never too hot in mid-day, the mornings and evenings were pleasant to a degree; indeed, towards the middle of December the temperature of the air was so reduced in the early morning as to oblige most of our troops to wear top-coats on the march. Such an atmosphere was particularly invigorating. As there had been abundance of rain prior to our leaving Mhow, the rivers, and tanks, and wells afforded us more than enough water for our use, and of the best kind. This is always a source of comfort to a camp, while well-filled tanks, clear flowing rivers and wells—ever the scenes of busy life—add a never-failing charm to the landscape. Malwa is a particularly picturesque country —one is never tired by the almost eternal level so striking in other parts. There are rivers, broad, deep, winding, and rapid; hills clothed with jungle and timber trees; miles of undulating grass land, and extensive plateaus of rich alluvial soil; in which are cultivated the sugar-cane, various cereals, every kind of esculent vegetable to be desired, and the opium poppy.

The grass-land, extending for miles in various parts, unbounded by any visible mark, save the distant hills, and studded here and there with stately forest trees that vie with the oaks of England in size and beauty, and clothed with grass from four to five feet high, in which antelope and deer roam in herds, gives one an idea rather of a princely, well-kept forest-land than of a country neglected and wild. The cultivated fields are very extensive, and their produce rich and abundant. The most important plant cultivated in Malwa is the Papaver somniferum—the opium poppy,—from the monopoly of which Government obtains a considerable revenue.

The culture of this plant is a laborious work—great care, constant weeding, and irrigation are needed. Around most of the villages are opium fields. Manure is stored for the soil and ploughed in. The whole field, however extensive, is divided into numberless little compartments by elevated ridges of earth, and into each of these compartments water is run night and morning from an adjacent well, drawn up by bullocks in a leather bucket. As soon as the bucket arrives at the top it is tilted over and the water falls into a small cistern, from whence it runs for the purpose of irrigation through divers channels into the opium fields. This is a tedious and long business, but since the ryot finds it profitable to produce a certain quantity of opium yearly for sale to the opium agents of Government, it must be done, for without copious irrigation the poppy dies.

The cultivation of the poppy gives employment to many of the villagers, and at the cutting season there is a good deal of life and excitement in these gardens of poison. After the opium has been extracted from the poppy it is amazing to see with what care it is packed up, blanketed, and transported to Bombay. The sowcars (money merchants) in Mhow, Indore, and other large towns make enormous sums of money by the opium trade. I have known as much as fifteen per cent. given for money by native merchants during the opium harvest, and if natives will give so much, and sometimes they give more—what must be the profit obtained by them upon this article of commerce? for we know that the native is not satisfied with a little.

We not unfrequently passed through fine groves of tamarind trees, mango trees, and peepul trees. In one of our marches I remember we halted near a village, beneath a gigantic banyan tree, at the foot of which ran a small stream. This tree had extended so far as to be fully capable of shading a thousand men lying at ease beneath its branches. Its droopers reminded one of the pillars of a huge gothic building, outside all was sunlight and brilliance, beneath the green canopy shadowy, cool, still, and murmuring with the hum of insect life. A little tomb lay at the foot of the trunk over which hung flags of red and white cloth.

Such trees are not uncommon, but I never saw

one so large or so well fitted for repose before or since.

The brilliant and gorgeous sunrises and sunsets at this season of the year were something astonishing. The most fantastic clouding, the most marvellous colourings imaginable, were there, grouped in such passionate minglings that seemed almost to defy description or copy. Burning red and gold, like floating molten masses of metal rolling and streaming in ether; bands of transparent yellow, tipped with crimson and umber, gliding over fields of delicate shadowy green; feathery cloudlets of rose and crimson and gold parting for ever in an ocean of purple, and dark angry mountainous heaps looking terrible with their fringes of deep red and tumbling heads of umber and purple and black,—all this, and a thousand times more, painted on the canopy of heaven, brightening, deepening, changing, dissolving for ever!

Nor are the nights less beautiful. Scarcely does the curtain fall ere the scene is changed as by the touch of a magic wand, and now we have a thousand brilliant worlds scintillating above us from their cold, deep-blue abysses of night. Awfully grand is the contemplation of heaven by night in India. The mind passes from the finite to the Infinite—the boundless—the eternal; time is forgotten—space and spirit appear only as one, until at last the soul shrinks back from its flights into the little fleshly world' it has leapt from, awe-stricken and chastened.

Often were the southern cross and the great bear visible in the heavens at the same time, and, as it seemed, only a short distance from each other. These two bright constellations divided, as it were, the beauty of the starry hosts between them. The pellucidity of the milky-way was most striking, vast masses of what appear only as faint nebulous tingings in other climates show themselves as well-marked clusters of stars infinitely deep in space.

Malwa, from the south of Jaôra extending to the west, is rich in fine-grained sandstone; there are also sandstone slates, and clay iron-ore. Very good iron ore is found in mammillated and reniform masses and is worked. Some very rich specimens are to be had in the bazaars, besides which are the rude masses which have been smelted of a *bright crystalline* form.

Basalt is found in the Chumbul in horizontal stratified tables and solitary boulders.

Some of the villages are particularly clean and well built, others very wretched collections of hovels; the people of the villages appeared in no wise to be badly off. The large towns, such as Dhar, Noli, Mundasoor, Mahidpore, Oojein, Seta-Mhow, and Indore are more or less imposing, and thickly inhabited by very wealthy merchants, shop-keepers, and numerous artizans of considerable skill. A feature worthy of notice during these troublous times was that *the peasant and agriculturist continued their ordinary labour as though nothing in the world was afoot of greater moment than the seed they were sowing or the crop they were reaping.*

A battle might be fought in one field, and in another was the ploughman with his plough and oxen. Occasionally we saw evidences of distrust in our route,—a well-rope and bucket and yoke all clean and moist by the well, but no oxen, no attendant; a plough just in the loam with oxen hard by, no ploughman. These were hard times for the ryot whose estate happened to be in the line of march. Many a carrot field was trodden down or well nigh consumed; many an opium field sadly injured by camels, elephants, and wanton camp followers; many a sugar-cane field looted by elephants and camp followers; many a hempen well-rope turned into a drag-rope; and I fear, also, that many of the poor villagers came off little better, for long lines of camp followers always straggle through the villages while the force passes by, and these creatures are always given to plunder. However stringent orders may be to the contrary, they cannot be enforced to the letter. These beings are the necessary evils attendant upon the march of an army in India; they act upon the rule of might, not right; and although no countenance is given to them, they plunder the poor villager, unoffending or otherwise. Each fellow manages to obtain a tattoo and a tulwar, and with these overawes the timid and defenceless. They are great scoundrels, but an army cannot get on without them.

One of the most marvellous things is the way in which women and children spring up with an army. A force may march out for the field with only, perhaps, a slight sprinkling of native women with them —such as milk-women and horse-keeper's wives, but, ere long, more and more women and children appear, and by-and-bye, on either flank of the force, there is a brigade of women riding tattoos astride, and chattering like parrots all the time. The milk-women are wonderful beings, they not only march with the force, carrying milk upon their heads— (where they get it from is a mystery)—to supply the men as they go, but after camp is pitched their voices are heard everywhere crying out *doodh* for the whole day long. One woman generally attaches herself to a particular corps, and thus each corps is supplied with milk. Although these women undergo considerable fatigue, they seem to thrive on the occupation.

Sometimes a horse-keeper has a wife and seven or eight children with him. How such a fraternity

INCIDENTS ON THE MARCH.

manage to live is a marvel. It frequently happens, too, that a poor man with such a prodigious family is a terrific drunkard. That his children should squint or do anything alike is not to be wondered at. A man with such a string of representatives has hard times of it. When it blows cold at night, as it often does, they make a fire near a cart, put up a cob-web kind of screen, cook their rice, eat, drink, and fight, and then, amid wailings and oxen, retire until the bugle arouses the camp next morning. If perchance he is overcome by Bacchus, as he often is, he lies down on the earth, abuses his wife and family and Government, and swears he'll be a sepoy, while his poor half-starved wife covers him up to prevent master seeing him, and master's horse neighs and paws to know why he is not attended to.

Another extraordinary accompaniment of a force is the number of dogs. Day by day as the march continues these creatures increase in numbers, and they are generally of the most wretched caste. Certain of them attach themselves to each corps, many others to individual camp followers, and the jealousy with which they look upon the intrusion of another of their kind into their ranks, when moving from place to place, is very striking. If a stranger attempts to join them, no matter how he fawns and cringes and snarls, he is summarily expelled in the most uncourteous manner, and hunted away as the veriest outcast. Notwithstanding this jealousy of cupboard, they multiply in direct ratio with our movements. On the line of march they are annoying, by the constant clouds of dust they create in their frolics and fights, in the camp they are far more serious evils. Their howlings, and snarlings, and barkings at night are most irritating. If it be a clear moon-light night they hold their orgies till grey morning. Sleep is out of the question, for they come screaming, snarling, racing, and panting among your tent ropes—sometimes through your tent—like wild beasts. By the time you are up and out, they are off among the ropes of another's tent; and thus, backwards and forwards, until you wish them all in Styx. Added to these nuisances, packs of jackalls and hyænas follow in our track, and invariably commence their demoniac concert about the hour one wishes to court "tired nature's sweet restorer," never content with indulging in their predaceous habits without announcing their presence by their fiendish wails and howls. I know nothing more horrible than to be awoke by the voices of these skulking carrion—cowards in the calm of night!

At Mundasoore and Oojein, many of the town's people came into our camp to sell their goods. They all appeared quiet and well to do. In the evening a considerable number of the merchants came out to hear the band of the 25th N. I. I do not imagine this was really to listen to the music, as the native considers our music execrable—nothing to be compared to his own tom-tom—I believe it was a demonstration on their part of good feeling towards the victorious arms.

There was abundance of every kind of game for the sportsman—water-fowl in great numbers. The starting of an antelope or hare in or near the camp was always attended with a good deal of excitement among the troops. However long the march had been men were never too tired to race bare-headed in the sun through the camp after them. The cry was no sooner heard than camp followers, sepoys, dragoons, and artillery men were out in the chase, and mingling with them were bull-and-terriers, terriers, and pariahs of all sizes and colours, dodging among pickets of horses, guns, tents, and carts, after the unfortunate game. Frequently at the same time a horse or miserable tattoo would get loose and scamper off with his head and heel-ropes flying about him into the midst of dragoon or artillery horses, whereupon a kicking scene would ensue, followed by other horses getting loose, and accompanied by universal neighing and screaming as they chased each other among the tents, breaking tent-ropes and upsetting everything in their way, while their keepers were vainly endeavouring to capture them. These scenes were always ludicrous, sometimes dangerous.

By the middle of December we had hoar-frosts in the mornings, and consequently the early morning marches were very invigorating. When we arrived at Indore we were agreeably surprised to find we could obtain ices at any time during the day. This was a luxury beyond expectation, and so long as we remained there we naturally indulged in them. The sites of all the larger towns and cities are generally well chosen. They are usually commanding, and built upon the banks of a river or on the side of a large tank. They are surrounded by thick, high walls, with strong bastions and gateways, and usually have a citadel or fort commanding the most exposed face. They are well stocked with cattle and grain, and in most instances have good encamping ground for forces, more or less shaded by extensive groves of tamarind and banyan trees. The rivers are invariably without bridges, and during the rains are almost impassable; at other times their banks are so steep and rugged as to require cutting before artillery and baggage can be passed over. The roads are invariably bad, broken up, and intersected by nullahs in the clay and alluvial soils, or rugged and stony in the districts of sandstone and trap; this naturally impedes the progress of a force; heavy guns and baggage-carriage are dragged along them with considerable difficulty and labour, and are often a day or two behind the advanced column. The whole of these city fortifications are now in a greater or less degree fast going to ruin. They would never give umbrage to a force opposed to Europeans, although an European force would sustain a long and triumphant opposition within them.

CHAP. IV.

Major-General reviews troops and inspects hospitals.—Preparations for campaign in Central India.—General events.—Siege train marches to Sehore to join second brigade.—Arrival in Sehore.—Execution of mutineers.—March for Rhatghur.—Bhopal.—Siege of Rhatghur.—Escape of rebels.—Affair of Barodia.—Death of Capt. Neville.—Relief of Saugor.—March to Gurrakotta.—Capture of fort.

INDORE AND PRELIMINARIES OF THE CAMPAIGN.

AFTER the advent of Major-General Sir H. Rose and Sir R. Hamilton, the Malwa field force changed its name. It was now styled the 1st brigade of the Central India field force; and the force recently assembled at Sehore, under Brigadier Stuart of the 14th Light Dragoons, was styled the 2nd brigade of the Central India field force, the whole now under the command of Sir H. Rose. The Major-General reviewed the 1st brigade on the morning of 17th, and in the course of the day inspected hospitals. On visiting the hospital of the Madras sappers, the General said that Government was highly pleased with the Madras sepoys, and on a wounded sapper begging not to be left behind if the force moved, Sir Hugh very kindly said that every attention should be given to him, and that

MAJOR-GENERAL REVIEWS TROOPS. 153

he should not fail to make particular inquiries about him when he visited hospitals in Mhow. When the General visited hospitals in Mhow some few days afterwards, he paid marked attention to the welfare of the sick of the Madras sappers.

For several days about Christmas week Indore was in a very unsettled state, owing to a show of resistance on the part of some of Holkar's troops regarding the summary way in which the Major-General was dealing out punishment to some of their brethren. The General properly assumed the right of dictating what he thought the miscreants deserved, which in several instances amazed the people of Indore, and Maharajah Holkar too; but in no instance can it be said that he more than fulfilled the wishes of every right-thinking officer and soldier, or answered to the loud cries of revenge from the nation one tittle too much. Vengeance—terrible and prompt—was called for, and in the person of the General we had one who was in every way suited to the occasion for its administration to a full and effective measure. The General not only displayed a polished *suaviter in modo* at once pleasing and attractive, but the *fortiter in re* that marked him as a man of promptitude, determination, and vigour, and one in whom confidence could be reposed.

At this period he had just arrived from England

with a bloom of health and elasticity of constitution seldom seen in men of his standing in India, and much, indeed, he needed these for the completion of the labour now before him, as we shall presently see.

There was much to be done and numerous arrangements required before the two brigades now under the command of Sir Hugh could again take the field, and this the General set about and accomplished to the amazement of all in an incredibly short space of time. He was laughed at and called a griff by a good many, and a good many others asked who he was and what he had done? About this time, too, an envious notice of the services of the General appeared in the papers from England. How their predictions have been fulfilled the world knows, and the wisdom of the choice of such an officer has been well proved. The idea of any one and every one being griffs unless they have seen the Indian world is, of course, Indian. The world has had a pretty good lesson in the late mutiny on griffs. One thing was quite evident, viz., that long residence in this country neither added to personal courage or wisdom, while it is patent that men who were denominated griffs were the very best leaders for these Indian wiseacres.

The troops had a little repose, and during this cool rest the sick and wounded derived much benefit. The whole country about Indore was particularly suited as a resting-place prior to the coming campaign. There was an abundance of the common necessaries of life, no lack of good water or fodder for cattle, and a climate for the time being of a most enjoyable nature. Towards the beginning of January 1858 there were rumours of a move towards Saugor, and eventually as far as Jhansi, of many sieges before us, and some whispered of the probability of our seeing the Ganges ere our work was ended! In fact, there was no end to the conjectures and rumours of war, so we looked anxiously every day for the orders that were to seal our fate for the year.

In the meantime I must not forget to mention the happy re-union we had on Christmas-day in Mhow. Almost every officer of the Malwa field force dined together that night. The room was decorated in a most becoming manner for the occasion with green leaves and the banners captured by our troops in their victorious little campaign in Malwa. The Major-General and staff came in from Indore—a distance of twelve miles—to the dinner. Every arrangement and detail was as well managed and imposing as the times would permit. Indeed, considering all things, it was surprising to see so goodly a *tout ensemble*. There was much cordiality and spirit; the position of Europeans under the trying circumstances of the times seemed to knit them together in a closer bond of amity; the work of retribution so well begun was an incentive to further and more brilliant conquests; all present felt the deep importance of the coming struggles, and how dear the honour and prestige of his fatherland were to him. "The maids of merry England" were not forgotten, nor were the heroes who had gone gloriously to their graves in the conflicts in Bengal and other parts of India.

It was a happy meeting; few, however, who were present then met together to celebrate another Christmas. It was a half serious, a half merry time. So unlike the cold, frost-biting time of year when old Father Christmas is welcomed with merry-sounding bells, huge blazing fires, and the time-honoured carol in old England, as he presides with his crown of icicles and wreath of holly in every home. In India our Christmas time is one of imagination when compared with that we joyed in in other years. Here all is sunny, warm, foreign. Though we imitate the holly and mistletoe boughs, though we strive to make all within look as like the season as mortals can, yet we cannot persuade ourselves that we are not imitators, for, save the good things of the table, everything wears the dress of a midsummer's day.

We were on the eve of a new year—a happy one

for some, a dark and shadowy one for many; not one among us then could realize the future, nor dream of which friend death would first deprive us. To look forward to the end of another year was like looking through a glittering halo of fire into the dark abysses of fate. Our work of retribution had but just begun, we had been baptized with fire, and now had a course of trying ordeals to run through until the goal should be attained and the sword sheathed in a crowning victory. By this time our enemies had rather multiplied than decreased; though victory after victory had been gained by us, they appeared numerically as strong as ever. An amazing thing to us was the amount of guns they had possession of. In almost every instance in which we had by this time opposed them we had taken all their guns from them, and yet in every engagement guns re-appeared as though by miracle. True, many of these field-pieces scarcely deserved the name; nevertheless, they were guns, and often did a good deal of mischief. I remember those we captured at the battle of Mundasoore were all antiquated things, honey-combed and worn out; how they dared fire them was a wonder.* Those they

* One of these guns, older than the rest, and with a vent like the muzzle of an old "brown-bess," they had facetiously named "*greased-lightning*," and bedaubed it all over with red and green paint. It was an old fourteen pounder of "G. Rex's" time.

had seized belonging to the different contingents and forts were, of course, the same kind as those used by us.

By this time we had the cheering news of the relief of Lucknow under Sir Colin Campbell. His masterly retreat from the residency of that city in the face of some 50,000 rebels can never be forgotten. The chivalrous way in which Sir J. Outram behaved towards that bravest of heroes, Havelock, when marching for the relief was only another instance of the many of its kind that have marked the long and honourable career of that General— the *brave des braves*, as he was once called.

Sir James had been appointed Chief Commissioner and General of that division, but as General Havelock had fought so valiantly every foot of the ground thus far, Sir James Outram felt he could not do less than allow General Havelock the honour of achieving what he had so nobly and manfully commenced, and the General thus writes in the order of the day :—

" Major-General Outram is confident that the great end for which General Havelock and his brave troops had so long and so gloriously fought will now, under the blessing of Providence, be accomplished. The Major-General, therefore, in gratitude for, and admiration of, the brilliant deeds of arms achieved by General Havelock and his gallant troops, will cheerfully waive his rank on the occasion, and will accompany the force to Lucknow in his civil capacity as Chief Commissioner of Oude, and tendering his military services to General Havelock as a volunteer."

What nobleness of heart and fine feeling are displayed in those words! How many, under similar circumstances, should we find do likewise?

Major-General Outram knew the character of Havelock too well, and was too interested in the cause, and too proud of the heroic deeds of a brother officer, to sully so bright a career by the assumption of command at such an hour.

General Havelock and his well-tried followers had broken the neck of the mutiny; they had paralyzed their enemies by their undaunted courage and endurance, and well, indeed, did he merit all that the world lavished upon him, but the honour and joy that were to follow he was not permitted to bear. He had toiled and marched, fought and endured, sounded the tocsin in the ears of the enemy and the trump of relief to the half-famished brave, and then, worn out and exhausted ere the little span of life was run, he lay down to depart to that " bourne from whence no traveller returns," while the voices of a nation echoed, " Well done, thou good and faithful servant!"

While we had brought our operations in Malwa

to a successful issue, other small forces elsewhere—west, north, and east of us—had been adding to the list of victories, for such they must be called, while at the same time, spite these repeated demonstrations of the utter hopelessness of their cause, regiments which had up to this period appeared staunch and had even received the thanks of the Governor-General for their loyalty, could no longer withstand the potency of the moral contagion, and one after another dropped away from allegiance, like gangrened members from a poisoned body, till at length the whole Bengal army and its contingents had passed away! The only regiment which had not openly mutinied or undergone the degradation of being disarmed was the 31st N. I., stationed at Saugor, of which we shall speak hereafter.

It was wonderful to know that even up to the period of the last act of mutiny, somewhere about the middle of November, that they refused to believe Delhi had fallen! How could it have fallen? Had not all the feringhees, men, women, and children been murdered? were there not now some two hundred thousand well-armed men against us in the field, and all converging to that centre of Mogul power? Had not Nana Dhoondoopunt issued a proclamation and told them that no assistance could come to the British from beyond the seas, for all their ships had sunk, and the Governor-General

MUTINY AT CHITTAGONG.

was beating his head? Verily the spirit of evil was walking the earth then! How is such insanity to be accounted for?

On they went in their choice, and in the meantime we were daily increasing in strength to punish them.

The Rhamghur battalion had been defeated near Chuttra; they lost their guns, baggage, &c.

The Mhow and Indore rebels were met by Col. Greathead near Agra on October 10th, and after a severe engagement, which lasted upwards of two hours, they were signally defeated with a loss of nearly fifteen hundred men, the whole of their baggage, and their plunder, amounting nearly to ten lakhs of rupees.

The mutineers who had taken refuge in the stronghold of Nana, Bhittoor, were expelled thence on October 18th, and with their expulsion the gold and silver plate of Nana was captured, the principal portion being found in wells. The tales of these treasures were extraordinary at the time.

On November 18th the three companies of the 34th N. I., who had up to this date remained faithful, could no longer withstand the temptation of rebellion. In the night they broke out in mutiny at Chittagong, fired their lines, set free the prisoners, robbed the treasury of about three lakhs of rupees, and then marched to Dacca. The news of their doings had gone before them, as it always did in some mysterious way or other, and the 73rd regiment there made a climax of the affair.

I had almost forgotten to mention the revolt of the Kotah Contingent, and the murder of the Political Agent, Major Burton, and his two sons, and their surgeon. The major and his two boys gallantly defended themselves for hours on the top of their house; at length the rebels got ladders, and then completed their tragedy. These blind fiends trooped also towards Delhi.

This was the state of the country when Sir H. Rose assumed command of the Central India Field Force, and, added to these rebels, we now had opposed to us most of the native princes, with their hordes of plunderers and cut-throats on every side.

The general having satisfied himself that all was in readiness for a move, the sick and wounded having been duly disposed of, and the disaffected in these districts awed, orders were issued to the effect that the force would move upon Saugor for the relief of that place; all heavy baggage was to be left behind, and as few bullock carts taken as possible. Our movements were to be rapid, and the general rightly wished not to be encumbered with baggage. The siege-train, with the Madras Sappers, and part of the Hyderabad Contingent under Capt. G. Hare, and a squadron of 14th Light Dragoons under Capt. Leith, were ordered to join the second brigade at Sehore, to which place the general had gone a day or two previous. The 1st brigade was to remain behind at Indore some few days, and then to march north, parallel with us, so as to fall upon Chandaree, a strong fortress then occupied by the enemy. The 3rd Bombay Light Cavalry, a company of the 3rd Bombay European regiment, and some Horse Artillery, with Colonel Turnbull, and other officers passed through Mhow on 2nd January for Sehore, *via* Simrole.

Opening of the Campaign of 1858.
March to Sehore.

About 5 A.M. on the morning of the 8th January the siege-train commenced its march from Indore to Sehore. We had scarcely gone four miles on the road, when a violent explosion was heard in our rear. For an instant we imagined ourselves fired upon from ambush, but on turning round we saw a great column of smoke among the artillery of the Hyderabad Contingent, and men rushing wildly about here and there. The halt was sounded, and we galloped to the spot, and a most melancholy scene presented itself. A limber of a 9-pounder was filled with loaded shell, and these had exploded through some accident in packing. There lay a human foot in one spot, pieces of flesh in another, burning cloth in a third; a wounded man here, another dying there, a third with the hair of his face and head singed off, and jaw broken! Two men were blown to atoms—the head with the right arm attached being all that was found. The limber had disappeared, and the gun, with its trail broken, was driven some yards back covered with blood. The oxen stood still as death, also wounded. The driver who sat upon the box was only blown off, while the second ahead of him was killed.

The wounded were sent back into camp at Indore, and when an advance could be made, we marched on from this awful scene, keeping well clear of tumbrels and ammunition waggons ever after. It was a sorry beginning we all thought.

Such are the uncertainties of life. In one moment these men who were marching cheerfully along in the pleasant hour of sunrise, full of life and hope and vigour, were blown into atoms, and their existences scattered upon the winds like breath. In this march towards Sehore we passed Ragooghur, situated near a pass over some hills. The little fort, if such loophooled mud bastions and walls deserve such a name, was partially destroyed in October last by Major Orr's force. The hills on either side were densely covered with jungle. At Peepliah, a town some twelve miles on, Major Orr had also chastised

ARRIVAL IN SEHORE.

the rebels. On our arrival at Ashtah, in the Bhopal territory, we heard that a large rebel force had collected beyond Sehore, and that the force there were anxiously awaiting the arrival of the siege-train.

We were now in the Bhopal state, and met a small force of the Begum of Bhopal encamped at Ashtah.

On our way to Sehore evidences of good management met the eye everywhere. The land was under the best cultivation, and looked quite refreshing.

We joined the force on the morning of the 15th, and were heartily received. Rather a laughable incident occurred on our marching into camp. The sappers had captured a standard at Mundasoore—a gaudy yellow and green affair, and as they marched on this thing was unfurled, and flying at the head of the company. When they passed the 24th N. I. the quarter-guard turned out and presented arms. Many wanted to know what it was, whether it was the colours of the corps, as they had never seen Madras troops before, and the sappers in dark grey jackets, pagrees blacker than their faces, and the *je ne sais quoi* air about them which no other troops have, arising perhaps from a knowledge of their own fame and scientific calling, were certainly a specimen calculated to excite wonder.

The Bhopal Contingent had been little better than their brethren elsewhere; a few, however, remained faithful, and of these few much was made, and well, indeed, did they deserve it. It was curious to find that those who had remained true to their allegiance were mostly Seikhs—true and tried men.

There was a long list of delinquents under guard in Sehore, and of these not fewer than *one hundred and forty-nine* were found guilty by the courts, and accordingly sentenced to be shot by musketry!

The duty of carrying out the extreme sentence of the law fell to the 3rd Europeans. The prisoners were brought out in the evening just as the sun was setting, were ranged in one long line, and at the given signal were shot, one man escaped.

Ere the execution was well over darkness had come on, and through the long, cold, dreary night an officer and men of the 3rd Europeans had to keep guard over this horrid line of dead. So ended this debt against this rebellious contingent.

The brigade moved off for Rhatghur at 3 A.M. on the morning of the 16th. This brigade, under the command of Brigadier Steuart of the 14th Light Dragoons, consisted of head-quarters of 14th Light Dragoons, 3rd Bombay Europeans, 3rd Bombay Light Cavalry, 24th Bombay N. I., a battery of Bombay Horse Artillery, B. Company Madras Sappers, detachment of Bombay Sappers, Hyderabad Cavalry, Infantry, and Artillery under Capt. Hare, and siege-train. The siege-train was permitted to halt one day, and then followed on the 17th; on the 18th we encamped near Bhopal.

Immediately before coming to Bhopal, we had to ascend a range of hills, and then we saw the fort and city behind, high hills to the south, dense topes of trees all round, and a fine lake also to the south. A more beautiful site for a city could not be imagined. It looked like a cluster of summer-houses in a rich garden.

As we approached, guns were fired from the fort. It was a salute on the departure of the force that had preceded us. The fort of Bhopal is built on a rock commanding the road from the south, and the lake, and the country to the north. The walls were very high, strongly built of fine-grained sandstone, loopholed, and strengthened by square and round bastions, upon which guns were placed. As we passed the fort, the bastions, gateways, and walls were crowded with soldiers of the Begum.

The gardens in the immediate neighbourhood were beautifully kept; and as far as the eye could reach green fields of wheat, linseed, dhal, and tobacco covered the earth, broken here and there by large shadowy clusters of tamarind and banyan and peepul trees.

I was much gratified by a stroll through this city. It was very clean, well-built, and evidently in a highly prosperous, progressive condition. The streets were clean, drained on each side, and lighted every alternate fifty yards by an oil lamp on the top of a post, as in the olden times in England. The shops were very numerous and well-stocked with goods. In the centre is a large mosque, with towering minarets tipped with gold, in the best condition; around this mosque is a large bazaar, and this was crowded with people, who, from their appearance, seemed well to do. There were poor, of course, but the only one I saw was a leper dressed in sackcloth. He was as white as an European, and an albino. He appeared very pitiable among people so opposite in colour—every one seemed to shun him, and he to avoid all as he strolled along turning his pink eyes here and there from the bright sunlight. The women were very fair and pretty, some even beautiful; the men well-made and handsome.

On the extensive lake close to the city is a steamboat belonging to the Begum. This steamer is managed by a well-educated Musselman. The lake supplies the city with fish and wild fowl.

The Begum of Bhopal is a shrewd, enlightened old lady. The people of Bhopal would, doubtless, have gone against us had it not been for the influence of this one person. She put off their mutinous solicitations from day to day, assuring them that the proper time for the expulsion of the British had not yet arrived. She knew too well her position, and the power of England, and rightly turned her back upon rebellion.

Her only child is a daughter, whom she has married to an officer of her own force,* and who was then in an interesting situation.

Her territory, though small, is a model one—a pattern principality. The little part of it we passed over was mostly a rich plateau, broken here and there by undulating hills, well clad with clean timber trees. There was but little jungle comparatively, and where this most prevailed it could easily be removed, for it was generally grass and the small palas trees—the butea frondosa. Indeed, it looked like a well-kept and very picturesque park. Around the city of Bhopal in particular, the groves were very beautiful and numerous. There were the banyan ; peepul—ficus religiosa ; mango ; kuthal— jack tree ; neem—melia azadirachta ; bele—cratæva marmelos ; tamarind ; mhowa, bassia latifolia, and many others blossoming or in fruit, some blossoming and fruit-bearing at the same time. Nothing could be more beautiful than these groves dotted about here and there in the midst of luxuriant waving crops, and this, too, was after a season of unusual dryness. It appeared as though little or no oppression marked the rule in this territory, though it is in the centre of Central India, far removed from any large river or other city. The condition of the

* "After the manner of Victoria and Albert," as the old lady remarked.

country speaks well for the administration of Sir Robert Hamilton and his assistants. I cannot say whether the very superior condition of the city was owing to the advice given by Capt. Keatinge, but I believe the presence of the little steamer on the lake, a thing so likely to astonish and stimulate and awaken the people of this far-removed state, was owing to the exertions of this officer.

On the 21st we reached Bilsah, famous for its tobacco, as its name implies, and topes. We were again in the territory of Scindiah. A little distance from the bungalow and encamping ground is an enormous rock of trap standing out from the plain around like a huge pre-adamite obelisk. There is a small temple on its top.

On the 23rd we were at Gwarispoore, a most solitary, cold looking spot.

We had had rather a quiet day, and intended marching early in the morning. So we enjoyed our dinner and retired early. However we were not permitted to enjoy what we had bargained for, for about 10 o'clock the bugle sounded, and we were all up again in an instant. Orders had been received from the force in advance of us to request our joining immediately, as a body of the enemy was on our left flank, and might delay the transit of the siege-train.

There was some slight confusion in our little

camp. An elephant belonging to the train broke loose, upset a cart and bullocks, and decamped to the jungle.

We marched *ten* miles in *three* hours, and joined the force at about 1 A.M. We lighted fires and consoled ourselves in the cold open as philosophically as could be expected, until our tents came up, and then we turned in for a nap. The force again advanced leaving us behind. This time the 8-inch howitzer and two $5\frac{1}{2}$-inch mortars accompanied the advanced body.

We assembled again about 10 A.M. on the 24th, and proceeded slowly, there was such an interminable line of baggage.

By 4 P.M. we had scarcely gone more than four miles from our encamping ground. The sappers were then ordered to advance ahead of this immoveable line to remove, if possible, the cause of obstruction. On they went and came to a river where there were hundreds of gharies jammed together, and unable to gain the opposite bank. And so they would have remained for months, for the drivers seeing the hopelessness of the case had taken the thing in the quietest possible way. There they were, abusing each other like pickpockets, squatting down, and smoking their hubble-bubbles, while the obstruction was getting worse and worse.

The sappers piled arms and went to work in good

earnest, felling trees, cutting the road, and carrying dry sand to cover the slippery path. The carts were got over after intense labour, then came the 18-pounders, and when they arrived at the slippery incline the elephants struck—they would not move an inch further with their charge, so the heavy guns were pulled up by the Madras sappers. When this was accomplished it was near 3 o'clock in the morning of the 25th. *We bivouacked in the jungle that night,* and were up again for the march at about 6 A.M., going in advance of the guns to meet any difficulties.

We marched on through jungle, over rough ground, nullahs, and hills, and at length arrived in camp before Rhatghur about 1 P.M. on the 25th. Nothing can be more harassing than accompanying a siege-train over such a country,—nothing more gratifying than to know that by the exertion of one's troops the labour is achieved. I am convinced that no men in the world could have done better (few so well) than did our Madras sappers in their voluntary labour in this instance. They had it all their own way, and be assured they spared neither voice nor arm in the work. I saw bullock drivers and officers' servants stand by in mute amazement at what they did; and the way they joked in Tamil and then in good *English* seemed to astonish them still more; however low-caste "sawmies," as they were called, proved their value in this instance as well as in scores of others to be mentioned by-and-bye. Soldiers are not wanted to be mere dandies and *show-men*, as the high-caste villains of the Bengal army were to a considerable extent. Government require workmen, and those, too, who will not be particular about what is expected of them. No better proof of the superior qualifications of the two kinds is needed than the universal eulogy paid to the corps of Madras sappers and miners wherever they have come into contact with troops of the other presidencies.

The Siege of Rhatghur.

The brigade arrived before Rhatghur on the morning of the 24th. The enemy appeared in the plain at the foot of the fort, occupied the town and banks of the river. After some brisk work they were driven from these positions into the fort, and there they shut themselves up to await the progress of the siege ; they however reoccupied the village. The fort, said to be larger and as strong as that of Mooltan, is situated on the spur of a long high hill, and commands the country around. The east and south faces were almost perpendicular—the rock being scarped and strengthened by a deep rapid river—the Biena—running close beneath from east to west; the north face looked along the densely jungled hill, and was strengthened by a deep ditch some twenty feet wide; the west face overlooked the town and Saugor road: in this face was the gateway flanked by several square and round bastions. The wall to the north side was strengthened by an outwork looking like a second wall. Along each face were strong bastions commanding various points, and also in the four angles. Approach from the east and south was next to impossible, approach from the west or town side almost as difficult.

After the affair of the 24th, in which we lost the subadar major of the 24th N. I., one dragoon and four sepoys of the 24th N. I., the major-general invested the place on all sides. On the east were about a thousand of the Bhopal troops; on the north and north-east were the 3rd Bombay Lt. Cavalry and sowars of the Hyderabad Contingent, the remainder of the force occupied the plain on the Saugor road and the south-west advances. To the rear of our camp were hills and jungle, and further off villages.

That all the rebels did not go into the fort on the 24th is certain, inasmuch as sundry camels, bullocks, and tattoes were captured by them on the 25th in the jungles in our rear, and several unfortunate camel drivers were killed.

About 3 P.M. some of the 3rd Europeans, horse

artillery, and dragoons went out in this direction, and drove them off. On the night of 24th, after the moon had gone down, the enemy attacked our pickets, and were driven back with some loss.

The enemy again attacked our pickets on the night of the 25th. Heavy firing was also heard from the side of the Bhopal troops.

Early on the morning of the 26th orders were out for the force to be in readiness for a move. The sappers and miners were ordered to prepare fascines in the jungle at the foot of the hill, and to have sand-bags in readiness. Almost before these were made the major-general and staff at the head of the 3rd Europeans came quietly from the camp round the Saugor road to the north of the hill, followed by the 18-pounders, howitzers, and mortars, and 6-pounders of the Hyderabad Contingent. The sappers then fell in, and the whole moved along from the road to the jungle. As we passed through the jungle towards the foot-path that was to lead to the summit of the fort-hill, we found ourselves in the midst of fire. The jungle-grass before, behind, and on both sides of us was in a blaze! what with the heat of the sun and the fire, we were pretty nearly roasted. The guide had lost the path, so we halted; the order to "right about face" was given, and by-and-bye we came upon the track. We had not gone far when we found ourselves jammed—

progress, save by single file, was impossible. The order "sappers to the front" was given, and away they went to cut a road up this hill for the guns. The Europeans continued to thread their way to the height, and the road was soon completed for the guns. The ascent, however, was so rugged and steep that much labour was required ere they could be dragged up to the summit.

During the time occupied in establishing ourselves on the hill, the other part of the force had moved out in three divisions. The town was then permanently occupied without resistance. A body of the enemy posted in a grove of trees to the right of the town showed some resistance, but were soon expelled after a few rounds of shot. The enemy kept up a sharp musketry fire from the fort, and from a gun on one of the bastions. By 3 P.M. the town and hill were in our possession. The fire from the north face of the fort upon the forces on the hill was kept up with great vigour the whole of the day.

The general was in the front the whole of the time, and had numerous narrow escapes of being killed. The sites for the breaching and mortar batteries were chosen under his own superintendence, and the batteries were soon erected. The mortar battery was thrown up in less than four hours. To the right of the mortar battery two six-pounders of the Hyderabad Contingent kept up a constant fire of shot and shell upon the fort, while the Enfield rifles of the 3rd Europeans kept down the matchlock fire of the enemy.

The quartermaster of the H. C., Mr. Thompson, had two narrow escapes. One musket ball struck his leathern helmet, and a second struck him in the chest, upon a pocket-book. Several others were wounded by musket-balls.

About 11 P.M. the mortar battery opened fire. The breaching battery was completed, and the 18-pounders opened fire about 5 A.M. on the 27th at a distance of about three hundred yards. Two eight inch mortars and the howitzer played upon the fort from the plain all day on the 26th.

As soon as the breaching battery opened, the enemy concentrated a very heavy fire upon it, occasionally the bullets whizzed by like hail, and now and then wounded some one.

On the evening of the 27th a mud-tower was taken by assault close beneath the gate of the fort. A private of the 3rd Europeans was shot dead, and as the place was too exposed, and valueless when held, it was evacuated.

All day on the 28th, the breaching went on. By 10 P.M. a breach which appeared practicable was made, and an examination was determined upon. Corporal Linahan, Subadar Seelovay, and two privates of the Madras Sappers, examined the breach under a very heavy fire from the enemy, who were evidently on the *qui vive*.

About 11 o'clock A.M. on the 28th while the breaching was steadily progressing there was a great uproar in camp. Camp followers and camel drivers came running in from the jungle in our rear almost frightened to death, and crying out that the enemy was coming down, which was indeed the fact.

On the hill and in the jungle in our rear a large force of the enemy were seen approaching with their standards flying.

The cavalry pickets engaged them. Their fire was very smart and in vollies, they also threw rockets among our men. The horse artillery, dragoons, and sowars, and 3rd Bombay Cavalry, and 5th Infantry H. C., moved out upon them. The guns could not cross the river in this place, and so opened fire from the camp side with shell and grape. They were too knowing to advance or remain in the position they had taken up, and accordingly fled back into the jungles again as fast as their legs would carry them, throwing away their muskets, flags, and other things. By the time the cavalry and infantry had crossed the river they were well off, though our troopers followed some six or seven miles, and cut up a few of them.

They managed to drive away two elephants, some dozen camels, and upwards of a hundred head of cattle they found grazing in the jungles.

These rebels were mutineers; they had the red coat, the percussion musket, and the cut of sepoys.

Among the things picked up on the pursuit were carved heads upon poles representing European ladies and officers' heads with bleeding throats! In the heads of the ladies they had imitated a back comb, from which hung real human hair, and which must have belonged to some unfortunate victim, as it was so different in colour and texture to native hair.

During the time this action was going on in the plain, the enemy in the fort redoubled their fire upon the batteries. They could see as well as ourselves how the day was going, and when their friends were put to flight, contrary to their expectations, they relaxed their fire as quickly as they had increased it, and we continued to pound away as though nothing had occurred to interfere with our pursuits.

After the breach had been inspected the firing went on as usual, everybody expecting the "storm" to follow the next day. It was a very clear moonlight night and very cold on the top of the hill. The enemy only fired an occasional shot at us, and we enjoyed a quiet chat, and at length retired to our beds in the jungle near the batteries. Our sleep was not much disturbed.

In the early hours of the morning we were up, looking about us, and speculating on the next move. We were surprised to find our enemy so very quiet; not a shot was fired from the fort, although shells were going in from our batteries every quarter of an hour.

Lieut. Strutt of the Bombay Artillery and I, noticing how quiet all was, thought we would go to the breach. We went, not a shot was fired. Lieut. Strutt jumped down into the ditch, scrambled over the rubble and up the breach, I followed. On looking into the fort not a soul was to be seen— the birds had flown; how was a mystery. One or two artillery men from the heavy-gun battery followed, and we were in possession of the fort, before a soul in camp knew they had escaped. The men of the 3rd European regiment who were posted behind the batteries began to rush into the fort. The commandant, Col. Liddel, was in a great rage, ordered them back, and placed Lieut. Strutt under arrest; he did not know who the other officer was, or I should have been in a similar position. There were only a few men left behind, and these were soon despatched. One of their sentries was found asleep in one of the bastions. There were two or three old men and women and

ESCAPE OF REBELS.

children in some of the houses, who informed us they had all gone away about midnight down the east face, on the side guarded by the Bhopal force.

There were a good many lying about dead in various places—also dead bullocks, horses, and ponies, yet it was astonishing to see how little harm our battering and shelling had done the many buildings.

They had a smith's shop, and were preparing to cast a gun; the stables were full of good horses, saddled and bridled, and among these was the charger of the late Lieutenant Redmayne, upon which he was killed at Mundasoore; tatoos and bullocks were chasing each other about; and among the trees and on the buildings were scores of huge monkies, chattering and bounding as though they considered our presence an intrusion; in the houses were all kinds of native camp lumber.

The news of the evacuation soon reached camp, and, by-and-bye, the general and his staff came in also by the breach.

The Hyderabad Cavalry were sent out after the rebels as soon as possible. They succeeded in cutting up a few, and making a few others prisoners. The two head men were captured. One was found squatting under a tree not far from the river, by an officer's servant. When the man went up to him, he whispered, "I am the Rajah, show me how to escape," and promised him money. The servant told him to remain quiet, and forthwith summoned his master, who captured him. These two men were hanged over the gate-way. The majority of the enemy got clear away. The most amazing thing was to see the place from whence they had escaped. To look down the precipitous path made one giddy, —and yet down this place, where no possible footing could be seen, they had all gone—men and women —in the dead of the night! One or two mangled bodies lay at the bottom, attesting the difficulty of the descent. Nothing but despair could have tempted them to have chosen such a way; this was the only one, and they chose it rather than the alternative of awaiting the events of the storm.

What the Bhopal troops were about to have permitted it we never could learn.

The view of the surrounding country from the fort was very beautiful. The river winding its way along the valley; the distant hills clothed with verdure; the rumbling of the stream from the falls and over the loose stones as it flowed round the fort and onward to be lost among other hills; the camp and all the variously dressed people belonging to it sauntering about in peace, bathing or washing in the clear river, presented a scene worthy the pencil of any artist!

On the 30th the sappers and miners occupied the

fort and commenced mining and demolishing the buildings. About forenoon Sir H. Rose received information that the rebels had taken up a position about eight miles off, had destroyed a village and posted themselves in another small fort. The general was soon after them with horse artillery, two five-and-a-half inch mortars, two guns of reserve battery, the 3rd Europeans, the majority of the cavalry, and a section of the Madras Sappers. About 4 o'clock we heard heavy firing.

Some short time after this we saw a line of dhoolies coming into camp with wounded; these were eight men of the 3rd Europeans, two of the 3rd Light Cavalry, and one of the H.C., more or less severely wounded. They informed us that the action had commenced on the banks of the river, which we had a few days previously found so great an impediment to our getting the siege-train to Rhatghur. About 10 o'clock P.M. a large supply of provisions came into camp from Saugor, under an escort of the 31st Bengal N.I. These men informed us that we might expect an attack upon our camp at any hour from the Saugor side of Rhatghur, as they had seen a large body of the enemy on their flank.

After crossing the river our force had had some sharp bush fighting up to a village called Barodia. The enemy were considerably cut up. They had sent away their women and baggage previously, and then came out of the village to dispute the passage of the river, and thereby facilitate their escape. Captain Neville, of the Royal Engineers, who had joined our force the day before, was killed by a round shot striking him in the head. He fell dead from his horse. The loss of this officer was much lamented by the general. He had been all through the Crimean war—had passed days and nights in the trenches before Sebastopol, and had escaped with much honour, and in so short a time to have met death in such a manner after such a career was indeed lamentable. He was buried the day after in a little mound near the camp, all the officers of the force having followed him to his grave.

The force returned to camp about 2 A.M., having given the rebels a sound beating, but without taking their guns from them.

Thus ended the operations connected with the siege and capture of the fort of Rhatghur.

This first achievement of Sir H. Rose was not quite so bright a beginning as the general might have wished. The grand object, however, was attained, and the work executed in a manner that foreshowed to every one better times under a leader of such energy and judgment. Not a man would have escaped from this fort had the general had a

DEATH OF CAPTAIN NEVILLE.

sufficient number of reliable troops. The place they chose to escape from showed how hard they must have been pressed, nor would they have given us the slip in this instance had Europeans been where the Bhopal troops were posted. An escalade might have succeeded where we breached, but this would have been attended with considerable loss to the Europeans, and at this season not an European soldier was to be spared over and above what prudence and necessity called for. The rebels were always cunning at escape, as we shall hereafter observe.

By the fall of Rhatghur we effected two most desirable objects. We could now march on to the relief of Saugor, in the fort of which city the Europeans had been shut up for an anxious period of *eight* months, constantly bordering on despair, and we had rid all the country south of Saugor of a cowardly tantalising foe, while the road from Indore thus far was again opened for communication.

For months past these rebels had been in the habit of threatening Saugor, plundering villages, and committing overt acts of villany, and again retiring to their stronghold confident of security. The *Feringhees* were no more, and they were lords of their castle, oppressing the poor and plundering the rich. The tide of affairs had at length turned, the storm that was ere long to engulf them had overtaken them, the simoon of British anger was now blowing upon them from all quarters in terrible blasts.

RELIEF OF SAUGOR.

On the morning of 3rd February we made our entry into Saugor. It was a bright, pleasant day, pleasant it must have been to the people in Saugor. As we neared the city the Europeans came out upon elephants, horses, and in buggies, to meet us; and on each side of the road there were swarms of natives in their bright and many coloured dresses. By-and-bye the guns of the fort fired a salute, and as we marched through the large town the bands played. The town was very crowded with people, and sauntering about the streets were the sepoys of the 31st Bengal N. I., the only regiment of the Bengal army which had remained faithful.

The Europeans looked very pale and care-worn, and well they might, after having endured so anxious an imprisonment, cut off from all escape, and packed together within the walls of the fort for so long, surrounded by bodies of the enemy who constantly harassed them, and living in the midst of a vast population of disaffected natives.

In some of the streets there were a good many sullen, diabolical looking fellows, who seemed to wish us anywhere else. As we marched past the fort, which is situated on a hill in the town in a commanding situation, its walls were crowded with Europeans, men, women, and children. The fort appeared a very strong one. Here and there were some new works upon the old, and from most of the embrasures guns pointed out. We passed through the town close to its beautiful lake, and encamped on the right of the road beneath a barren belt of hills. The cantonment, which was in perfect repair, was in our front to the left of the road.

Small-pox was in the town, and accordingly orders were issued forbidding any one in camp to visit the place.

The Preliminaries and Capture of the Fort of Gurrakotta.

On February 6th there was a parade of all the troops. On the 8th fifty rank and file of the Madras Sappers, with an engineer officer, marched out of Saugor for a fort and works lately occupied by the enemy at Nurraullee, some fourteen miles off. They were accompanied by details of the Bengal 31st N. I. and 42nd N. I. In September 1857 a body of bundeelahs took possession of the place, and threw up a strong stone work, about a mile in length, on either side of the village gateway, and strengthened this work by bastions. The troops from Saugor went out for the purpose of dislodging them, and were repulsed with the loss of their commanding officer, Col. Johnson of the 42nd N. I., who was shot dead. The detachment of sappers now left with the force were then ordered out to Sanoda, about ten miles, to destroy another fort recently held by the enemy, and to cut a road for the siege-train to cross the river Beeas. Close to our encamping ground was a beautiful suspension-bridge spanning the river. It was in excellent repair, but not considered sufficiently strong for the passage of heavy guns. The whole of the materials for this bridge were obtained and worked up in the neighbourhood. The appearance of this structure, so familiar to one in England, was quite a novelty to one in this country. The river itself in this spot is very picturesque, but the addition of the elegant suspension-bridge considerably enhanced the natural beauty of the landscape.

It is surprising that this kind of bridge is not oftener met with in India, for it appears to possess great advantages over the ordinary ones. In the present instance, although the siege-train did not pass over it, I have every reason to believe it would have borne the weight of the guns separately with perfect safety. The field-batteries, and horse artillery, and baggage crossed it in one continuous stream with very little alteration in its plane.

The villagers about Sanoda appeared to be in the deepest distress. They had been plundered of everything by mutinous sepoys and bundeelahs for months past, and were reduced to such an extreme condition of poverty as to wander through our camp seeking the undigested grains from among the dung of our cattle, and then and there to eat them !

Large quantities of grain were distributed among these poor sufferers. In one of the villages near our camp we captured a cotwal who had given the enemy every assistance in his power for months, and had exercised most undue severity towards the unoffending peasants about. This man at first told Capt. Hare he would give him much valuable information concerning the rebels in case his life was spared, which was accordingly promised on the condition that he did so the first thing in the morning.

When the morning came he denied being able to say anything, and maintained a dogged silence. Three hours were allowed him to reconsider the value of his existence, at the end of which time he was to be hanged if he persisted in the lie. What effect the night's sleep had had upon him it is hard to say, at the end of these three anxious hours he chose rather to die like a dog than tell the truth.

He was accordingly marched to a tree, an empty bullock-cart was driven under it, into which he mounted, and, blindfolded, waited the horrid moment of strangulation. The noose was arranged around his neck, the bullock's tail screwed and away went the cart, and he dropped dangling from a mimosa branch, and thus died. Probably he discredited such summary punishment.

The force was now on the march for the fort of Gurrakotta, in which the mutinous 51st and 52d Bengal regiments, with large bodies of other rebels, had made a stand, and from whence they had annoyed this part of the country for a long time past.

After a very fatiguing march of about 25 miles we sighted the fort, having halted on our way at Shapore to breakfast, and hang a few more rebels. When we arrived at Shapore we learnt that the enemy had only left that place some two hours before, so the general determined to push on, and leaving the ordinary road to our left, we forced our way through a very difficult jungly path over some hills, and at length came up on a cavalry picket of the enemy, some four or five miles from Gurrakotta. While we were passing over the hills we surprised an infantry outpost. They were driven before us by the Bombay 24th N. I. and the 3rd Europeans, leaving their kit behind them. The day was well nigh spent when the column halted ; marching through the jungle, skirmishing and halting, and stealing upon the enemy, was most trying to the troops ; the sun was very powerful, and there was scarcely a shadow to creep into, and having to halt every thirty or forty yards from hour to hour eventually overpowered most of the men.

The Bombay 3rd Light Cavalry, the 3rd Europeans, and 24th N. I. preceded the column when we neared the fort. 'The cavalry captured five men of the enemy's picket. These the major-general ordered to be taken to the rear and shot. They were taken some distance on our left flank, and despatched by the Bombay Cavalry as desired.

By 3.30 P.M. we were on our encamping ground. The general was making a reconnaissance, and about 6 P.M. we marched to our places, got our tents pitched, and made the best of a very rough dinner. Our baggage arrived after midnight.

Soon after our camp was pitched, round shot came in among our tents from the enemy's guns in the fort. They also fired rockets at us.

The general did not return to camp till nearly 8 o'clock that night. How he endured so much was surprising to every one, nor was it the most agreeable thing for his staff. The enemy had erected some very creditable earth-works upon the road to the south, from whence they *expected* our arrival, and they occupied the village near the fort in some force. To oust them from this position the horse artillery took ground upon an open and rather elevated spot in front of our camp, and commenced a brisk cannonade upon them. The enemy sounded their bugles and advanced in force at a double upon our guns ; they were, however, repulsed by the 3rd Europeans ; they again formed up and advanced in great steadiness, and this time got very near to the guns, but again gave way and fell back in great disorder, some flying towards the fort, others to the south ; these the Hyderabad Cavalry followed and cut up. A breaching battery was then erected opposite the west face. The 24-pound howitzer was at work all day on the 12th, and soon silenced the enemy's guns. One large gun annoyed us a good deal. It was worked well, and we could see the enemy in their red coats loading and firing it. Lieut. Strutt of the Bombay Artillery fought this gun admirably, and at length knocked it from the embrasure. After this no further annoyance from them was experienced. The 18-pounders played upon the fort all the evening and through the night. Early on the morning of the 13th we could see the enemy escaping in great numbers from the fort gate. We ceased firing, and by-and-bye marched down with the 3rd Europeans to the fort, to find that all had escaped in the night-time. Capt. Hare, with

CAPTURE OF THE FORT.

the Hyderabad Cavalry, pursued them some twenty-five miles and completed the work. A great number were slain and made prisoners, as was also a good deal of their plunder captured. Thus, the 51st and 52nd mutinous sepoys were punished, and the beautiful little fort of Gurrakotta fell into our hands.

A guard of the 3rd Europeans occupied the fort, and the Madras and Bombay Sappers commenced the work of demolition.

It was abundantly stored with grain, flour, cloth, sugar, spices, and other commissariat articles. There was an infinitude of such lumber as natives love to hoard : bags full of bangles, bracelets, anklets, and rings ; boxes full of miniature mariner's compasses, English loot—steel pens, and paper. The sacks of flour were the largest I ever saw in my life, they resembled huge hogsheads, men must have mounted ladders to have filled them. Here and there was a dead bullock, tattoo, or man, and everywhere little heaps of bullets and gunpowder.

Several of the dead sepoys wore their medals round their necks, and we found the buttons of some seven Bengal regiments upon various shell-jackets about. Near the gun from which we had been so annoyed, and which was silenced by Lieut. Strutt, were three bodies ; one of these was the ·body of a havildar, the other two were privates. The last shot from the howitzer had killed these men.

o

The enemy had evidently provided for a long sojourn in this place, and from its natural position and structure it appeared eminently suited to the purposes of guerilla warfare. The fort stands upon an elevated angle of ground, the wide deep river Sonar washing the east face, a tributary stream—the Gidaree nullah—with precipitous banks flowing around the west and north faces, to the south is the strong gate-way flanked by bastions, and a ditch about twenty feet deep and thirty wide. This ditch ran round the west face also. On the opposite side of the river is the well-built town of Gurrakotta, about one mile from the fort.

Report says that this fort stood a three weeks' siege some forty years ago, and that the garrison eventually capitulated to Brigadier Watson, C.B., who, with twenty-eight pieces of ordnance, found it impossible to effect a breach. Marks of shot still were visible in several places, and in others the present enemy had repaired the damages done to its walls and bastions.

The south-west wall of the fort was blown down on the evening of the 15th, and a company of the 31st Bengal N.I. under Lieut. Dickins, remained in charge of the enormous heaps of grain which still remained after our force had conveyed away to Saugor as much as they had carriage for.

In a conversation with this officer upon the pro-

POSITION OF THE FORT.

bable cause of this regiment not having joined in the general rebellion, he stated that the only reason he could give was the fact that the officers, perhaps, understood their men better than others. The company under his command had all through evinced a willingness to obey to the letter, and had on several occasions met small bodies of the enemy, who had taunted them with their allegiance, and had in each instance behaved as well as men could be expected. He was an excellent linguist, and appeared to be thoroughly acquainted with the native character, and the native officers to appreciate his.

There appears to be a good deal of reason in this simple statement. As a rule I fear we do not enter into a sufficiently exact analysis of the native character, while it is well known that no one in the world forms a quicker or juster estimate of our actions than they do.

An unfortunate private of the Bombay Sappers got into disgrace here. He was found leaving the fort in charge of a camel upon which a few handsful of flour and a little ghee and other trifles had been secreted. Looting of every kind was strictly prohibited by the general—even the few ounces of flour and morsel of ghee were not to be appropriated, and so the man in charge of the camel was placed in arrest to await his trial for disobedience of orders.

We returned for Saugor, after the column, on the

16th. As we passed along the road we had marched on a few days before, we came to the spot where the five men had been shot, and there lay their five skeletons bleaching in the sun in the same position as they had fallen, and we were again surprised to find the poor villagers in our route back picking among the dung on the road for grains to convert into food. Destitution could scarcely be worse than this! The poor wretches appeared verging on the last stage of starvation! As we re-crossed the suspension bridge, the body of the budmash we had hanged upon the mimosa tree, the day we cut the road for the siege guns at the river Beeas, still hung there, and the jackalls had eaten away the two legs as far as the knees. It was a horrid sight!

We rejoined the force in Saugor on the 17th, and *now had a few days rest before us.*

The capture of the fort of Gurrakotta, and the escape of the enemy, was another instance of the difficulty formerly experienced of totally entrapping our foe. Here, again, the position of the fort was so admirably chosen, that nothing short of a far larger force than the general had at his disposal could have ensured such an investment as would have prevented the escape of the enemy, favoured as they were in their flight by the river and the densely wooded undulated ground south of the fort. The fort, however, fell into our hands in a short time, and the enemy on this side of Saugor was disposed of, so that the major-general now had an unopposed basis for the important operations that were to follow in the campaign.

In almost every instance of encounter with these once famed Bengal sepoys, we observe that they always supposed we should attack them in *one* direction only, and they accordingly threw up works to oppose us in that position they imagined we should of necessity choose. Of course, the general had information of this, and then painfully proved to these rebels the feasibility of operating from quite a contrary direction, and when they saw this, and the utter uselessness of all their works of defence, they no longer attempted an opposition—the little sneaking ambush courage they possessed speedily oozed away, and like assassins and thieves they made the best use of their heels in the dark hours of night.

CHAP. V.

General prepares to march upon Jhansi.—Court-martial on Bombay sapper.—March of the force.—Affair at fort of Barodia.—Troops benighted.—Forcing Malthon and Mudanpore passes.—Defeat of the Rajah of Shahghur.—Fort and garden of Sorai.—Murrowra.—Annexation of territory of Shahghur.—Baunpore.—Destruction of palace.—Tal-Behut.—Capture of fort of Chandaree.—Investment of Jhansi.—The siege.—Arrival of Tantia-Topee.—The " Battle of the Betwa."—The " storm."—The capture.—The palace.—Escape of the Ranee of Jhansi.

Sir H. Rose was now preparing for a long march to the north, and a scarcity of provisions was anticipated by large supplies daily arriving in camp from Bhopal and other places. All who could get boots laid in a stock, and the messes provided themselves with all kinds of European articles, and beer, soda water, and wines as largely as possible. The Parsee shopkeepers at Saugor proved most invaluable friends to us; although they charged us exorbitantly then, as the future proved, they were most moderate when compared with other merchants further north. Those who laid in what would appear an *excessive*

PREPARATIONS FOR MARCH ON JHANSI.

quantity of beer at that time were truly fortunate in the hereafter. The little experience we had already had of the state of the country beyond Saugor was very ominous. The season was becoming hotter every day, and we had every reason to believe that the districts we were about to march through would afford us little or nothing in the way of commissariat, as almost all of them, from Saugor to Cawnpore, were in the hands of the rebels and disaffected chiefs, and their enmity, added to the withering effects of a hot season, would not be likely to leave us a blade of grass, or a grain of corn in a few weeks hence. The general wisely foresaw all this, and took means to provide for his force accordingly. Sheep and goat, and oxen, and grain and flour, and large supplies of tea, and soda water for the sick and wounded, were collected together with all possible speed. A military train had been established from Bombay, which was to follow and aid our force in many various ways.

The sick and wounded were transferred to the field-hospital in Saugor, to be sent away at a fitting period, or to rejoin the force when opportunity presented.

The siege-train was re-supplied from the arsenal with a large amount of ammunition, and strengthened by the addition of other heavy guns, howitzers, and large mortars. Many more elephants were obtained, and the ordnance and engineering parks were especially strengthened. The 3rd European regiment changed their relaxing and highly injurious uniform for one especially adapted to the season and country, and they now dressed in a loose stone coloured cotton blouse and trousers, and pagree of the same colour. This was a most judicious step, as the men could bear considerably more fatigue with comparative comfort while at the distance of half a mile they were almost invisible.

Nothing can be more baneful to European troops in India than the dress worn by them in England and other temperate climates. It is amazing to think that the authorities did not alter this a century ago. We cannot be surprised at the excessive mortality of British troops in India, when we reflect that they have had to combat the fearful effects of a tropical climate from year to year trussed up in uniform only suited to England or the Polar regions. Not more ridiculous would it appear to see an Icelander enveloped in his furs in this country, because such is the uniform worn in *his* mother country, than it is to see our poor fellows buttoned up to the chin in a heavy tight-fitting dress, such as they wore in chilly and frosty England.

It is to be hoped that all European troops coming to this country will be permitted to leave their useless and enervating dress behind them, and have one of a light and suitable material provided in its stead.

During the time these preparations for the march towards Jhansi were maturing, a district court-martial had been held upon the private of the Bombay sappers who was under arrest for looting at the fort of Gurrakotta.

Lieut. Dick, Bombay Engineers, was in command of this detachment of sappers, and from his investigation of the affair, firmly believed the man to be innocent of the crime imputed to him. The man was in charge of the camel coming out of the fort, but asserted his total ignorance of the loot in question being upon him. Another might have done this, it was true, but as there was no proof of his innocence, further than his own word, the evidence appeared much against him.

At his trial the poor fellow was frightened by the ordeal and pleaded guilty, and, it would appear, contradicted himself.

Lieut. Dick was called upon for his evidence, and left the court fully impressed with the belief that the man would be acquitted.

Shortly after dinner the order book was brought in, in which a parade of troops on the following morning was ordered for the punishment and dismissal of the prisoner.

This astonished most of us, and Lieut. Dick, sincerely impressed with the innocence of the prisoner, declared that he could not conscientiously see a good man thus disgraced, without further protesting in his behalf, and using every lawful means for his honourable acquittal.

Some technical informality appeared upon the face of the proceedings, and after consultation with other officers, he sent in an official to the brigadier that night, requesting a postponment of the parade that the man might be tried by an European court. Lieut. Dick was evidently much affected, and awaited with some anxiety for an answer to his communication—none came.

On the morning of the 22nd, the troops paraded and formed three sides of a square.

The preamble of the crime, and the sentence was read aloud, and translated to the native troops. Then Capt. Todd, the brigade-major, was seen to read a paper and to go up to the brigadier, who then read it. He seemed much disconcerted by its contents, and then the prisoner said aloud that he desired to be tried by an European general court-martial. The brigadier then rode up to Lieut. Dick, and said, " Lieut. Dick, I've to thank you for this," and the parade was dismissed,—the man still a prisoner, and Lieut. Dick ordered under arrest by the brigadier ! This surprised a good many, but mostly Lieut. Dick, who had acted all through with so good a motive.

Another court sat upon the prisoner, and this day's order book informed us that he was sentenced to receive fifty lashes, to be branded with the letter " M," for mutinous conduct on parade, and to undergo *seven* years' imprisonment—every other of which was to be solitary, and the medical officer in charge was ordered to " be prepared to brand the prisoner with the letter ' M ' ! "

Poor Lieut. Dick was much affected by this extraordinary decision of the court, and more particularly so since the prisoner's antecedents had been unblemished. He had served Government *nine years* and some months, without a single default as a sapper, and it seemed improbable that a man of such good conduct should lay himself open to such disgrace for so paltry an offence as the one he now stood sentenced upon ; and there was reason to believe another was guilty of the crime. But the sentence had gone forth, and the man who had thus served Government was to be branded as a mutineer, flogged, and imprisoned for seven years !

Mutineers and murderers have since fared better.

Early on the 25th the troops paraded again for punishment, and branding of the prisoner. There was no mistake this time. The troops formed three sides of a square as before, and in the centre was an empty cart. The sentence was read out as before, and the prisoner led to the cart. The brigadier then inquired of the medical officer in charge if he had "come prepared to brand the man with the letter 'M?'"

The medical officer replied that he had not. When asked if he had seen the orders directing him to do so, he said that he had, but that as the art and science of *branding* formed no part of *his* professional education, and as an order to the effect that it formed no part of a military surgeon's *duty* had long ago been issued from the "Horse Guards," he had only come prepared to *superintend* the infliction of the punishment, and if the prisoner were then capable of undergoing the branding to superintend that also. The man was then flogged *secundum artem*, and the troops marched back to camp.

The health of the troops continued very good; the bands played every evening; a few evening parties were got up in the station; there was a picnic to the beautiful lake near the fort; and great and constant conviviality in the various messes and camp.

We were on the eve of a long and trying march north—months would pass away ere another such respite could be dreamed of, and if we could place any reliance on the reports in camp of the work in store for us, we certainly had every reason to take pleasure by the hand and "be merry while we may;" so there was music and feasting in all due order; and days of promotion, and days of receipt of gratuity for service wounds, and birth days, and other memorable occasions, were celebrated with rejoicings.

These scenes were soon to change to the "roughings" and night bivouac of the jungle, to the hurried cup of tea and hard biscuit before starting on the mid-night march, and to the unremitting fatigue of a harassing campaign in a scorching season and wasted country.

MARCH TO JHANSI.

By this time everything was arranged for a start on the march—the city of Jhansi being our destination. Accordingly the camp was roused at 2 A.M. on the morning of the 27th, and the force moved off over a belt of hills through a narrow pass to their first halting ground at Raneepoor.

Major Orr's column of the Hyderabad Contingent started the evening before upon another route to march parallel with our own. Directly our force had marched off the ground at Saugor several large rockets were seen to shoot up into the dark sky from the centre of the city. The enemy had evidently had their spies in our camp, who were now telegraphing the departure of our troops to their friends north of us.

After the march was over a parade of the officers of the force was ordered to assemble at the brigadier's flag-staff in the afternoon. This was for the purpose of publicly reprimanding Lieut. Dick for his conduct in the late business of the court-martial at Saugor. A most severe and lengthy reprimand, delivered in very caustic strains with much agitation of manner, was then read out to the assembly by Brigadier Steuart, 14th Lt. Dragoons.

Lieut. Dick was told that summary dismissal from the service could alone have answered the ends of military law, had not youth, ignorance, and inexperience pleaded in extenuation of his conduct. He had, it was remarked, struck at the root of all good military order and discipline, to the subversion of the most important duties of a soldier; he was then released from his arrest, and deprived of his command.

From that hour every spark of honourable ambition and military ardour seemed quenched in his breast; he appeared to give over his papers and charge like a man who signs his last will and testament, and quietly awaits the hour of death.

Lieut. Dick's grave misdemeanor lay in pointing out a few informalities, and in recommending a good man to the judgment of an European court more likely to do justice to a prisoner than a native one ; and this he did with the noblest possible motives couched in terms of respect, and prompted by a deep sense of his own conscientious behaviour. His lot was indeed a hard one.

The next morning we were roused by the bugle at 2 A.M. The column had not pressed off the ground more than a mile when rockets again were seen shooting up into the sky at regular intervals in front of us.

A mile or two ahead of our force, on an elevated piece of ground, a bright beacon fire was blazing up and then some seven or eight hundred yards in advance of this another burst up in flames, and as the column marched on and on, another and another bright fire shone out of the dark masses of jungle on the different hills, first on our right, then on our left, until the morning rendered them useless. Around each of these fires were three or four natives, suspicious looking men, but they swore they were only preparing for a feast when captured by the dragoons. No doubt this was a well-devised means of warning the enemy of our approach ; nothing could be better than a chain of these fires for the purpose, and few things carry an air of such apparent innocence and simplicity, for what more natural than that men should make a fire in the jungles in the cold hours of the morning, or one for a feast! The road was tolerably good, though up hill almost all the way. The plains on either side were generally well cultivated, and the hills covered with dense jungle. We were now nearing the *Malthon-pass,* where strong opposition was expected from the enemy, who had placed guns so as to command the pass, and had a strong body of infantry and cavalry posted there. We halted near the village of Rajwas, and pitched camp in a flat surrounded on three sides by high hills.

About two miles from our camp to the north was another village and a small strongly-built fort on the spur of a long hill above the village. This fort immediately commanded the road leading to the pass, and was named the fort of Barodia. Towards afternoon some one who had been out looking about the neighbourhood of the camp went so close to this fort, which was thought deserted, as to call down the matchlock fire of a body of the enemy, who still kept possession of it. This signal was enough, and about 3 P.M. a few guns, a couple of mortars, infantry, and cavalry were sent out to drive the enemy out of this little den.

After some shelling and knocking open the gate, the enemy were seen escaping over the fort wall into the jungle on the hill.

A good deal of musketry firing then took place in the jungle, and the enemy there sustained some loss. The 3rd Bombay Light Cavalry pursued around the hill by the road, but failed in doing much on account of the dense jungles.

When the fort was taken possession of, only one or two men were found inside; one had both legs recently broken, and his friends had cut his throat before parting!

By this time the sun had set, and dark masses of clouds rolled thicker and thicker over the sky; flashes of lightning were followed by deep peals of thunder, and then the rain began to pour down unmercifully. We had scarcely turned our faces towards camp when we found ourselves enveloped in darkness dense as Erebus. We lost our road, although we were so short a distance away, and went on stumbling through nullahs and bushes, while sheets of lightning flashed over us, frightening our horses, and rendering the path doubly difficult to find. The cavalry and artillery bugles were sounding in various directions, we could see the camp fires, hear horses neighing, but could not get into camp. At length, after blundering about till nearly 9 o'clock at night, we passed the sentries, and eventually found our quarters, wet through and tired. Long after we were comfortable under our canvas, we heard the imploring cries of the cavalry bugles from those who could not find their way home. Some, I believe, did not get into camp till past midnight. Such a circumstance is hardly credible, nor could we credit our own difficulties while the camp fires were so plainly visible to us, but of one thing I am quite certain, viz., that nothing is more difficult than to find one's way home at night through a camp, particularly if it be a large one.

We halted the next day on account of the good folk who lost their road that night, although the general had determined to push on, and had issued orders to that effect.

At first it was determined to destroy this fort, and then it was thought advisable to put it into a state of defence as a postal station from whence to keep up communication with the marching column and Saugor.

Accordingly, Lieut. Prendergast, Madras Engineers, with a section of the Madras Sappers, and a company of Khoonds—a semi-barbarous, undisciplined body of levies recently raised from the hill districts —took possession.

These Khoonds* were most extraordinary fellows. When they marched they seemed to keep on the jog-trot, laughing and joking, and carrying their arms as one would imagine of a wild Irish mob; they seemed possessed of no scruples of caste, and

* A hill people from the jungles, about the source of the river Nerbudda

were always willing to go anywhere and do anything where there was a chance of looting a rag or a lota. They appeared to be the very best of material from whence to mould a useful corps, but at present, as might be expected, were in the roughest possible form.

With these Khoonds, then, Lieut. Prendergast was left in charge of the hill fort of Barodia, with a few sappers to put it in a state of repair and defence.

He posted guards for the night, and in his rounds invariably found them asleep and had to kick them up. They seemed never to imagine that they were not to sleep on their posts! What did they think of or care for any enemy? They were inside a fort, had shut the gate, and that was enough. With such a garrison one may imagine that an European officer would scarcely feel at home or very comfortable, and would be happy to get off to safer and more civilized company.

On the morning of the 3rd March the general devised a movement against the enemy in our front of a very important kind. The Pass of Malthon, naturally a very strong obstacle to the advance of an army, was held by the enemy in force; every day was of importance, so that the general determined to gain the table land above these hills by a flank movement through the Pass of Mudanpore into the territory of the Rajah of Shahghur, who was in arms against us, while he made a feint in the enemy's front at the strong Pass of Malthon.

Accordingly, about 2 A.M. the 24th Bombay N. I., three guns, Bhopal Artillery, and a howitzer under Capt. Lightfoot, a body of 14th Light Dragoons, and 3rd Cavalry, all under the command of Major Scudamore, moved off for the Malthon Pass, while the remainer of the force, again strengthened by the junction of the Hyderabad Contingent, moved quietly from the encamping ground about 5 A.M. for the Mudanpore Pass.

Forcing the Pass.

We marched along the foot of a long range of hills for a distance of about five or six miles, and then began to enter upon the almost pathless route for the Mudanpore Pass. As the column moved quietly along into a horse-shoe kind of plateau with hills densely clad with jungle on both sides towards the gorge, a heavy fire was opened upon the leading bodies from the enemy's guns and infantry in their front.

This was rather a surprise to us, and the news quickly passed along the long line that our artillery and infantry were already engaged with a strong force of the enemy.

FORCING THE MUDANPORE PASS.

As we gradually neared up towards the front the fire of our guns rapidly increased, and in the intervals we heard heavy vollies of musketry. The hills on our right and our left were crowded with the infantry of the enemy; the pass and the brushwood immediately before it were held by their artillery, cavalry, and infantry in force.

By this time we had arrived within sight of the engagement, and then we saw our horse artillery blazing away into the masses of their infantry in our front near the pass, while the infantry of the Hyderabad Contingent and 3rd Europeans were clearing the hills on our flanks.

The enemy held their cover with considerable firmness for a long time, and their fire was so galling and heavy that our guns were ordered by the general to retire some yards. Ere this could be done the fire was so fierce that the artillerymen had to take shelter behind their guns; several were wounded, and the general had his horse shot, and narrowly escaped death several times.

The bullets fell about like hail-stones. The artilleryretired and re-opened fire, and by this time the guns of the Hyderabad Contingent opened with shell upon the enemy's masses in the jungle left of the pass. Then the 3rd Europeans and Hyderabad Infantry charged into the jungle, while the guns poured shell upon the enemy over their heads.

They were now seen flying in great numbers over the hills to our right and left and through the pass. The Hyderabad Infantry and 3rd Europeans were upon them, while the Hyderabad Cavalry and dragoons dashed across the plain and through the pass after them.

The day was now ours. The main body of the enemy had fled through the pass with their guns, around a large tank, and into the town of Mudanpore. We then moved on quickly through the pass, brought up our howitzers to the front, and again the enemy opened their guns upon us from behind the tank wall. Their fire soon ceased, however, and the troops advanced through the town, and halted to breathe awhile and quench their thirst. The hills all round were scoured by our infantry, and the rebels found in their jungles were despatched.

After a short halt, the Hyderabad Cavalry were sent in pursuit, and right well did they do their work. They came up with the tail of the enemy's force, cut up a great number and captured many— among others, the astrologer of the Rajah of Shahghur. They followed the enemy some miles over hills and through jungle, and at length came up to the fort of Sorai, where their work ended. They were reported to have slain upwards of three hundred of the enemy.

As we marched through the pass, many of their bodies lay about; some were those of sepoys, some of bundeelahs. While the fighting in the jungle was going on, several characteristic incidents relating to the Khoonds occurred. No sooner did one of them or anybody else shoot down a rebel, than three or four of them rushed upon the fallen foe, threw down their muskets, and commenced forthwith a scramble for the belt and pouch, the pagree, the jacket, the waistband, and the pice it might contain; and there they were in the midst of fighting, bawling away and laughing, like human vultures; then they shouldered arms and trotted off with a couple of pouch belts, perhaps, over their shoulders, and two or three pagrees on their heads. When they got into the town, they seemed to think there was nothing more to be done than to batter open the cottage doors and hunt out the vile rags and broken pots left behind by the inhabitants, who had fled also to the jungles.

I remember while we sat down to rest a short time near the town, a shot was heard immediately in our rear. On looking round to the spot from whence the sound came, I saw a man drop down from a high tamarind tree on to the roof of a cottage; he fell like lead, and died a moment or two after. The man who shot him thought he had achieved a great feat, and reloaded his musket with considerable resolution, while he repeatedly impressed the fact upon his bronzed brethren, "I killed him."

As soon as the troops had rested, we moved off again to end a glorious day in the most wearisome after march perhaps we ever endured. The sun was very hot; the late excitement had done its work, and as the troops marched and countermarched, halted and crept along, examining villages, sheds, and jungles, they began to fall out in twos and threes, to cry frequently for the water-carrier, and to go into a sound sleep in the sun if a ten minutes' halt occurred. At length, weary and foot-sore, parched and exhausted, we halted near the village of Pepeeria, where the artillery and infantry, dragoons, camels, carts and followers all got jammed together in a confused mass for a long time in a kind of horse-shoe piece of ground below the village, around which ran a deep wide stream; this continued to get worse as the baggage poured in, and there seemed no end to our present woes at hand. At length the camp-markers marked out our camp above the village, and little by little we wound ourselves back from the maze we had got into, and in the dark groped our way to our respective places, waited till about 9 o'clock, and then threw ourselves beneath our tents, glad to lie down anywhere without our beds, and rest our wearied limbs—for we had marched close upon twenty miles. Although the troops had gone through a very hard day's work, they bore all their fatigue with the best possible spirit. Sir Hugh Rose was heard to say he had never been under hotter fire in his life, for the time it lasted, than he was in while forcing this pass. The infantry opposed to us were mostly mutinous sepoys. Capt. Abbot of Hyderabad Contingent obtained several of their medals, which he took from the slain after their pursuit.

Their leader, once a havildar major, was slain. He was so enormously fat that his tattoo could not carry him quick enough to elude our cavalry. The Rajah of Shahghur had escaped, and his astrologer, who was now in our hands, confessed that he had been mistaken in his prediction of the fitting day for the annihilation of the Feringhees. He evidently had read the stars through a glass darkly that night, and had woefully proved himself a false prophet.

We were now encamped within sight of the fort of Sorai, which lay some three miles east of our camp, on the top of a solitary hill. The sappers marched to this fort the next day for the purpose of destroying it. The general and his staff also rode over to examine the place.

The fort was a little well-built keep on the top of

a hill, commanding an extensive view of the surrounding plains. At its foot was a small deserted village, and on the north side of the village was the beautiful garden and the *sarai* of the Shahghur Rajah. The fort was very filthy, and full of rubbish.

A more lovely place than this garden was could not well be imagined for a country like India, and I cannot pass on without giving something of a picture of what it was when we resided in it, while the work of destruction was being carried on in the fort.

In the centre of this extensive enclosure was the seraglio of the Rajah, overshadowed by mango and guava trees, and embowered by groves of orange and citron trees, laden with golden fruit and sweet-smelling blossoms.

In front of the doorways were jessamine and myrtles, and roses, oleanders, and camellias and pomegranates in full bloom, and in tiny and tastefully laid out flower beds, reaching away on all four sides, were variegated poppies and marigolds, verbenas, hollyhocks, lilies, and feathery larkspurs, interspersed with little plots of sweet-smelling thyme, mint, borages, and Damascus roses; and in and out of these beds partridges, minars, and parrots strutted and fluttered about as though they alone were the lords of this Elysium. Then there were bowers of roses and jessamine, and, further off, clusters of orange, and citron, and peach trees, all in blossom, hedged in by long lines of rose bushes. Then beyond these were beds of " Windsor beans," trellis-work covered with "French beans ;" then onion, lettuce, beet-root, and asparagus beds, long rows of plantains, and a host of other good vegetables for the table. The whole was enclosed by fine tamarind and mango trees, in which scores of enormous monkeys kept up a constant " hoo-hooing " and chattering all day. I never saw such huge specimens of these before ; some of them were as large as calves, and " hoo-hoo'd " as loud as any asthmatic old man, from sunrise to sunset. In the garden there was also a pretty little temple, a large bowree, from whence water was drawn all day by bullocks for the purpose of irrigation and drinking, and a large stone-built, corridored *chahbachcha*, or cistern, self supplied with most excellent water ; this made a capital bath.

This garden was the pleasantest spot we ever had the good fortune of pitching in during this campaign. We were cool all the day ; enjoyed all that the garden produced for table *ad libitum* ; the wood doves cooing in the early morning ; then the songs of other birds, and the plaintive notes of the bull-bull at night.

The little fort was rendered useless in all due time.

The force marched next upon Murrowra, about twelve miles north, where there was another large fort, and a deserted town of some size, full of Hindu temples. The fort had been recently repaired by the enemy, but was deserted. South of this fort is a large tank of *very* pure water, and good encamping ground. On the 7th the British flag was hoisted upon a bastion of the fort, a proclamation of annexation of the territory was read, the artillery fired a royal salute, the bands played "God save the Queen," and the Rajah of Shahghur was disinherited!

The force under the command of Major Scudamore, 14th L. Dragoons, rejoined after having had a slight engagement with the enemy at the Malthon Pass. The flank movement of the major-general and the defeat of the army under the Rajah of Shahghur at the Mudanpore Pass fully accomplished his designs. The enemy at Malthon received early warning of the results of the battle; they could hear our firing, and, when the enemy at the pass before us gave way, they fled through the jungles over the hills towards Malthon, and then their friends there joined them in a general flight, a few only remaining behind to oppose the advance of the force sent against them by the major-general.

A few miles from our camp was the town of

Shahghur, and the little independent state of Theree, friendly towards us.

It was feared that the enemy would march upon Theree and loot the town of the Ranee, so the Hyderabad Contingent was ordered to march upon Shahghur and Theree to afford assistance in that quarter if needed.

On the 9th March we started for Baunpore. The villages we now passed were all deserted, a few half-starved oxen and pariah dogs appeared their sole occupants. We met some twenty villagers, who stated that they came from Chandaree, and had left the town on account of the fighting going on between the first brigade and the enemy who held that strong fortress. As we neared our encamping ground opposite Baunpore, we heard the sounds of very heavy firing at regular intervals from the west. This came from Chandaree, and was the sound of the siege guns of our first brigade breaching the fort there.

The town of Baunpore was almost as deserted as the villages we had passed on our march. The palace of the Rajah was a very extensive building, and in it were found great quantities of property belonging to different officers of the Bengal army—boxes and clothes, books, and surveying instruments, private letters, and beds. Besides these things there were heaps of tents, palkies, broken carriages, moulds for guns, and palace lumber.

Dr. O'Brien, formerly in the Gwalior Contingent, and now doing duty with the Bombay 3rd Europeans, which corps he joined at Saugor, discovered among the recovered loot a camphor-wood box, mathematical instruments, and letters belonging to him, which he had left in his flight from Lullutpore many months before. He had suffered severely, with several others, in their long flight to Saugor; had since been paralyzed, and was now on his way to Calcutta for England. His tales of woe were very sad indeed, and it appeared a marvel how they had endured their privation and suffering as fugitives so long.

Major Boileau was ordered to destroy this palace, and accordingly, in the evening of the 11th, part of it was blown down, and huge fires lighted in other apartments; by nightfall it was burning brilliantly —like a grand bonfire.

One of the rooms of this palace was covered all over with allegorical pictures painted upon the plaster; some of them were historical and fierce enough, others highly obscene, others eminently childish. The relics of women and children always abounded in these places; no room was without some plaything or bangle, or hand punkah; and

BAUNPORE — DESTRUCTION OF PALACE. 223

reams of native paper and manuscripts lay strewn about everywhere, and the atmosphere of the whole place smelt strongly of frankincense and myrrh, aniseed, benzoin, and other delicate native perfumes. Sounds of heavy firing continued to reach us from the west, and were heard all through the night.

We marched from Baunpore at an early hour on the morning of the 12th, the palace still a burning pile, for the town and fort of Tal-Behut. The Hyderabad Contingent preceded us. We arrived before Tal-Behut about 6 A.M. on the morning of the 14th, and found Major Orr's force encamped on the plain west of the fort.

When the Hyderabad Contingent arrived at Tal-Behut, a body of the enemy held the fort; they exchanged a few round shot with Major Orr, and then at night made the best of their way from the place, so that when we arrived there we found our progress north, to our astonishment, unopposed, although, perhaps, no fort we moved against in this campaign presented greater difficulties for an army to surmount than did that of Tal-Behut, had it been held by a determined foe.

I scarcely remember ever having seen a prettier natural picture than the fort of Tal-Behut, occupying the whole of one extensive hill, mirrored on the bright surface of the large lake which spreads from its foot far away to other distant hills rosy and blue in tufts of soft jungle foliage, with the white tents of our troops pitched in the high grass to the westward, the bright sunrise flooding the heavens with crimson and gold in vivid fan-like beams of light, while our troops marched along the border of the lake, and the wild fowl flew in hundreds above it, screaming and darting into its quiet, weedy waters!

It seemed a pity that the ruthless hand of rebellion should have touched such a spot more favoured by nature for romance than the dread realities of war; and yet war would add interest to its history by new deeds of tragedy as it had done in years gone by, for there is a story of how it had withstood a siege against the Scindiah of former days, and how they erected batteries upon rafts on the lake for its reduction under a famous General Yacob, and how it fell into this general's hands after a weary resistance.

The fort works occupied the whole of the hill. There were two strong lines of works strengthened by bastions and loop-holed, and above these the citadel and fort buildings, temples, and towers. The lowest line ran along the margin of the lake and round the whole hill. From this line to the second there were gardens and pasture-grounds and jetties leading into the lake; a sort of palace also looked into the lake from this range. Between the second and the fort proper were other gardens, temples, and jungle, and high above all was the citadel commanding the town to the north-west, and the surrounding country. The whole was well built and in good repair.

The temple in the fort was full of little gods in all possible postures; these were generally brass. Some of them had tiny silver anklets and bangles on, and little nose-rings of gold on which hung pearls and rubies; there was also a vast collection of brazen pots and cups and bells, and gods of stone and gods of wood, and several Brahmin priests.

The town was almost deserted, though it had every appearance of being inhabited by people of the better class of natives. During our halt here a breach was made in the fort wall on the north side, and some guns found there were burst. Two Europeans were sadly blown up in this latter business by the explosion of some loose gunpowder. There was also some little hanging of prisoners carried on.

We were superabundantly supplied with snipe and teal, and duck from the tank, and peacock from the jungle. The wildfowl were more numerous here than we had known them anywhere, the "bags," accordingly, were overcrowded with spoil. However, they were purchased at some expense, for the sun was now more than hot, and this had to be endured in a little open boat upon the lake for the game in quest. When the sportsmen returned to camp, soda-water and beer to a vast amount disappeared, and much they needed and deserved it. The objects of their toils graced our table in the evening, and nothing was more acceptable when one reflected on tough goat and tougher stuff called beef. We had not heard from Chandaree for some time. The letters sent from either camp must have been stopped by rebels on the road, for none reached us. The major-general naturally became anxious about the first brigade, and despatched Capt. Hare, with the Hyderabad troops under his command, to communicate with them; this was effected, and Capt. Hare returned to Tal-Behut the next day.

On the 16th the Madras and Bombay Sappers with the Hyderabad Contingent marched off to the left bank of the river Betwa, about eight miles from camp, Tal-Behut.

The general had ordered the chief engineer, Major Boileau, to construct a bridge across that river, as it was thought the artillery could not pass.

On arriving at the river we found it fordable, with a capital shingly-bottom, so the men had

CAPTURE OF FORT OF CHANDAREE. 227

simply to raise the road to and from it, and pitch camp on the opposite bank. At another time the general would have experienced great difficulty in crossing this river in the face of an enemy; fortunately, however, the cessation of rains and a long continued hot season favours a rapid movement of troops. The whole force crossed the Betwa the morning of the 17th March, St. Patrick's day, and encamped on the left (north) bank.

Thus far the major-general's progress from Mhow had been one series of rapid and successful movements against numerous bodies of the enemy. He had swept the whole of Central India thus far without a single check, in every instance driving the enemy from their strongholds further and further north, and spreading terror by his unrelenting punishment of mutineers, and restoring confidence by his masterly tactics in all the districts he had passed through. The successful issue of his career thus far was doubly insured by the fall of the Fort of Chandaree, captured by storm by his first brigade, commanded by Brigadier Stewart of the Bombay army, on the morning of St. Patrick's-day, about the same hour the general had crossed the Betwa. This good news arrived in our camp on the 18th. The rebels were reported to have escaped north towards Jhansi; accordingly a body of the Hyderabad Contingent was sent out to intercept them. They came up with some few in the jungles west of the Chandaree road, and cut them up and captured some camels and tattoos.

The first brigade had had very hard work at Chandaree, and the enemy in that fort had evinced considerable determination to hold out to the last. The breach, which had been made through an almost solid rock, was stormed by the 86th, while a feint upon another side of the fort was made by the 25th N. I., and afterwards converted into a real attack. A good deal of resistance was made at the breach, and just as the storming party entered, headed by Capt. Keatinge, of the Bombay Artillery, the enemy exploded a mine. The casualties in the capture were between twenty and thirty. One officer, Royal Artillery, Lieut. Morsby, was shot dead, and Capt. Keatinge severely wounded. When the enemy saw the 25th coming in over the walls, they gave up resistance and hurled themselves over the parapets headlong into the deep pits and broken jungle outside. Every living soul who could not escape was bayoneted or cut up by the "*Royal County Downs*" and the 25th, for it was St. Patrick's day, and as I afterwards heard one of them say, "*Sure, they had had a thdram, and the raal blood was up, and by St Patrick they couldn't spare one of the murtherers!*" "*Why should they, when they remembered the* little babbies *and the poor ladies who were butchered in Cawnpore and Jhansi?*" Such were the sentiments of the 86th,— how could an enemy stand against old soldiers like these with such hearts? An Armenian rebel—a Christian too—who had led the Bhopal troops to mutiny, came into camp to-day and gave himself into the hands of Sir R. Hamilton, expecting pardon for all his villany.

This fellow instigated the rebels to plunder the treasury, and then went off with them. He was a good looking, fair-complexioned young man, and was dressed in very gaudy apparel.

Sir Robert told him he would be hanged at sunset with other rebels. He then requested to know if he could leave his property and valuables to his friends. He had a good deal of gold about him and other things, which were forfeited, and about 5 P.M. he was hanged upon a tree in company with several other rebels. By this time the heat was becoming intense. Every day we found hotter than the preceding one, and the marches began to tell perceptibly upon the troops and cattle, while the whole face of nature appeared to put on the seared and barren garb of winter. The roads were dusty, the wells almost dry, the grass bleached and withered away, the dry yellow leaves rustled beneath the jungle trees, and the branches above were naked and bleached, and the cattle crept in vain beneath these for shade. The winds began to blow as though they had just escaped from the hitherto-closed door of Pandemonium, and they swept over us, scorching up every pore of the body, and making the eyes feel as though they had been blistered. The thermometer stood in the shade of our tents at 110°, in the open at 130°! Nothing was cool, the chairs we sat on felt as though they had just been baked, the tables and tent poles were too hot to touch without necessity; cold water was a luxury, and the necessity of having one's beer cooled for the evening became one of the great and momentous objects of our existence. Each bottle was carefully enveloped in a wet cloth and assiduously punkahed by a servant until required, or when a breeze blew was hung up and constant evaporation encouraged. By this means we generally had a *cold* drink at night after the heat of the day.

The heat indeed was so great, that even the hair of the head became a burden, and many officers placed themselves in the hands of the barber, and came out cropped to the scalp— a sort of stubble field pate, deliciously cool, and favourable to the constant immersion we were now obliged to practise, and bad colds in the head which were soon to come. This gave a very comic air to the *personnel*, but then brushing and combing were dispensed with—a great consideration on the march—while it became a very easy thing to water the pate and allow evaporation to go on steadily. Indeed, anything and everything was done to counteract the heat and its effects upon the body, but to very little purpose, for as the month sped so the thermometer gradually and alarmingly rose, and the hospitals began to fill with sick with abdominal complaints, affections of the liver, and derangements of the head.

When night came on our beds were always brought outside; this was the only cool time, but this we never enjoyed long, as we were roused at all hours for the march.

On the evening of the 19th, orders came round that the force would march at twelve o'clock that night for Chuchunpore—fifteen miles. When we arrived at our encamping ground the sun was getting very powerful; we were now only about eight miles from Jhansi. After a rest of about two hours the cavalry, horse artillery, and light field guns were ordered on to Jhansi for the purpose of investment and reconnaissance. Major Boileau and Lieut. Prendergast accompanied them; the whole under command of Brigadier Stewart, 14th Light Dragoons.

At 2 A.M. on the morning of the 21st the

column marched upon Jhansi, and arrived before that city about seven o'clock. The cavalry and artillery had bivouacked on the plain about a couple of miles from the city; the enemy's cavalry retired to the town on the approach of our troops.

The troops piled arms on the right of the road about a mile and a half from the fort, and the general and his staff rode off for the purpose of reconnoitring the city and surrounding country. They did not return till past 6 P.M.! Here we found we were short of water, firewood, and grass, and there was not a tree to give shade to the troops, who remained out in the open till the return of the general.

In our front between our force and the fort and town were the ruined buildings of the civilians, the officers' bungalows, the jail, the "Star fort," and the lines; nearer the town wall were several large temples and topes of tamarind trees; on our right, stretching to the north and east of the city, was a long belt of hills through which ran the Calpee and Oorcha roads; to our left were other high hills and the Dettiah road, and due north of our force was the fortress on a high granite rock overlooking to the north the walled-in city.

The enemy had taken every possible precaution to remove all cover they thought likely to give shelter to our troops; they had cut down trees and broken down walls wherever these were thought by them likely to derange their plans; they had built up the old bastions of the fort and mounted large guns upon them, thrown up batteries in other commanding positions outside the fort, and mounted guns upon other works erected upon the town-wall, so as to command every possible approach, and admirably to enfilade each other. The town-wall had very strong bastions at intervals, and upon all these were guns, and the wall itself was very high and loopholed all round.

There were four strong looking bastions or towers on the south face of the fort—one had a white top looking towards the east, above these was a high square looking tower, and from this the standard of the Ranee of Jhansi waved. Along the east face of the fort were other towers overlooking the lines and city, and square buildings. Along this face we could see a good many of the enemy promenading.

Soon after our arrival we saw them busily engaged in constructing a three-gun battery on the wall a little to the east of the south face of the fort. They worked like bees, and quicker than I ever saw natives before. The battery was soon made and finished off in a proper engineering style. From this battery they would command any approach in this quarter; — still further east along the wall, at a salient angle, was another battery, which they were now finishing off with chunam—this commanded the Saugor road; from another bastion they had guns pointing along the Oorcha road; to the west of the fort, in a garden, was another two-gun battery commanding the approach to the city-gate. Every tower of the fortress had its guns pointing east, south, and west. On the east side of the city was a large tank, numerous gardens, and temples; on the west another large tank, gardens and temples; on the north, gardens and maidan. The whole city was surrounded by the wall before mentioned, which was some twenty-five feet high, built of granite, loopholed and bastioned, and outside the wall to the north were some miserable lines of native houses crowded together.

This, then, was the city of Jhansi and its fortress, full of rebels, who were evidently determined to stand to the last by the Ranee in the struggle which was about to commence, and which it was now the onerous duty of Sir H. Rose to terminate.

They were evidently on the *qui vive*, for whenever an officer rode towards the different buildings they had destroyed, down came round shot from the fort and various batteries on the wall, bouncing along his path or whistling over his head in unpleasant proximity. They had the range of these various buildings exactly, and it was dangerous to pass them carelessly.

The whole day passed away before the general and staff returned, and, as they came round the east side of the city, the enemy opened fire upon them from the guns on the *white* tower of the fort : their elevation was too high.

The camp was then pitched, and about eight o'clock we sat down to dinner. The cavalry of the first brigade came into camp late that *night* from Chandaree.

Tantia Topee was reported to have left Jhansi the day before our arrival for the purpose of bringing down a large army from Calpee to the assistance of the troops of the Ranee. Whether or not this was his real intention was not known to us, and it was more generally believed that he had sought safer quarters than Jhansi under this bombastic excuse. There was a large rebel force at Calpee well supplied with all the munitions of war. This body of the enemy consisted chiefly of the famous Gwalior Contingent, infantry, cavalry, artillery, and siege trains, and mutinous regiments and bundeelahs, and altogether they formed a very formidable army likely to oppose our further progress if they did *not* attempt a relief of this city.

The horrid massacres at this city, instigated by the Ranee, had only been exceeded by the bloody deeds at Cawnpore under the orders of Nana. The same course of events had marked the mutiny here as elsewhere—extermination of every soul, followed up by general spoliation and ruin, so as to obliterate every trace of British existence. The fire-brand had destroyed every house formerly inhabited by the officers of the commission and the military, and this followed by heavy rains, and months of total neglect, had left most of them little better than crumbling heaps of masonry.

Ten moons only had shone upon the gory pit in which the seventy-four mangled bodies of our fellow countrymen had been thrown, and the day of avenging had arrived; their spirits had risen up against their murderers, who were now hemmed in on every side, and the voices from the grave were soon to be answered by the deafening roar of cannon and the shouts of vengeance falling with the merciless sword. No maudlin clemency was to mark the fall of this city. The Jezebel of India was there—the young, energetic, proud, unbending, uncompromising Ranee, and upon her head rested the blood of the slain, and a punishment as awful awaited her.

This she well knew, and—not one iota undaunted—prepared a commensurate resistance, such an one, indeed, as would have shed honour and fame upon the name of any princess, whose hands were unstained by the blood of the innocent and unoffending. In Jhansi there were said to be about 10,000 troops, and numbers of these were mutinous sepoys, and there was to be no quarter !

The country about Jhansi was as bare as a desert; they had evidently done all they could to starve us, but we found friends in Scindia and the Ranee of Theree, and from them we obtained grass and firewood and vegetables for the troops. A few days prior to our arrival here the Ranee of Theree with a small force was said to have marched upon Jhansi with *one gun*, and proclaimed that she had come to fight for the Ranee of England ; they then fired a few shots at the fortress, and departed.

On the 22nd the city was thoroughly invested by our cavalry, and then commenced in good earnest

THE SIEGE.

About 9 P.M. on the evening of the 22nd, the Madras and Bombay Sappers moved silently from camp in company with two 18-pounders, howitzer and mortars, and a company of the 24th N. I. for the purpose of throwing up a battery near the Oorcha road on the east side of the town-wall. A little while before some horse artillery and dragoons had passed along the same way, skirting the hills, towards the north-east side of Jhansi.

All was dead silence, and we could hear the tom-tom and hum of voices of the enemy in the city, and occasionally see the glimmer of a torch or lantern passing to and fro in the fort. An occasional flash and rattle of a matchlock fired by a sentry from the wall towards us told us that they were on the watch. As the heavy guns rolled silently along towards the spot indicated by the chief engineer, Major Boileau, for the battery, a light flashed a few yards in our front, and as quickly disappeared. At first it was supposed to come from a body of the enemy, and the men halted and prepared to resist. Then several officers dashed their horses forward to find that the light had come from a body of the 3rd Europeans, who already held the position, and had an extended line along this face. The men worked hard all night without interruption from the enemy; a mortar battery was thrown up upon a little temple, and the heavy gun batteries upon a rocky eminence about three hundred yards from the wall. At dawn the enemy opened fire upon us from the fort guns, and from two or three batteries upon the wall. At first their shots passed over us, but by-and-bye they got our range exactly, and then their shots struck the sand-bags, and the temple almost every time. There was generally time to bob one's head beneath the bags when they fired before the shot reached, but one of their guns, which we named "Whistling Dick," never gave us time for this precaution—for the puff of smoke was scarcely seen before the shot whizzed over your head, or came with a heavy *thud* against the battery.

All day the enemy were at work behind a screen throwing up a new battery on the wall to their left to enfilade ours.

On the evening of the 24th we had four batteries ready to open on this "*the right attack*," as the general had named it, and at daylight on the 25th the guns opened fire. The howitzer and mortars threw shell into the fort, and every part of the town, while the 24 and 18 pounders poured their contents against the works upon the wall. Several of the enemy's guns were silenced, and their battlements torn down.

After shelling and carcassing for a few hours a large fire broke out in the town beneath the east face of the fort, and by-and-bye other fires broke out in various spots, so that Jhansi began to look awfully panoramic.

All this time there was constant rattling of musketry firing from the enemy, and from our infantry who occupied various advanced positions behind boulders of granite, cottage walls and temples. We already had several wounded, and lost a Bombay sapper, whose arm was torn off by a round shot.

The first brigade from Chanderee had now joined Sir H. Rose, and the general forthwith instituted a "*left attack*," from a position immediately south of the fort, and commanding several of the enemy's works upon the wall. With the first brigade there was a company of Royal Engineers under Capt. Fenwick, and a detachment of Bombay Sappers, horse artillery, and a field-battery, so that the general was now sufficiently strong in siege *materiel* to push on the offensive operations with vigour to a speedy conclusion. And much indeed was an end of these affairs to be desired, for the heat was daily increasing—in fact, it was terrible, because we had to endure it from sunrise to sunset without a morsel of shade to creep into, and this among great boulders of granite, themselves heated as with an internal fire from which they never cooled, and from which radiated an unbearable glare and dashes of heated air all day.

But there was the excitement of the enemy before us, and the work of destruction to go on with, so by the constant applications of cold water to the head upon a towel, and frequent large draughts of cold water from the *musuk*, we managed to endure for long consecutive hours what one would imagine would kill one in half the time.

THE SIEGE.

On the morning of the 26th the Madras Sappers marched with a working party of the Royal Engineers to erect batteries on the "*left attack,*" upon a rough rocky eminence about four hundred yards from the fort and the new three-gun battery we had seen the enemy throwing up on the wall the day we arrived.

Below this hill was a small defile and a little nearer to the enemy other elevated ground. This was taken possession of under a very galling cross fire from the fort-guns and those on the bastions on the wall. The Royal Artillery, commanded by Capt. Ommaney, soon got a ten-inch howitzer into play, and the Hyderabad Artillery brought up other smaller guns.

This position was held, supported by the 86th Royal County Downs, the 25th Bombay N. I., and the 5th Infantry H. Contingent.

The greatest annoyance was experienced from the *white* tower guns, as from this bastion the enemy quite commanded our position.

The general was very particular in ordering the parapets of the fort bastions to be battered down.

A round shot from the fort killed a subadar, and a havildar of the H. C. Artillery as they were laying a gun. A sepoy of the same contingent quietly remarked, "*there's luck for somebody!*"

All day on the 26th the troops were hard at

work on this attack, while the guns on the "right attack" continued to pour upon the city.

Great numbers attempted an escape and were cut up by our cavalry, who also seized several cart-loads of vegetables and fruits going to Jhansi. On the 28th there was continued heavy firing from the batteries on both attacks, and the enemy kept up a very smart fire upon our various works from their guns and from the whole line of the wall reaching from the fort to the right attack. We had silenced several of their guns, and as often as they were silenced so often did they re-open from them to our astonishment. In the midst of this din and roar, flash, and smoke, a great explosion occurred in the fort on the east face. This followed the constant shelling from the *right* attack. Every ten minutes in the twenty-four hours shell and shot fell in various parts of this doomed place, and fresh fires burst out among the different buildings—each fire greeted with loud hurrahs by the men in our batteries. The excitement frequently became intense, and the gunners continued their work in the scorching sun as though it were winter time. By the 29th the parapets of the fort bastions were torn down from the left attack, and the enemy's guns were accordingly rendered useless.

At the same time a breach was commenced in the town-wall near the fort. The cannonading went on with great spirit, while the enemy continued a determined opposition from the "garden battery" on the west side, and from musketry and light guns along the wall.

During the mid-day heat scarcely a shot was fired by the enemy, but about 3.30 P.M. every evening they re-opened upon us with considerable spirit. Round shot of various sizes bounced over our heads, and matchlock balls whizzed like hail about us. From this hour till sunset was always a dangerous time, and our poor fellows were severely tried. The "garden battery" and guns on the fort gate pestered us a good deal. Near the former battery we could see scores of the enemy among the trees, sauntering about as though they were superintending a quiet every-day matter of business, although our shells occasionally dropped in the midst of them.

In one of these evening resuscitations their shot came among us with most disagreeable severity. In the defile between the two eminences on the left attack, scores of our infantry and dhooly-bearers took cover, but this place no longer afforded shelter from their fire. Our men got out of it quickly, but a round shot killed a poor dhooly-bearer, and, as he was being carried away, another shot smashed the dhooly in which he lay dead. The breaching and shelling were continued with unabated spirit on the

30th and 31st, and the enemy kept up a fearful fire upon us. Notwithstanding the damage done to their fort and works upon the wall, their vigilance and determination to resist abated not one iota; on the contrary, their danger appeared to add to their courage.

Arrival of Tantia Topee and Gwalior Contingent.

Soon after the major-general had invested the place he had taken the very wise precaution of establishing a telegraph-post upon one of the hills, east of Jhansi, which commanded an extensive view of the country, north and east. It is unnecessary to dilate upon the *sagesse* of such a step; suffice it to say, that on the evening of the 31st, flags were flying from the telegraph-post indicating that "the enemy were coming in great force from the north." The general was in the battery on the right at the time, and when his aide-de-camp rode up to communicate the news, he rode off as quietly as though nothing of importance awaited his orders. Now, perhaps, a more anxious time never fell to the lot of a general. Here was the city of Jhansi crowded with a determined foe, and a fortress of great strength before him, which must be captured at all risks; and around this city the general had of necessity dis-

ARRIVAL OF TANTIA TOPEE.

posed of the majority of his force, from whence it would have been fatal to have withdrawn them, and now on his right flank, in the maidan between the hills and the river Betwa, was an army of 20,000 strong, almost within hail of their friends in Jhansi —the redoubtable Gwalior Contingent, who had recently destroyed the British camp at Cawnpore under General Wyndham, were now marching to the relief of Jhansi under Tantia Topee. This was the position of affairs on the evening of 31st March, and now the military skill of Sir H. Rose was about to be tested by no mean ordeal, but his resources were equal to the occasion, the more he was tried the greater brilliance he displayed.

Soon after the departure of the general the first brigade struck camp, and moved off along the Calpee road on the Jhansi side of the telegraph-hill. The sun was down, and it was now dark, and they marched on over against the right flank of the enemy unobserved, and remained there under arms all night. By-and-bye elephants came silently up to the battery and took off two 24-pounders, which were placed upon the Oorcha road near the hill, so as to check the enemy making for the city this way; the second brigade remained under arms in their camp, which was only separated from the rebel army by the Oorcha road; and the pickets along the whole British line were strengthened and ready for action. The general did not weaken his investment of the city by the withdrawal of a single picket for the opposition of the relieving army, and the shelling and siege operations went on from both attacks with the same vigour and determination all that night.

The force at his disposal, for the battle about to be fought against such odds did not number over 1,200 men of all arms, and out of these he had not 500 British infantry !

But Sir Hugh Rose knew his men, and they trusted implicitly in his genius, his intrepidity, his unwearying vigilance, while individually they determined to die or conquer. By-and-bye the enemy made a bold reconnaissance of our position from the telegraph hill. That was enough (Sir Hugh had deceived them by striking the camp of the first brigade), they saw the few tents only of the second brigade, and what was such a force against theirs ? They accordingly marched in masses and took up a position close in front of our camp, lighted great fires, killed their cattle, and ate ! The enemy in the fort could see all this, and they shouted, and fired a salute, while the tom-toming and bugling went on at a Bedlam pace all night, and the matchlock-men along the wall wasted a proportionate amount of ammunition. The camp-fires of both forces burnt all night, and our sentries were often taunted by the enemy's, who told them that they would all be sent to *Jahannam* (hell) on the morrow. "What was the handful before them to the Paishwa's thousands! wah!"

Night wore on apace, and our troops longed for the hour that was to decide the fate of so many!

" From camp to camp, through the foul womb of night
The hum of either army stilly sounds,
That the fixed sentinels almost receive
The secret whispers of each other's watch:
Fire answers fire; and through their paly flames
Each battle sees the other's umbered face:
Steed threatens steed, in high and boastful neighs,
Piercing the night's dull ear."

Battle of the Betwa.

It was an anxious time for most of us, and glad were we when early dawn came on. Between 4 and 5 A.M. our pickets retired upon the main body, and then commenced the terrific roaring of our heavy guns and field artillery, answered by those of the enemy. Vollies of musketry rattled from both sides for some time, then the first line of our infantry were ordered to lie down while the horse artillery poured awful destruction upon the left flank of the enemy's infantry. No sooner was a tendency to waver seen in their ranks than the general and Captain Prettyjohn, each at the head of a body of cavalry, charged their right and left wing, and broke their dense masses into pieces, and in a moment turned their position ; then our little line of infantry dashed forward, and put them to flight, dealing death on every hand, while the cavalry and all mounted officers charged through and through them, fighting like Trojans !

The dense blue clouds of smoke had scarcely cleared away when we found, still pursuing and slaying the enemy in masses, that they had fallen back upon their second line of infantry, artillery, and cavalry, commanded in person by Tantia Topee, and which stood drawn up upon jungly-rising ground about two miles from their first line. They opened their guns upon our rapidly-advancing troops to no purpose, for onward they dashed, already flushed with victory. The first brigade had by this time moved round the hill into the maidan on the enemy's right flank, had encountered a large body of them who were moving off towards Jhansi while the battle was raging in our front, and had swept them before them like chaff. They fled back upon their reserve and into the jungle to the north, while the 86th, 25th Bombay N. I., and the cavalry, pursued so hotly that they had no time to re-form, and gun after gun fell into our hands, while tens, twenties, and fifties died in nullahs, or among bushes, or around their guns. Their front line being broken and destroyed, their right flank turned, and our forces now moving upon the reserve body from two points, induced Tantia Topee to retreat as fast as he could upon the river Betwa, their artillery constantly pouring shot into our advancing columns. It *now* became a cavalry and horse artillery fight, and while he crossed the Betwa he used his remaining guns well. Nothing, however, could stop our troops until they had taken every gun, and swept the enemy away like a whirlwind. They were too exhausted to continue the pursuit much farther ; by sunset this victorious little band returned over the conquered field, where upwards of 20,000 of the proud Gwalior Contingent with Tantia Topee at their head, had drawn up in battle array at sunrise, confident of victory and relief to the doomed city : now they were no more ! No sooner did the roaring of the cannon announce the commencement of the battle, than the enemy in the fort and town opened fire upon our batteries like demons. They mounted the bastions and the wall, and shouted and yelled, and poured down vollies of musketry until it was thought they intended to make a sortie, while every tower of the fort was enveloped in flame and smoke.

But the fort commanded a view of the maidan whereon their friends were proving their faith, and the men in our batteries were not to be deterred from their important work by shouts, yells, and wild waste of powder and shot: the breaching went on, perhaps, with more vigour than heretofore, and so the enemy at length gave over their firing and the tom-toms ceased, and the city din was hushed to a whisper.

This was a bloody day, for not a man of the enemy asked for quarter or received it. Our cavalry suffered the most, as they had dashed through and through their ranks, a mere handful, combating as many hundreds of well-armed and disciplined sepoys. But the danger of the field lay not in the forward charge alone, for long after the enemy had given way, and our force had advanced some miles over the plain, our infantry came upon large bodies of them secreted in the various nullahs and behind rocks, and in these instances a combat as deadly followed. I saw one serjeant of the horse artillery hewn in pieces in one of these nullahs, while numbers of our troops were close at hand. He had cut down two of the enemy, and was then attacked by others from behind; he fell in the ditch, and was there sadly cut up, while numbers of the enemy were being slain beside him. The man who had cut him down then ran among us, and figured away like a mad dog, first stepping one way, then another, and another—brandishing his bloody tulwar—until he fell, shot by a 3rd European. Escape was out of the question for hundreds of them, and they hid behind stones and bushes to have one dead shot before they died; and herein lay great danger. By the time the battle was over nearly a thousand of the enemy lay dead on the field. We captured all the guns they had brought from Calpee, and among these was an 18-pounder, drawn by elephants, like our own; two were brass 9-pounders, thirteen were native pieces of various sizes, also a brass mortar mounted on a gun-carriage; besides these a good many bullocks and a large amount of shell, shrapnel, and carcase, and heaps of kit. The 1st of April had passed away gloriously with the well-fought "Battle of the Betwa;" few instances in the annals of Indian history can be brought forward to eclipse the military genius of the general who planned and carried out so perfectly the defeat of such a foe, or the valour of the handful of the brave troops who fought under him that day. Weary, but *morally* stronger than ever, they returned to camp to rest and recruit awhile, yet to pour their unexhausted wrath in a few hours more upon the city that was now more than ever in our hands.

On the 2nd April orders were issued for the storming of the city on the morning of the 3rd. Scaling ladders were prepared for the storming party on the right attack; on the left attack a breach had been made in the wall sufficiently large. A feint was to be made on the west face by a body under Major Gall, 14th Dragoons, and when the sound of his guns was heard by the storming party, they were to debouch from cover, escalade the wall at various points, and carry the breach at the same time.

The major-general came down in the afternoon to one of the batteries on the *right* attack to look to the ladders which lay below under the cover of the hill. He then went to the left attack, and inspected, as far as possible, the condition of the breach. Up to this time the siege had been carried on with such unabated vigour that the whole of the towers on the south face of the fort had been rendered useless, and the works upon the walls quite battered down. The kindness of the major-general to his men was most marked. He constantly visited the sick and cheered them up, and never failed to notice any good conduct. He frequently rewarded men on the spot, and often distributed money from his own purse among them when they pleased him by accuracy of fire or other gallant acts. He expected much of them, but never failed to show them that he, too, could bear the hard and harassing duties of the field. Every comfort for the sick and wounded was at hand, and the contingencies of the coming "storm" were provided for in every possible way. Great numbers now attempted escape from the northern gate of the city, but were all cut up by our line of cavalry pickets or fell by the rifle.

Unfortunately the nights were brilliantly moonlight, so that we should have no opportunity of stealing to the walls unobserved; however, the hour was nigh at hand, one more dinner together, one more "good night," a few short hours' sleep, and then to the fearful work of the "storm."

The Storm.

About 3 A.M. on the morning of the 3rd we marched off in dead silence from our tents to the two attacks from whence we were to debouch in two strong storming parties at the moment of the given signal sounding from the western side. The right attack was to be by escalade, the left by storming the breach. On the right attack were the Madras and Bombay Sappers, the 3rd Europeans, and Hyderabad Infantry; on the left attack the Royal Engineers, the 86th and 25th Bombay N.I.

The moon was very bright; too light, indeed, for the coming work. We waited some time in terrible suspense for the signal, as morning was fast approaching. At length the word to advance was given in a voice a little above a whisper, the ladders were hoisted upon the shoulders of the sappers, preceded by the 3rd Europeans and Hyderabad Infantry as a covering party, and away we marched from our cover in three bodies—swords and bayonets glistening in the pale light.

No sooner did we turn into the road leading towards the gate than the enemy's bugles sounded, and a fire of indescribable fierceness opened upon us from the whole line of the wall, and from the towers of the fort overlooking this site. For a time it appeared like a sheet of fire, out of which burst a storm of bullets, round-shot, and rockets, destined for our annihilation. We had upwards of two hundred yards to march through this fiendish fire, and we did it, and the sappers planted the ladders against the wall in three places for the stormers to ascend, but the fire of the enemy waxed stronger, and amid the chaos of sounds of vollies of musketry and roaring of cannon, and hissing and bursting of rockets, stink-pots, infernal machines, huge stones, blocks of wood, and trees,—all hurled upon their devoted heads,—the men wavered for a moment, and sheltered themselves behind stones. But the ladders were there, and there the sappers, animated by the heroism of their officers, keeping firm hold until a wound or death struck them down beneath the walls. It seemed as though Pluto and the furies had been loosed upon us; and inside bugles were sounding, and tom-toms beating madly, while the cannon and the musket were booming and rattling, and carrying death among us fast. At this instant on our right three of the ladders broke under the weight of men, and a bugle sounded on our right also for the Europeans to retire!! A brief pause, and again the stormers rushed to the ladders, led on by the engineer officers. In a few moments more Lieut. Dick, Bombay Engineers, was at the top, fighting bravely, and calling on the 3rd Europeans to follow him; Lieut. Meiklejohn, Bombay Engineers, had gained the summit of another ladder, and boldly leaped over the wall into the midst of the enemy; Lieut. Bonus, B. E., was upon another. In a few seconds more, Lieut. Dick fell from the wall, bayoneted, and shot dead; Lieut. Bonus was hurled down, struck by a log of wood or stone in the face, and Lieut. Fox, Madras Sappers, was shot through the neck; but the British soldiery pushed on, and in streams from some eight ladders at length gained a footing upon the ramparts, dealing death among the enemy, who still contested every point of the attack in overwhelming numbers.

Now we heard the victorious shouts of the 86th and 25th, who had carried the breach, and as they rushed along the ramparts, driving the enemy before them from every spot, the two streams of the stormers met, and the air resounded with yells and huzzas!

> "The rampart is won and the spoil begun,
> And all but the after carnage done."

The wounded and dead who fell beneath the walls were very numerous, and the onerous and dangerous task of looking after these men under such a murderous fire for so long a time, too, was no enviable duty. Several times did I cross the line of fire to look after the wounded, and while bullets and rockets were bouncing all around I went to the front to attend Lieut. Fox, and under that fire staunched his wound, which was apparently bleeding him to death, and then conducted him back to the shelter temporarily taken up for the hospital.

A doctor's duty with the storming party is a dangerous one. Dr. Stack, of the 86th, was shot through the heart on the left attack, and Dr. Miller severely wounded on the right attack.

As soon as the wounded were attended to and sent to the field hospital, I hastened among the stormers up a ladder to render aid to those inside, for the shouting and rattling of musketry were going on as hard as ever. Soon after I gained the bastion over the Oorcha gate the general and staff came along the rampart, accompanied by Col. Turnbull, commandant of artillery. Street fighting was going on in every quarter from the wall to the palace. Heaps of dead lay all along the rampart and in the streets below, and screams and groans were heard in every house. By this time the town near the wall and along the main street was pretty well cleared of the enemy, and the general with some sappers then went off to the palace, which by this time was in the hands of our soldiery. In a few moments afterwards, numbers of wounded and burnt men were brought along the street—the enemy had exploded some powder in the palace.

While these were being looked after as well as circumstances would admit of, Col. Turnbull was brought back upon a charpoy—shot through the abdomen from a window in the palace. The blood welled out from his wound, and I knew he would die. Then there were many others along the ramparts lying wounded, and near these the body of poor Lieut. Meiklejohn cut to pieces, and robbed of everything, even to his socks! But death was flying from house to house with mercurial speed; not a man was spared, and the streets began to run with blood. Ere long the houses on both sides of the street leading to the palace were on fire. The heat from the sun and these flames was fearful; and as we passed from beneath the cover of these burning buildings to get into the palace yard, we had to make a rush, for the gateway was immediately commanded by the fort, into which the enemy had fled, and from which they kept up a constant heavy fire upon this spot. When I got into the palace I found it crowded with our soldiery, some lying down worn out with the heat and hard work, some sauntering about with two and three pagrees upon their heads and others round their waists, some lying down groaning from their wounds or the explosion, and others busily engaged extinguishing the flames in the rooms where the explosion had taken place. The whole place was a scene of quick ruin and confusion; windows, doors, boxes, and furniture went to wreck like lightning. The jewels had been found, and these, too, would soon have disappeared had they not been secured. The officers and men needed rest during the mid-day heat, for there was yet enough to be done ere Jhansi was captured. We had been some two hours in the palace when it was discovered that a large body of the enemy had shut themselves up in the stables. The 86th and 3rd Europeans rushed in upon them and slew every man—upwards of fifty, but not before they had cut down some dozen Europeans. The wounded men came staggering out with the most terrible swordcuts I ever saw in my life. Here was found the British flag, and when it was brought out into the yard, how the Royal County Downs yelled and

THE PALACE.

cheered! It was instantly taken to the top of the palace by the adjutant of the 86th and put up, under a heavy fire from the fort. The street fighting went on all this time in a terrible way. Those who could not escape threw their women and babes down wells, and then jumped down themselves; they were dragged out, the women and children taken care of, and the men then despatched. Every house, almost, had its inmates of rebels, who fought to the death like tigers, so the bayoneting went on till after sunset.

About 4.30 P.M. a message came to the general that the enemy were again coming down upon our camp. He moved away from the palace with some men of the 86th.

About 400 of the enemy had escaped from the west face of the town, and gained a hill, where they were surrounded by our cavalry. Then the horse artillery and a body of the 24th N. I. went out to them; the artillery were not of much use on account of the stones; then the 24th went in at them and slew them all save about twenty, who gained an eminence difficult of approach. Lieut. Parke, of the 24th, was shot dead with many others, and about twenty of that regiment were brought into camp wounded. Those who retreated to the top of the hill then blew themselves up! To the west side of the palace about 1,500 men collected in a place called the new Pettah, and here they determined to stand or die. After some hard fighting a good many endeavoured to escape, but the cavalry cut up some 300, and the rest then moved beneath the fort in which the Ranee and, as reported, about 500 followers, had taken shelter.

A report was circulated that the Ranee intended committing suttee if she could not escape from the fort.

All the day on the 4th there was a good deal of street fighting going on, and we lost great numbers of men in one way or another. We took possession of their gun-carriage factory and foundry, and exploded two magazines and captured a good many elephants and horses.

On the morning of the 5th, Lieut. Baigrie, 3rd Europeans, went up to the fort gate and found it open; he then went on from gate to gate, peeping and seeing no one, and at length found himself in possession of the fort of Jhansi.

The Ranee and her followers had fled in the night from the gate near the garden-battery, and were off long before we knew of it. Our cavalry went in pursuit, and caught up some 200, and slew them to a man. Street fighting continued on and off all the day.

On the 6th, the last desperate body, which had collected in the Lane-Bagh was disposed of, after hard fighting and considerable loss on our side. Lieut. Sinclair, Hyderabad Infantry, was shot dead; Lieut. Simpson, Bengal Army, shot through the throat; and many rank and file killed and wounded.

After four days' hard fighting, Jhansi,—city and fort,—was in our hands, and a hard gained prize it was; for, considering all difficulties the general had to combat,—the heat, the want of provisions, a large fortress and city crowded with the enemy, an army of their best troops beaten on 1st April in the face of the enemy,—their friends in Jhansi,—it is not to be wondered at if our list of killed and wounded numbered upwards of 300 !

In Jhansi we burnt and buried upwards of a thousand bodies, and if we take into account the constant fighting carried on since the investment, and the battle of the Betwa, I fancy I am not far wrong when I say I believe we must have slain nearly 3,000 *of the enemy.*

Such was the retribution meted out to this Jezebel Ranee and her people for the heinous crimes done by them in Jhansi.

They had luxuriated for nine long months in our travail; they had defied our authority; they had fattened on our spoil; they had twisted the moustache in contempt of our rule; they had laughed at our power, and basked in the sun of their long unopposed tyranny; they had stepped from peace and security into the vortex of rebellion, and dyed their hands in the blood of innocents; but the avenging hand was stretched out, and their puffed up thousands were swept to the grave! Jhansi will never be forgotten. Next to Cawnpore the massacre was the largest,—certainly as awful, for only five escaped to tell the tales of woe,— Mr. Ryves, Mr. Tyrwhitt, and Mrs. Scott, an East Indian, with her two children. The latter had been hidden by a gardener, and were rescued by us when the city was stormed.

The fall of Jhansi was more than successful, for not only did the general capture their stronghold, but he so completely hemmed them in that escape to the mass was next to impossible. Death stared them in the face on every side; no quarter was awarded them as a word of warning to others. I exaggerate not when I say I saw the streets stained with blood, but I also know that the rough and bearded soldier behaved most kindly to the women and children. It was an awful sight to see these poor creatures follow out of their houses some rebel husband, brother, or son, who was at once shot, and then to see them huddled together, pale and trembling, beneath the walls, helpless and alone in the world! But the soldier was as compassionate to these poor wretches as he was unrelenting to all male inhabitants found in arms. Many I saw dividing the contents of their havresacs among these half-starved women and children, and every woman was treated with kindness and respect. How different to the conduct of the brutes who had murdered our women and children in cold blood, beside perpetrating other iniquities, a few months previously!

The enemy had occupied the palace to the last, never dreaming that we should so soon force them from it. In the first moments of excitement our troops smashed and destroyed everything before them. Doors inlaid with plate-glass, mirrors, chandeliers, chairs, and other native furniture, went to a thousand pieces in a moment; every room was ransacked and covered with heaps of things broken and torn to atoms; carpets, mats, velvet and satin beds, bedsteads with silver feet, velvet cushioned chairs, a brazen throne of excellent old workmanship, golden and silver handled tulwars, spears, silver mounted sticks, silver birdcages, ivory footstools, lamp shades, marble slabs, dozens of pagrees and shawls, silver candlesticks, crockery ware, and a thousand other things such as a luxurious woman would have, lay here and there in chaotic confusion in every part of the building.

The soldiery went to and fro tramping over and

through these things, and kicking them about as they would any heap of rubbish, until order was somewhat restored.

A good many of the jewels had found their way into their pockets, but, considering the temptation, one must say that they were more than obedient to the order to keep their hands from picking and stealing under the trying and exciting circumstances of the day.

In most of the rooms we found some relic or other of the unfortunate officers who perished here in the mutiny. In one room I found the portmanteau of Mr. P. S. York, containing sundry things, and, among others, a copy of Horace, which the general allowed me to retain. Copies of Longfellow and Byron, and other books, and clothing and plate, were found in other places; these things showed that the Ranee had not only participated in their murder, but had positively shared in the plunder of their property. The palace, as a building, was the most beautiful and richly furnished I have seen in India; exquisite taste and luxury combined to make it a fitting abode for a worthier princess, although it was surrounded by filthy hovels and in the centre of the city.

Other large houses we found stocked with loot from the dwellings of Europeans who perished in the massacre. Why they did not destroy these things was a mystery to us, for wherever they were found, death paid for their presence. The palace was turned into an hospital for the European wounded and sick. The heat in tents was by this time fearful; I had seen the thermometer in the shade of a tent as high as 120° in the open, and in the batteries it was almost insufferable. Men fell sick from the heat alone, while the wounds received in action soon mortified, and fatally prostrated the sufferers.

In the fort about *forty* guns were found and a large amount of ammunition. Major Robertson of the 25th was made commandant for the time being.

The prize agents were busily engaged daily in taking stock of the money, jewels, and other valuables found in the palace and town, and sales were going on daily in camp for the disposal of prize goods and the property that once belonged to officers who had died in action.

Fabulous sums were paid for most trivial articles. Boots had become very valuable indeed, and all kinds of "ol clo" were bought at amazing prices. Medical committees sat daily upon such officers as were wounded and no longer able to carry on their duties; and the two chaplains of the force, the Rev. Mr. Schwabbe and the Rev. Father Strickland, had their hands full in consoling the wounded, sick, and dying, and in burying the dead.

We were now encamped for several days upon the old cantonment ground, the general awaiting the arrival of a large supply of commissariat stores, and a reinforcement of troops, before he made another move after the enemy.

After the storm the bodies of those officers who had fallen were consigned to their mother earth. They died as soldiers should die,—in the hour of victory, and for their country's sake.

Such are the chances of war! While we laugh in the face of peril, death hovers above us, and snatches us away to that "bourne from whence no traveller returns," and where din and strife are no more.

During this time the sick and wounded were sent into the field hospitals in the city, for the heat was too much even for strong men to bear in tents, and every day now the list of sick was swelling. A field hospital after an action, in a tropical climate, established as this was, is at the best but a sorry apology. At this season it may be well imagined how the poor wounded and sick suffered from the heat, the atmosphere tainted by noxious effluvia, the swarms of flies, mosquitoes, and other vermin which ceased not to pester them by night or by day. Anxiety, sharpened by pain, sat on

THE HOSPITALS. 267

many a fine fellow's pallid face ; the sunken eye and fallen cheeks of others showed how rapidly vigour and life *may* wane away in such a country ; despair spoke in the trembling lip and appealing eye that had vainly searched for hope.

To see many of these men at prayer was, indeed, a gratifying spectacle. Sorely stricken, yet there were the God-fearing and trusting sons of Britain praying to their all-kind Preserver in the palace of the heathen ! And what prayers, we may be sure, these men mutely offered !

On the 14th the Christian burial service was read over the pit near the Jokun-Bagh, into which the enemy had thrown the European bodies after they had massacred them in a nullah close by. Horrid accounts were given by one or two natives of the prior treatment and butchery of the Europeans here ; these have been contradicted since, but I am more inclined to believe the story of their villanies than one since concocted to show that they only fell upon them with swords and slew them ; the latter suits the present times and our hopes, but I fear the old men's tales were too true. The father of the Ranee, and the Jhansi *bakhshi* (paymaster), were captured by a zemindar some twelve miles to the west, and brought into camp on the 18th ; the Ranee's father had been wounded in the leg in Jhansi. They were in a miserable condition, and on the evening of the next day they were both hanged on a tree near to the nullah where the murders had taken place. The campaign was beginning to tell fast and heavily upon our men and officers. The mess of the sappers and miners, which numbered eight before the battle of the Betwa and the storming of Jhansi, was now reduced to two! Lieut. Prendergast, who was always foremost in the fray, was most severely wounded in the cavalry charge in the battle-field on the 1st April; Lieut. Fox, who had slain eight men in the same battle, was dangerously wounded in the storm by a musket ball which lodged in his neck; Lieuts. Meiklejohn and Dick were both slain; Lieut. Bonus wounded, and Captain Brown too sick to continue on duty any longer; Lieut. Goodfellow, who had assisted in carrying a ladder on the right attack, and afterwards a powder-bag to blow open the gate in the face of the fearful resistance from the enemy, escaped unhurt, as did also Lieut. Gordon.

Poor Lieut. Dick had evidently thought his time was come, for in his desk we found a will, written in pencil, apparently the night before the storming of Jhansi, in which he left his rifles to Lieut. Strutt, forty rupees to a gunner who had behaved kindly in attending to Lieut. Christie after he was wounded at Dhar, a lock of hair for his mother, and his property to his brother, an officer in the Royal Navy. He was disheartened, and said he would do something to show he did not merit his disgrace, and he fell, bravely leading on the Europeans in the "storm."

By-and-bye the arrangements for garrisoning Jhansi had been made, and the general, although considerably crippled, was preparing for a move towards Calpee. The garrison under command of Col. Liddell, 3rd Europeans, was to consist of,—

> Head-quarter wing of 3rd Europeans.
> 4 companies 24th Regt. Bombay N. I.
> 3rd Light Cavalry,—left wing.
> Hyderabad Cavalry, 100.
> ½ company Bombay Sappers.
> 3 guns, Bhopal Contingent.

About midnight on the 22nd, Major Gall, 14th Light Dragoons, marched out with a small force to a place called Mhow, to reconnoitre the position of the enemy. The first brigade started for Calpee at midnight of the 25th,—the second brigade to follow

CHAP. VI.

March to Calpee.—Poontch.—Capture of fort by Major Gall.—Koonch.—The battle of Koonch.—Defeat of rebels.—Dust storm.—Destruction of fort of Hurdooi.—Orai.—Effects of the sun upon the troops. — Camp, Calpee.—The Ravines.—Battle of Golowlee.—Capture of Calpee.—Calpee, town and fort.—General Rose's "order."—Rebels capture Gwalior.—Scindiah flies.—Sir Hugh Rose defeats the rebels, and reinstates the Maharajah Scindiah.—Remarks.—Journey from Calpee to Cawnpore and Calcutta.—Mutilation.—Allahabad.—Dâk to Calcutta.

On the 29th, after several midnight marches, we moved on Saurie, where we found a powder manufactory of the enemy, and made some prisoners.

The country through which we marched was one continuous flat, the wells were almost dry, and the water filthy. The heat became more and more oppressive, and the cattle began to emaciate and die. Our speedy arrival at Calpee became a paramount necessity, for it was quite evident that unless the troops could ere long lie quartered beneath buildings and be supplied with plenty of good water, the sun would prove a fiercer and deadlier enemy than the rebels; and the state of the country was such that the general was precluded concentrating his troops. When we arrived at Poontch we heard that the enemy had occupied strong positions all along our front, and that they had harassed Major Gall's party a good deal.

On Sunday 2nd May a strong party of the 25th and 3rd Europeans, under Major Gall, went out a few miles from camp at Poontch to a fort wherein some 500 rebels had collected; the place was surrounded, the gate was blown open, and, after considerable resistance, every man was slain. This was a very complete affair.

About fourteen miles in our front was Koonch, and here the rebels had collected in great force, determined to give us battle. The Ranee of Jhansi, the Rajah of Baunpore, the Nawab of Banda, the Rao Sahib, Tantia Topee, and other great folk, were there! To effect a stand at this place was one of their last hopes; if they were driven from Koonch, death in the field or the waters of the Jumna would be their portion. They knew full well how the climate was weakening Sir H. Rose's forces, and how difficult a thing it would be for him to unite his two brigades, on account of paucity of water and fodder for the cattle. It was no uncommon thing now to see our horses picking up the dried sticks and leaves blown over the barren wastes upon which we encamped, or to find the wells drawn dry in less than an hour afterwards. The nearer we approached the famous valley of the Jumna, the more critical our position became, and yet the troops bore all their sufferings, induced by deprivation of sleep, intense heat, and the harassing works of the campaign, with a cheerfulness and spirit beyond all expectation.

We were joined by the 2nd brigade, strengthened by the 71st Highlanders, on the 5th May; the 1st brigade then moved off again, and encamped about ten miles nearer Koonch. The next march would bring us before the enemy. The 2nd brigade took a route to the south of Koonch, and the Hyderabad Contingent one more easterly, while the general with the 1st brigade was moving to the west of that place.

The whole district was studded with forts, every village we passed by had its fort, and in these little strongholds the enemy had posted themselves for months past; they had, however, deserted them on the approach of our forces, doubtless with the intention of re-occupying them after they had given us a beating, as we found most of their gates locked.

The Battle of Koonch.

Another day of extreme heat, paucity of water, a few hours of unrefreshing dose, (sound sleep was

SUFFERINGS ON THE MARCH.

impossible from howling dogs, jackals, and beasts of burden chewing their cud and jingling bells with every move of the head ;) and then another march and a battle ! We marched most of the night, and how long the hours seem in night marches ! The infantry were fatigued before they started, but they began to try hard to bear up against it. In the first halt they sit down and are soon asleep, then they awake, nod off again, and awake again several times. The bugle sounds, and they are up and off again, but before a second halt is sounded they begin to fall out, and must be carried in dhoolies. An occasional joke passes off among the older campaigners, and the hopes of meeting the foe keep up their flagging spirits.

The sun gets up, and then the heat and clouds of white dust well nigh overpower them, and the men begin to cry out, almost hysterically, for water. Water ! but the bag is empty ! and they look round imploringly and keep on a little longer. By-and-bye a village and a large tope of trees is seen, and then the bheesties rush off for water, and the men expect a halt. Long continued excitement, like this, soon begins to tell upon the best of them ; a shadowing of delirium begins to show itself ; there is a nervous restlessness, and a wild glare from the dry red eye, and awful vengeance is vowed against the foe ! Men begin to talk of home, and cool shady places, and brooks, as the hot air begins to blow over them, parching up every drop of moisture in the body; and dogs rush past with great raw wounds in their backs, like sabre cuts, caused by the sun, howling for water and shade; the patient camel cries and grunts, and the intelligent elephant tries to rest the raw soles of his feet, and big tears trickle from his eyes as the advance continues; at length the head of the column has halted, there is a village, and the men are blessed with ample shade and water for a time!

Tea is soon made, and the jaded troops begin to revive. A hurried breakfast is ordered by the kind-hearted general, and the troops told to rest themselves, while he dashes off across the burning plain, now trembling in dense mirage, to communicate with his 2nd brigade.

Koonch is in our front, about two miles off, and looks like a garden suspended in the sky, and the plain around like a soft rippling lake beneath it. An hour passes away, and the general returns; bugles sound! and the troops are again on foot. The artillery move off, supported by cavalry and infantry through the mirage, and the rest of the column follows. There is no more shade yet, and before the action commences the general makes sure that no enemy are in the villages on our left. By and-bye we move opposite Koonch, and there are the enemy's red and blue-coated cavalry and infantry drawn up under trees below the town; then they open a battery upon our centre, which is speedily answered from our guns by shot and shell; then their cavalry waver, and disappear among the trees, and our column advances. Now distant sounds of musketry and artillery firing come from the Calpee side and our right; and news arrives by-and-bye that the enemy are escaping towards Calpee.

It was past mid-day when the 86th and 25th, and guns, and sappers and cavalry, advanced upon the place.

In less than an hour after the advance of the 1st brigade Koonch is in our hands, but the majority of the rebels are gone.

Then the dragoons and irregular cavalry and horse artillery pursue them, and cut up a considerable number of their infantry.

So ends the opposition against the advance of our forces upon Calpee! It was said much more might have been effected against the enemy, had the 2nd brigade been permitted to advance by their brigadier. As it was that brigade had the honour of standing fast in the position they had taken up, "like greyhounds in the slip straining for the start," until the enemy were off, while the poor men of the 71st and 3rd Europeans dropped down in numbers upon the field, *struck by the sun*, without being in a position to punish the enemy before them. Lieut. Macquoid, with his Hyderabad Infantry, charged a large body of the enemy's infantry, and routed them from an enclosure they held in the face of that brigade, but was not supported, and had to retire. The cavalry, however, made a good account of the enemy in their pursuit, and among the dead was a woman dressed in male attire who was flying astride upon horseback when she was slain. The sun had been a deadly enemy to us this day, for there was no shade. While the action was going on, dhooly after dhooly was brought into the field hospital with officers and men suffering from sunstroke, some dead, others prostrated, laughing and sobbing in weak delirium. The general himself had fallen three times, but he continued to struggle against it until the victory was won; and as the sun was setting the men moved off towards the encamping ground on the Calpee side of Koonch.

From the midnight before the whole force had been under arms, marching and fighting under a terrible Indian sun, and soldiers and followers, horses, elephants, and bullocks, appeared worn out, and heavily sauntered over the heated ground to their resting places; but the sun went down so quickly that long before the encamping ground could be gained it was dark, and everybody and everything

DEFEAT OF REBELS.

went wrong. We could see camp fires springing up in various directions, but no one knew where to find his place; elephants and siege-guns were moving about backwards and forwards over nullahs, utterly lost; baggage carts were getting overturned here, there, and everywhere; every one was crying out for his friend; and soldiers parched with thirst, hungry, faint, and footsore, were seeking their quarters almost dispirited. Camp followers had squatted down in groups anywhere, and began to make fires and cook, determined to wait till morning revealed their proper whereabouts.

I had wandered about till midnight, without finding my quarters, and then, completely worn-out, I made my bed upon the plain for the night, not to enjoy much sleep, however, for cattle and followers continued to pass and repass me until the bugles sounded in the morning.

We captured from the rebels at Koonch eight guns, a good deal of ammunition, and a large quantity of grain; but the cavalry, who had fled early in the day, had taken away most of their artillery. The number of the enemy who opposed us here was said to be nearly 20,000, out of which there were about 7,000 cavalry!

Their resistance in this instance showed much less determination than they had displayed previously. It seemed evident that the battle of the Betwa and the capture of Jhansi had had their desired effects upon both *men* and leaders.

Again we were on the march, and on the 9th encamped at Hurdooi, where there was another little strong fort. We found a good deal of grain, and a couple of guns in it, and the sappers commenced to demolish it.

The mines not being ready for explosion, the general and column moved off and left us, a solitary company of sappers, all alone in our glory in the plain before this fort.

A most extraordinary dust storm caught us up while we were encamped here. At first a general darkness came over the camp accompanied by a howling hot wind from the west. Then the whole sky to the westward appeared as though huge flames and massive pillars of black smoke were ascending from the still darker horizon, and continued to roll and tumble about in most turbulent disorder. A deep growling of distant thunder reached us, and then hot blasts of suffocating wind, and the tent tops began to shake, while this war of scorching elements went on veering to the south, south-east, and east, and alternately to the north ; then tiny whirlwinds passed through the camp, big drops of rain fell, the dark lurid clouds of dust were dissipated, and the sirocco had passed by us, curling up writing paper, and leaves of books, and drying up one's skin like parchment ! The highly electric state of the atmosphere in these regions was marked by one or two curious phenomena.

When the hair of the head was combed, a crackling sound followed the course of the comb, and hundreds of tiny sparks were visible in the dark ; the tails of our horses stood out in most grotesque positions, like an angry cat's ; and otherwise unaccountable furors seized the cattle, and they broke loose from their pickets, and caused constant uproars in different parts of the camp.

Beer was becoming now a most precious possession. No one can imagine the value of a bottle of beer in such a climate save those who have felt what it was to be without one ; but one may form a pretty just estimate when I state that as much as eighteen, twenty, and twenty-six rupees (52s.) were given, and gladly too, for a single dozen of this *sine quâ non* British beverage !

Brandy, arrack, and wines of all kinds are comparatively worthless adjuncts to a campaign in India, particularly if it be in a hot season ; there is nothing quenches the burning thirst and revives the flagging spirits so satisfactorily as a bottle of *cold beer*, which becomes the very nectar of existence in camp.

The 2nd brigade remained a day behind the 1st. Brigadier Stewart 14th Dragoons, had reported sick after the action at Koonch, and the command devolved upon Lieut.-Col. Campbell of the 71st Highlanders.

Having destroyed the fort of Hurdooi, we started on the 11th, about sunrise, to join the major-general's force. On our arrival at the town of Orai we found, to our surprise, that the force had marched off that morning towards Calpee. We had already gone about twelve miles, and the heat was becoming too much to bear, but there was no help for us, and so after a short rest we determined to push on, and, if possible, catch up the column, or at any events join them in camp, for we were not in a position to be left alone any longer in a country swarming with the enemy, and inhabited by people who appeared to be anything but friendly towards us. Orai is a large town, and appeared to be thickly populated. The people told us they had suffered much by the overbearing of the rebels at Calpee, and that their bazaars had been repeatedly looted by them. They also informed us that Tantia Topee had passed through there a short time before from Calpee with a very fine army and lots of guns, but that he came back by-and-bye without any guns, and that his troops ran off at our approach like pariah dogs!

The officers' bungalows and the sepoy lines of Orai were all in ruins. It appeared as though it had once been a pretty cantonment, but now the sun was so burning hot, and the plain so arid and glaring, that it was hard to imagine any one could exist in comfort in such a country.

About 9 o'clock we set off again along the beautiful macadamized road leading from Orai to Calpee, and after going about two miles we found a sudden cessation of foot-prints and wheel-marks upon the road, and then we saw that they turned off to the right across country. The force had evidently changed route, and, after grilling in the sun some time, we learnt from a villager that they had gone to a place called Sundee, eight or nine miles off. We went on, a fearful hot wind blowing behind us all the time, without being able to procure a drop of water, until the men began to cry out, and our dogs to drop down dead.

As we passed along we saw several camels, bullocks, and tatoos, which had fallen dead from the heat, but *there was no decomposition going on—* they seemed to be drying up like mummies in this intensely powerful sun! It was almost too much to endure, and as we marched on one felt obliged to gallop from bush to bush to gain a moment's shade, for one's mouth was parched, and one's head began to feel like a ball of fire, while rings of light danced before one's eyes. We had now caught up the rear guard, and followers of the column; it was past

1 o'clock. Scores of poor sepoys, who could go no further, had taken off their belts and horrible *red cloth coats*, and lay down gasping in any morsel of shade; others, jaded and worked up to intense nervous irritability, were dragging themselves along —limping onwards with drooping heads, or staggering with a gait like an idiot, a paralytic, or a drunkard. We had marched upwards of *twenty miles* this day in the sun, and when we arrived in camp, about 2 o'clock, I felt blind, and a sensation of swimming in the brain like approaching delirium came on. Copious effusion of cold water over the head and neck relieved this, and deep sleep followed, and thus I escaped a stroke of the sun.

Every day we began to grow weaker in all arms of the force, and the difficulties of taking care of the sick, and of transporting them from place to place, increased accordingly, and this, too, at the very hour the general required a greater force, for the strength of the enemy's cavalry, and their position in Calpee, rendered them much more annoying and daring. They knew full well how the sun and scarcity of water would tell upon Europeans, and they harassed us for the purpose of drawing out our men in the mid-day heat. They had been routed in every instance by Sir H. Rose and his valiant troops, and driven day by day further and

EFFECTS OF SUN UPON TROOPS.

further north; their strongholds and cities, their artillery and ammunition, their commissariat and cattle, had fallen into our hands; from the Nurbudda to the valley of the Jumna they had no longer a place of refuge if they lost Calpee; this city and fort was their last great stand-by, and here the Ranee of Jhansi, Rao Sahib, the Nawab of Banda, Tantia Topee, with the Gwalior Contingent, Bengal infantry regiments, Banda troops, rohillahs, and budmashes, with an enormous arsenal and commissariat at hand, and an almost impregnable position, had determined to contest our advance mile by mile, and to harass us hour by hour.

Col. Maxwell was on the north side of the river Jumna, and the general wished to communicate with him, for by this time our ammunition was well nigh exhausted; and on the 15th we gained Golowlee, distant about six miles from Calpee, to the east, and pitched camp along the bank of the Jumna. On our march to this position large masses of the enemy's cavalry and guns were observed along the Calpee road on our left.

They expected we should march direct along the high road into Calpee, and in this position among the tombs, on either side, and in their front, they had posted large batteries, and dense bodies of infantry and cavalry; but we left the road and took one across country between villages, marched on their left flank, with ravines between us, and thus rendered their offensive position a nullity.

After our arrival in camp the cavalry of the enemy came down in force upon the baggage and rear guard. Several men of the 25th N. I. were killed and others wounded, and the enemy were driven off with loss. In the onslaught they were heard to say, " You have looted Jhansi, and now you are come to loot Calpee, are you !"

The 2nd brigade with Major Orr's force had a smart encounter with the enemy on Sunday, 16th. Our force got under arms about 10 A.M., and remained in the open upwards of two hours. They were then told to take off their dress and remain in readiness; they had scarcely done this when heavy firing was heard in the position of the 2nd brigade, and the bugles again sounded for the troops to fall in. The general and staff then rode off over the plain towards the village of Diapoora. Shortly after this their infantry came swarming up the ravines between our camp and Calpee, and a brisk musketry firing ensued between them and the 86th and 25th, the enemy being driven back with loss. The 2nd brigade had had a hard fight for their post, but, as usual, it ended in the discomfiture of the foe—the 71st Highlanders dealing death among them at wonderful distances, by their splendid rifle practice.

Between our camp and Calpee was a most extraordinary labyrinth of ravines reaching for several miles from the Jumna, south, over which artillery and cavalry could make no progress, but which afforded an interminable cover of the most formidable description to the enemy's infantry. These deep rocky ravines rendered Calpee on this side almost impregnable ; in the rainy season, when the Jumna would be swollen, they would be full of water, and a greater obstacle than any river or lake ; in this hot dry weather they were so many covered ways for the approach of the enemy upon our positions, and from their number necessitated a great drain upon our suffering infantry to watch them. To the south of Calpee, along the sides of the main road, there are great numbers of huge sombre-looking tombs, capable of affording shelter to large masses of troops, and, save a few tamarind topes and babool bushes, the whole country around is the most wretched, sterile, sun-blighted desert I ever saw.

Sickness and mortality were fast on the increase —Europeans and natives, and beasts also, fell victims to the incessant toil, anxiety, and heat. But there was no rest for us, and we were fighting against enormous odds, despite these drawbacks, every day. On the 17th heavy firing again told us that the 2nd brigade was attacked ; it did not cease till about 8 P.M. on the 19th; these troops joined our camp, on account of the wells being emptied at Diapoora.

On the 20th the enemy made another attack upon our positions from the ravines, extending all along our front as far down as the village of Golowlee, and our officers and men suffered much from the sun.

The same evening two companies of the 88th, the camel corps, and 120 Seikhs, crossed over the river from Col. Maxwell's column.

We had been shelling the town for two days now from a mortar battery on our right front; on the 21st the batteries from Col. Maxwell's camp opened upon the fort and town, and continued shelling without cessation.

BATTLE OF GOLOWLEE.

Between 8 and 9 o'clock on the morning of the 22nd large bodies of the enemy were seen advancing in order of battle from the Calpee road, round the villages in our front, while our pickets in this direction retired in order upon their supports. The bugles sounded, and the whole force was speedily under arms.

It was reported that the enemy had sworn to drive us into the Jumna or die, and from the dis-

BATTLE OF GOLOWLEE.

position of their forces, which now began to show themselves in dense masses along our right and front, it appeared that a general action of some import really was about to ensue.

Their right, consisting chiefly of large masses of cavalry and horse artillery, came boldly to the front resting on the villages of Tehree and Golowlee ; and our right extending along the ravines to the Jumna appeared for a long time to remain unthreatened. Along this face was Brigadier Stewart, with the 86th, 3rd Europeans, four companies of the 25th N.I., half a field battery, a troop of dragoons, and one of 3rd Light Cavalry ; on the right of our centre were half a field battery, the Royal Engineers, and a body of the 25th, under Lieut.-Col. Robertson ; in the centre were the siege guns, howitzers, and rocket-tubes, with the Madras Sappers, under Lieut. Gordon, supported by a wing of the 71st, detachments of the 3rd Europeans, a squadron of the 14th Dragoons, a troop of 3rd Cavalry, and royal artillery guns ; to the left of the centre were horse artillery and two troops of the 14th ; and beyond these, the camel corps, and a field battery, supported by the Seikhs ; and to the extreme left the Hyderabad Contingent.

The enemy continued to advance in great force along our front, and seemed to take some pains in getting into array. Then they extended along the plain to our extreme left, and opened fire from their guns upon our centre. Their shot either went over our heads into camp, or struck the plain in our front, and then ricocheted among us. By-and-bye they moved a battery very coolly into a tope of trees near to our left, and their cavalry rode forward almost within musket shot of ours, but when the Hyderabad Sowars made a move towards them, they fired their carbines and quietly retired.

Our shot, shell, and shrapnell began to tell upon them from the heavy guns and howitzers, and now we could see horses dashing about riderless, and evident confusion among their cavalry, who first moved to the right, then the left, and wheeled about and began to retire. Our fire was too true and too heavy to allow them to answer it from their guns any longer, and by-and-bye, after several ineffectual attempts, they limbered them up and began to retreat, while at the same moment a dense mass of their cavalry and another field battery endeavoured to get to our left flank; but the Hyderabad Contingent were too quick for them, and turned them again. Our rocket firing was a perfect failure. One or two rockets hissed off from the tubes towards the enemy, and then suddenly buried themselves in the ground, and one or two others whizzed about erratically in the sky, and then turned back upon their friends who had wished them good speed, so the general ordered these dangerous things to the rear.

BATTLE OF GOLOWLEE.

We had been upwards of two hours pounding at the enemy, then the general saw the moment for advance, and with the horse artillery, field batteries, and cavalry dashed off towards them; they then turned round quickly and fled, vast masses of their infantry making for the villages and the ravines towards Calpee, others flying south and across country over the Calpee road, while our guns and cavalry continued to rout them. In the meantime terrific vollies of musketry firing and a brisk cannonading was going on all along the ravines. On our right, while we battled the enemy in our front, their infantry advanced with such determination and in such overwhelming numbers through these ravines that our men were well-nigh overpowered. At one moment they were close upon our light field guns and mortar battery! The 86th and 25th had weakened themselves by being obliged to extend their line all along this face against such odds; but they fought bravely and disputed every foot of the line, dealing death among the dense ranks of the enemy, until reinforced by the camel corps, who trotted round from our left, dismounted, and, at a quick double, charged down upon the rebels with the general at their head, in concert with the 86th, 3rd Europeans, and 25th N. I. A yell, a dash forward from our whole line along the heights, and down the enemy went headlong into the ravines below! flying from the British bayonet, and dropping dead in every direction.

> "Stroke, and thrust, and flash, and cry,
> Mingle with the volleying thunder,
> Which makes the distant city wonder
> How the sounding battle goes,
> If with them, or for their foes."

Some of them were so bhanged, or overcome by opium, that they lay down like drunkards with their muskets in their hands unable to move; but, with eyes glaring and bright like owls, they lay cursing the Feringhees until death ended their rebel course.

The 25th, who extended towards the village of Tehree, met the rebels, who taunted them for their allegiance, with a volley rushed on with a cheer into the ravines, and carried everything before them, driving the enemy back into the village, through it, and over the plain towards the Calpee road.

They saw that the day was lost, their dense masses of infantry were broken up and totally disorganized and flying, some towards Calpee, some towards the tombs and Jaloun; our cavalry and horse artillery and field guns had turned their right and completed the general rout, and away they went, infantry and cavalry and guns, all mingled together in a pell-mell over the heights, up and down the ravines, and along the high road! On our

BATTLE OF GOLOWLEE

extreme right, resting on the Jumna, Lieut.-Col. Louth, with a few of the 86th and a company of the camel corps, cut off a body of the rebels ten times their number, and either killed them in the ravines or drove them into the river, where they perished.

All the time the battle was raging on this side the Jumna, Col. Maxwell was pouring shell into the fort and town of Calpee without intermission, so that the enemy found but poor shelter and no rest in this place after their defeat in the field.

Our cavalry and artillery pursued them, and cut them up until men and beast could go no further and do no more.

This was a hard day's work and a glorious victory won over ten times our numbers under most trying circumstances.

The position of Calpee; the numbers of the enemy, who came on with a resolution and display of military tactics we had never before witnessed; the exhausted weakened condition of the general's force; the awful suffocating hot winds and burning sun, which the men had to endure all day without time to take food or water, combined to render the achievement one of unsurpassed difficulty. Every soul engaged in this important action suffered more or less,—officers and men fainted away, or dropped down as though struck by lightning in the delirium of a sun-stroke, yet all this was endured without a murmur, and in the cool of the evening we were speculating upon the capture of Calpee on the morrow.

Capture of Calpee.

On the morning of the 23rd the camp was struck, and the force moved off in two divisions—the first brigade towards Calpee through the ravines and along the Jumna, under Brigadier Stewart; the second, under Sir H. Rose, to the left along the Calpee road.

It was yet dark, and the shell from Col. Maxwell's batteries continued to pour into Calpee and upon the village of Tehree as we advanced along the interminable network of ravines. By-and-bye this village, which the enemy had hitherto held, was set on fire by his shell, and ere long we passed by it, and found the commencement of a battery and large quantities of ammunition in Agra boxes lying about the ravines. Morning soon broke, and as we continued our advance we caught sight of Sir Hugh Rose's column debouching from the village of Tehree and the ravines between it and the road. We halted a little while in these gullies and on their heights, and the sounds of the bugles echoed a thousand times through them. We could see large bodies of the enemy in the maidan below Calpee and near the tombs, but they made no show of opposition, rather seemed inclined to fly.

As the second brigade advanced the enemy opened fire from a masked battery among the ravines upon them, but they were soon silenced, and speedily limbered up and fled towards the tombs, as the columns advanced.

We nearly captured four of their elephants in our front, but the men were called back; and as we were going up and down these ravines, some of them forty feet deep, we saw the enemy behind the walls in the town and the smoke from a heavy gun which they continued to fire over the river at the mortar batteries still shelling the place. We halted again in front of the town nearly an hour, then the general's column came up in a line with ours; the advance was sounded, and away we went into the town without further resistance—the enemy had fled, and Calpee was at length in our hands.

They were then pursued by Col. Gall with cavalry and horse artillery, and the Hyderabad Contingent under Captain Abbott, for many miles. All the guns they had carried away with them were captured, with many camels, elephants, and horses, and great numbers of them cut up; and so hot was the pursuit that they not only threw away their arms, but stripped themselves of their clothing to get away faster.

We remained in the town till about 5 P.M. and then pitched camp among the tombs; but the baggage had great difficulty in getting up to camp, and many of us had the pleasure of a bivouac upon the plain without dinner, without cover—a deplorable condition after such a day's work and in such a place! Early on the morrow the troops paraded and a royal salute was fired, for it was the 24th of May—our Queen's birthday! and the troops rejoiced in the prospect of going into quarters, and the sick and wounded of going *home*.

A flying column of all arms, under the command of Lieut.-Col. Robertson, 25th regiment, left camp to follow up the rebels, who were reported to have gone towards Jaloun, and would in all probability make for the Sheer-ghaut, and so cross the Jumna and get into Oude.

Calpee, Town and Fort.

After a twelvemonth's anarchy, one ought not, perhaps, to expect to find a town in very good condition, more particularly at such a season of the year as this, but I must confess I never saw a place altogether more filthy or miserable than Calpee—a fitting habitation for rebels, outcasts, murderers, and jackals!

Most of the houses were ransacked, most of the

CALPEE, TOWN AND FORT.

streets filled with lumber and dirt; in numbers we found all kinds of English plunder,—enormous masses of sugar, corn, and oil, and pieces of tents.

In the fort we captured an astonishing amount of ammunition and all kinds of military stores. Standards, tents, barrels of blank and ball ammunition, gun-barrels, locks and stocks, shot and shell; saltpetre, sulphur, charcoal, and *coal;* heaps of old brass, lead, and iron for casting; gun carriages in all stages of completion; moulds for guns, mortars, shot, and shell; tools of every description looted from our arsenals elsewhere; bales of cloth, military caps, boots, and jackets; medical stores looted from Cawnpore and Agra; surveying instruments, Government books, reams of paper, official documents, and placards proclaiming Nana Sahib the ruler from the Jumna south!

The enemy had erected houses and tents in the fort, had their smiths' shops, their carpenters' shops; their foundries for casting shot and shell were in perfect working order, clean and well-constructed; the specimens of brass shell cast by them were faultless. They had constructed new embrasures overlooking the Jumna, and pointing from some of these were well-made *wooden guns*. In the arsenal were about 60,000 pounds of gunpowder, outside it were large heaps of shot and shell ranged after the fashion of our own. The value of the stores captured in this fort was said to be upwards of 20,000*l*.!

It would appear from the general aspect of the place that the enemy had prepared for a long stand here. Had they expected the rapid reverse they met at the hands of Sir Hugh Rose's force, they would never have allowed so large an arsenal to have fallen into our hands in such perfect condition.

The total defeat of all their arms in the general action before Calpee on the 22nd was more than they had calculated upon, and when they returned, crest-fallen and broken, they found no safety in either town or fort. We had looted Jhansi from them, we had driven them at the bayonet's point through the fearful chain of ravines of Calpee under a sun they expected would destroy us, and the next morning we marched upon their lair, confident of victory, and verified their predictions to the letter; we at length "looted Calpee" from them!

Preparations were now hastening for the transport of the sick and wounded from camp to Cawnpore. The force was to be quickly broken up, a part to remain at Calpee, part to go to Gwalior, where our staunch ally, Scindiah, was preparing cover and stores for their reception. Every one rejoiced at this, for a more sombre and detestable

SICKNESS.

place than our camp among the tombs cannot be imagined. Well may Richardson have written of Calpee,—

" Ye mouldering fanes, and melancholy tombs,
　　Sun-blighted wilds, where parched famine reigns!
A weary exile marks your mournful glooms,
　　And heaves a fond sigh for his native plains!
But vain the wish, and seldom cherish'd here :
　　Hope swiftly flies the soul-degrading clime,
While listless Apathy or wild Despair
　　Chill fervid Patriotism's glow sublime."

Hardly can I imagine a place on the face of this earth more likely to induce such feelings in one compelled to make his home in such a spot. Thankful, indeed, were we to know we were going. Most of the officers and men were sick, and the whole force needed rest.

The general himself was very ill; his chief of the staff, Col. Wetherall, C.B., was in a raving fever; his quartermaster-general, Captain Macdonald, was worn out, and among the list of others going away; the chaplain of the force, the Rev. Mr. Schwabbe, had lost his reason and was apparently sinking fast; and other officers, wounded or exhausted by their long and arduous duties and disease, brought on by these and the terrible sun, had been ordered to England !

Such was the state of the force after the capture of Calpee, when the major-general, who was about to depart on sick certificate, issued the following order :—

" Field Force Orders by
" Major-General Sir Hugh Rose, K.C.B.,
" Camp, Calpee, 1st June 1858.

" The Central India Field Force being about to be dissolved, the major-general cannot allow the troops to leave the immediate command without expressing to them the gratification he has invariably experienced at their good conduct and discipline, and he requests that the following general order may be read at the head of every corps and detachment of the force.

"Soldiers! you have marched more than a thousand miles, and taken more than a hundred guns; you have forced your way through mountain passes and intricate jungles and over rivers; you have captured the strongest forts, and beat the enemy, no matter what the odds, wherever you met him; you have restored extensive districts to the Government, and peace and order now reign where before, for twelve months, were tyranny and rebellion; you have done all this, and you have never had a check.

" I thank you with all my sincerity for your bravery, your devotion, and your discipline.

" When you first marched I told you that you, as British soldiers, had more than enough of courage for the work which was before you, but that courage without discipline was of no avail, and I exhorted you to let discipline be your watchword; you have attended to my orders. In hardships, in temptations, and in dangers you have obeyed your general, and you never left your ranks.

" You have fought against the strong, and you have protected the rights of the weak and defenceless, of foes as well as of friends; I have seen you in the ardour of the combat preserve and place children out of harm's way.

" This is the discipline of Christian soldiers, and this it is which has brought you triumphant from the shores of Western India to the waters of the Jumna, and establishes, without doubt, that you will find no place to equal the glory of our arms!"

The Fall of Gwalior and Final Defeat of the Rebels.

The long-dreamed-of repose, however, was not yet at hand. Scarcely had the sick been sent away ere the trumpets to arms! were again sounded. The rebels had marched upon Gwalior, defeated the troops of Scindiah, and captured his fort, guns, and treasures, and he was a refugee in Agra.

For a moment the fast drooping energies of the

general were forgot, and, though sorely stricken in body, he again buckled on the sword and was off, determined to leave the rebel no resting place.

After a rapid march of unparalleled hardships the general and forces sat down before the cantonment of Gwalior on the 16th June. The jaded troops had scarcely rested after their march, when the order to "stand to your arms" was given; the general had determined to give the enemy battle, and at once opened fire and advanced. The enemy were driven from the cantonment with great loss; then they occupied the heights, the town of Gwalior, and the fort. Another four days of hard fighting, glorious deeds, fearful and determined resistance from the enemy, and Sir H. Rose had the satisfaction of crowning his many victories by restoring the Maharajah Scindiah to the palace of his ancestors.

Sir Hugh Rose's work was now ended, and accordingly on the 28th he resigned his command, and started on the 29th for Bombay, a salute of guns from the fort of Gwalior announcing his departure.

The reduction of Calpee, the capture of this splendid arsenal; all the horse artillery and field and siege guns of the rebels, their tents, elephants, and baggage animals; the junction our general had at length effected between the British forces of Central India and those of Bengal, coupled with the rapid dispersion of the foe from this focus of rebellion, and the re-establishment of communication on the high roads, was a consummation of the most brilliant character. Nor did the victories achieved over climate and foe end here, the *chef d'œuvre* of the campaigns in India against our ubiquitous foes was the wresting of Gwalior from the hands of these desperate leaders and their well-trained army, in which victory their most determined, spirited, and influential head—the Ranee of Jhansi—was slain, and *upwards of fifty guns captured !*

On consideration of matters connected with this last great victory of General Rose, one is tempted to dwell upon it, not as a feat of arms only, which in itself were enough to raise the commander to the highest pinnacle of military fame, but as the grand check by which the policy of that able and cunning intriguer, that bold and powerful rallier of rebellious forces—Tantia Topee, was paralyzed and destroyed.

Had this intrepid, subtle, and really talented leader established himself in Gwalior, the probability is, that Indore would next have opened its gates to his forces, and the tens of thousands in the Deccan shouted for the Peishwah. We know how Hyderabad, with its hosts of malcontents, has quivered while the struggle for power has been convulsing the land, and recent events have proved to us how great a victory was gained by our forces over the rebels at Calpee and Gwalior.

Since then, Tantia Topee has hurried from city to city like an evil spirit; his followers have dropped off by hundreds; his sun has set, and he is now a miserable wanderer, flying from jungle to jungle, dreading the light of day like a murderer; houseless, friendless, penniless, and with a price upon his head!

No excessive amount of caution, no disposition to play at hide and seek with the enemy, no inclination to allow the lustre of one victory to be dimmed ere another was won, marked the military genius of our able commander, though he started upon a work of almost appalling magnitude, deficient, in point of force, in all essentials, save courage and discipline; with no naval brigade to fall back on, no new levies of chivalrous Seikh cavalry at his call, and with an European force lamentably small in numbers.

From the first hour the general rightly appreciated his foe. Months prior to his assuming command in the field, the British "pluck" had done wonders. Day after day we had seen what a dozen individuals could do against ten times their numbers of the enemy. Delhi had fallen into the hands of a body of British infinitely too small to have captured such a city in the face of the hordes who held it. There were the deeds of Clive, Wellington, and Malcolm to show how the valour and dash of our troops had swept away armies ten times their number. We had the same type of foe before us now—perhaps less brave, although better drilled—and the same onward, irresistible quick march and dash would lead us to the same goal.

No one knew this better than our foe; his system, accordingly, was one of much ostentation so long as we were a long way off. No one delights in playing "a game of long bowls" more than Pandy, Rohillah, or Bundeelah, by which he may harass our troops, and always keep out of harm's way; and no one knows better how to make use of dense jungle-land, high-standing crops, loop-holed villages, and hill forts.

A guerilla warfare is their delight, and they certainly excel in the requisite qualification—light of body, quick to perceive their own danger, thoroughly acquainted with every mile of the land they infested, and, ever ready to profit by these advantages, they gave us the opportunity of proving which was the better man as seldom as possible. The British soldier delights in a good, open, stand-up, hard fight; he is at home when he can see where to hit his man, and then he does it hard, and to some purpose; the native knows this to his sorrow, and always evades the tug of coming to. Behind a wall he is doggedly annoying; *there* his person is not in immediate danger, and, like a pariah dog, he snarls, and growls, and looks very savage, but the instant he sees the determined rush of his antagonist, down goes his courage, like the dog's tail, and he is off like a shot, to snarl and growl, and annoy again.

Sir H. Rose well knew all this, and was determined to act accordingly. He always showed a disposition and determination to fight, whatever odds were against him; in his fights he always punished severely; he marched without cessation from the Nerbudda to the Jumna, following on the heels of the murderer with the certainty and rapidity of the blood-hound; he caught them in their lairs, broke down their fastnesses, and stripped them of their weapons; when confronted by their thousands he met them with his hundreds, never yielding an inch, and, as at Marathon of old, laid their cohorts low in the dust; by day and by night, through the perils and dangers of disease, fatigue, the battle-field, and the burning sun, he led his overtasked squadrons from victory to victory, never sheathing the awful avenging sword until he had strewn the plains of India with corpses, and scattered the enemy like the four winds.

In the vallies, on the mountains, in the city, on the plains, the whitened bones of mutineers and rebels lie to tell their tales to all who pass by, and remind them of the avenging march of Sir Hugh Rose's army through Central India.

JOURNEY FROM CALPEE TO CAWNPORE AND CALCUTTA.

On the opposite side of the Jumna there were great numbers of bullock carts for the conveyance of the wounded and sick from our camp to Cawnpore.

We experienced considerable difficulty in getting the whole of these poor fellows over the river and into these carts before starting; the men were irritable, petulant, and stubborn, and some so sick and badly wounded as to move about very slowly —poor fellows!

A strong escort of Seikh cavalry, under the command of Capt. Matheson, was in readiness, and, after passing through the camp of Col. Maxwell, we got fairly on the road, and went off at a fine rate. This bullock train is an admirable organization for the speedy conveyance of troops and sick. The night was very cool and moonlight, and by about 3 A.M. we sighted the camp prepared for our reception at Akberpoor.

About 5 P.M., the sick having rested and refreshed themselves, the cavalcade again moved off, preceded and followed up by our Seikh guard. About 6 A.M. the next morning we made Cawnpore in safety, and the sick were disposed of in the field hospital in that station, which was already crowded.

Cawnpore presented a thorough picture of war in all its din, excitement, and horrors. Miles of ruins, cavalry dashing about in all directions; bodies of European infantry marching in and out at all hours; hotels, crowded with sick and wounded officers; dâk-gharies rattling in and out from all quarters of the country, trumpets and bugles perpetually sounding; salutes firing from the newly made fort; everybody in a state of highstrung anxiety; the Commander-in-Chief expected hourly; and constant news arriving of more rebels on the Grand Trunk Road, more murders, more battles.

No rain had yet fallen, the thermometer stood at about 120°, and the glaring sterile earth appeared only fit for salamanders.

I visited the entrenchment of General Wheeler— a marvellous thing to have kept off the masses of rebels thirsting for the blood of our people, for an hour, for a child might have walked over it. I saw the well into which the murdered were thrown from the "slaughter-house," but the house was no more; I saw the place where General Wheeler— brave old man—was slain, and the house from which the rebels fired upon our countrymen with

MUTILATION.

grape-shot (the Rev. Mr. Moore then inhabited it), and below, a short distance off, there was the holy river of India—the Ganges—rapidly flowing onward to the sea, laden with tons of putrescence, and, swinging on its mighty bosom, were numbers of the dead bodies of those who had ceased to worship it, floating downward to the ocean to be driven back again and again, until vultures, alligators, and crows have consumed them!

To digress a little—I ought not to forget to mention that Capt. Matheson who commanded the Seikh escort to Cawnpore had a servant who had been a faithful sepoy, and who for his faith to his old masters had lost his *nose and both hands* among his sable brethren, by order of Nana Sahib, when it was discovered that he was a spy in our pay.

Several of the Hurkarus sent from our camp at Jhansi, Calpee, and other places met with similar treatment from people of their own creed, colour, and country, and I am credibly informed that when Sir Hugh Rose's victorious army marched into Gwalior, to reinstate H. H. the Maharajah Scindiah, numbers of people by the roadside greeted their approach, some with their hands, some with their feet, some with their noses cut off by the rebels who had recently fled, and one of our lancers was found hanging up by his feet with his head severed from his body!

This is the common revenge of the people of India; it has been their custom from time immemorial, and I believe there can be little doubt that the people who practised these mutilations upon one another *could* feel any compunction in mutilating the helpless and hated race who were for a time exposed to all the outpourings of their vilest passions. I am at a loss to know why we should imagine it otherwise for a moment.

To return to my journey. By-and-bye the time to start for Allahabad arrived. The Trunk Road all the way was infested with large bodies of rebels constantly crossing the Ganges into Rohilcund, and recrossing into Oude; for a body of troops it was safe enough, but for solitary travellers eminently dangerous, as the many instances of murder fully attested.

Between Cawnpore and Futtehpore we passed the Pandoonuddee, the scene of Havelock and Neil's victorous encounters with the enemy in their splendid march to the relief of Cawnpore and Lucknow. Below this, some few miles, the Madras Rifles held the road. At Futtehpore we found the railroad, and after brief sojourn at the hotel, away we went on the incomparable iron-way to Allahabad. We passed the "Tank House," *where some fifteen of our countrymen had held out only a few months before for three days without food or water in a burning sun against three thousand rebels!* Relief fortunately came at the end of the third day to these brave people. We arrived in Allahabad at 9 o'clock at night, and again put up at the railway hotel, a straw house, crowded with officers going from and coming to the seat of war. Everything was very dear and very miserable, and the house very badly attended to, but even this, under the present circumstances, was a relief, for the constant din and strife of the field had at length lost its charms ; but even here, the fights were fought over again, and the excitement in the change was almost as quickening as that of the battle-field we had so recently left. The road was the chief topic, and how to get down so far as Calcutta in safety. The Dâk-ghari was the quickest, and the river steamer the safest ; but most appeared to choose the road. Allahabad was also in a constant state of military ferment. The fort—a most important one—was garrisoned by Europeans ; the cantonment had been burnt to the ground by the rebels, and a new one had sprung up, larger and better than the former. It was the head-quarters, for the time, of the Governor-General — "the Lord Sahib"—as the natives called his Excellency. The church had escaped destruction, and I can never forget the first time I heard its chimes on a quiet Sabbath morning. Years had passed since I had last heard this sweet church-bell music; for eighteen months the Sabbath had almost been forgotten in the constant toil and din of war, and when their sounds came floating on the soft wind, a thousand memories of by-gone years awoke by their magic tones, and war and bloodshed, the fire and the sword, vanished before the sweet remembrances which came crowding around me!

Verdant vallies and golden waving corn, babbling streamlets and flowery banks! the plough-boy's whistle and the lowing kine, the woodland cottage and the village spire, with its merry sounding bells; the silent breathing of a Sabbath morn, the cleanly rustic, the village school, the young and happy, the old and holy, all peacefully and humbly thronging to hear some soul-inspiring godly words from the lips of the good old vicar, while the church bells are softly and sweetly calling to worship; these and a host of other memories, and the life-time of my youth, all passed before me in an hour, when the spell was broken by the fierce rays of a June's sun—I was in India again, and *the Sabbath* was gone!

Journey to Calcutta.

From Allahabad to Calcutta by Dâk-ghari in these days was a terrible undertaking. From the moment the man sounded his horn at starting to the time one arrived at the railway station at Raneegunge, the journey was one continued gallop and dash.

The Ganges, bridged by boats at Allahabad, takes an hour to get across. Here is the first toll-house. From the Oude side the fort of Allahabad looks a very formidable, dark, frowning place. Once across the river and upon the Trunk Road, and off we start at a gallop for Benares. Occasionally a stubborn horse is put into the ghari, and lies down the moment he is harnessed; then he is goaded up again, and pushed on for a mile or two, kicking the vehicle all the time, till at last he is conquered, and finishes his run like a fiend, all in a lather, trembling and ready to drop when he is changed. The poor wretches are awfully punished, but the journey must be done, and, live or die, they are made to do it.

At Benares—this famous old Hindu city—there is a good bungalow, and here one gets a halt and a little rest; we cross the Ganges again over another bridge of boats, from whence we obtain a fine view of the celebrated ghaut, and the city full of temples. Another rush along the Grand Trunk Road for the river Soane, this part of the journey being enlivened by the close proximity of large bodies of the rebels on either side.

At the Soane there was a camp of Peel's famous naval brigade. Crossing this river, swollen by the late rains, was a very long and difficult business.

Then the gallop to Raneegunge, diversified by kickers, run-aways, and beasts little better than asses, occupies another day, and at last we arrive at the railway hotel, as usual crowded with officers going to the wars, and coming back, wounded or sick, for old England.

Another day passes, and in the evening the train is ready, and in a few hours more we are in Calcutta, and at last have fairly bid adieu to our campaigning, with all its hardships, dangers, excitement, pleasures, and trials.

———

Campaigning in India has its pleasures and attractions as well as its hardships and dangers.

It has not, fortunately for us, always been the lot of our armies to pass through two hot seasons in tents constantly on the march, fighting and re-establishing British supremacy. Campaigns usually began and ended in the cold season; one or two decisive battles in the open plain, a siege, a treaty, and all was over, followed by brevets, medals, and honours.

Not so with us in the late mutiny and struggle. Our arms had scarcely proved their power on the soil of Persia, when they were called away to fight for their own, and all that was dear to them in India.

From January 1857 to June 1858 our existence was one series of battles, stayed neither by rains, distance, nor an Indian sun, until the mighty powers arrayed against us were crushed almost to annihilation. During the long-continued marches of our troops from Arungabad to the Jumna, we occasionally had times of pleasure and incidents of an attractive kind to break the monotony of war.

Shooting of every description of game, large and small, may be enjoyed to the heart's content from October to the end of March, and while this affords an endless amusement to the sportsman, it supplies his table with viands in a truly princely style.

The early breakfast, after the march is over, under the cool shade of the banyan or tamarind tree, is always the pleasantest of repasts—nothing is more grateful, few things more enjoyable in this life; almost free from care, as jovial as Robin Hood's band, as hungry as hunters, voluble over passing events, and always hopeful of the future. The joke passes round,—cold peacock and ham, cold beef and cold beer are discussed,—the jam-pots emptied, pipes and cheroots, a lounge in the shadiest spot, the camp is pitched, and, by-and-bye, we retire to our respective tents, for a bath, a newspaper, a letter from home, or to write one from camp to our anxious friends far away.

Then there are sights to see, old forts to examine, large and small towns to walk through, Hindu temples, gorgeous mausoleums, Mahommedan churches, famous caves, palaces, and a score of other things to interest one, if one so pleases to use his limbs and eyes.

The natural scenery of the country; the glorious sunrises and sunsets; the peculiar geological and botanical features; the natural richness of the soil; the apathy, indolence, and indigence of the people, their pursuits, their features, their policy; the difference immediately perceived on passing from one native ruler's territory to another, from anarchy to order, and *vice versâ*; the ruined condition of what once were mighty cities; the marks of British supremacy and improvements through the whole length of the land, and the power of our local political administrators; all these strike the eye, and leave impressions upon the mind never to be effaced.

Then after a siege or battle there are happy reunions. Some have done gallant deeds and will be rewarded. Some fancy they have been slighted, and fear they won't be rewarded, and some are content to allow things to take a quiet course, while others fight and worry themselves into useless fevers about trifles.

But the marching goes on, and the enemy is always beaten, and the dinner hour comes, and there is general conviviality. The good old patriotic songs are sung, we forget our woes and troubles, there will be an end of them all soon, and then our well-earned honours will be enjoyed, while we remember our trials no more, or only as the few dark spots that tend to relieve the bright and pleasant picture of the past.

A camp life at all times, save the awful season of heat, is a most agreeable one to my thinking, and for a bachelor I know nothing in this country to compare with it. The energies of body and mind are always brought into full play, and if a man be a soldier and have any metal of worth in him, he is sure to shine. The disagreeable, querulous life of a cantonment is well nigh the most odious of existences; the *ennui* resulting from it is as inimical to mind as to body. In the field there is stir, bustle, and vitality that increase all one's energies, while they make the time pass pleasantly—sometimes too swiftly—on the wing.

A man learns to endure and find contentment in privations that would speedily end his days in luxurious cities, and then he begins to appreciate the things he left behind him at home as only one can do under such circumstances. He sees as much of the world, social and physical, as will lend him unceasing pleasure in the quiet days of old age; he realizes the dreams of his youth, and learns to disrobe his mind of false imaginations, and to estimate facts and things by what they are in reality, and nothing more.

The awful din and horrors of the battle field, the siege, the storm, are only so many realizations of youthful fancies robbed of their false colourings. We see how a name is made, a fame won, by wondrous little incidents, day by day.

But all days are not alike sunny, nor all paths equally smooth in the changing of camp life. Sometimes a sweet harmony of surrounding happiness gladdens the heart, sometimes scenes of horror bring a deep sorrow among us; then we glide along on the stream of time with gentle zephyrs and silvery ripples and flowery banks, and anon we are hurried in darkness and storm—lowering clouds above and destruction around!

The charms of a camp life are soon experienced by most who are in it. War is a terrible necessity, but the Englishman's feeling, with the Roman of old, is—

"Dulce et decorum pro patria mori,"

and the burden of his song—

"Might I march thro' life again,
In spite of every bygone ill,
To the end of life's campaign
I would be a soldier still."

CHAP. VII.

Collateral Notes.

HAVING detailed thus much of the actual campaigning, at the termination of which, happily, we found ourselves once more the lords and masters of the great tract of our Indian empire, called " Central India," I turn again to my journal to record in this place, in one connected whole, much that was noted down by me at the time in scattered portions, and which may not be deemed uninteresting, as it naturally sprang forth from the rebellion itself, without which, perhaps, in all probability, I should have remained as thousands of others are to this hour, ignorant of the habits and customs of the people of India, of the vastness and wonderful beauty of our own territories, of the mighty resources undeveloped, and as useless as the *buried talent* of old, of the cities, now desolate and mouldering, where once regal pomp and beauty reigned, of what has been done by former rulers, can be done, and is not accomplished by us; in a word, ignorant of almost everything pertaining to the country, and foreign to our immediate personal interests.

Happily, campaigning, and such a campaign as ours was, brings with it now and then opportunities of observation and incidents at once exciting and instructive, peradventure, never otherwise obtained. One drawback we must acknowledge is inseparable, that is, want of sufficient time to devote to the study of things apart from duty, and the constant fatigue induced by marching in the face of a foe in a tropical climate. And this daily fatigue is no mean obstacle, requiring no little moral courage to combat, if one would do more than the simple march.

Many a time I have been almost too weary to indulge in the pleasure of taking notes, a neglect rarely allowed, and when unavoidable always regretted afterwards, and this must plead for many short-comings ; at other times I have been struck down with fever,—cold, shivering, aching, while a burning sun shone, and hot and delirious in the cold nights,—and these days were blanks I could not fill up save by a fruitless memory of sufferings. Campaigning, however, in my humble opinion, brings with it advantages which tend to counterbalance most of its disagreeables. While it gives opportunity for the full development of individual talents and British prowess, it unveils, in all their hideous realities, the treachery, cunning, lying, cowardice, and unmanliness of the Hindu races as a mass, and their total unfitness to govern themselves. Steeped in ignorance, bigotry, and crime, swaggering in pomp and pride of *caste*, though poor as Job, lazy by nature, and beaten down by a scorching sun mentally and bodily; totally blind to the appreciation of the value of time; never understanding why knowledge should be gained by study for its own value, and the pleasure it may bring; it cannot be expected that they should be otherwise than what they are, and that the British rule, with its determined course of justice, love of truth for its own intrinsic worth, and hatred of perjury (which the native sucks from his parent), and the foul treachery which marks all their acts, should be other than a most distasteful sufferance, to be got rid of at any fitting opportunity, no matter by what crimes or at what price.

No one would be guilty of the temerity to say that all the acts of the late Government, individual and collective, were wholly righteous—in what land have they ever been so? but we may be almost bold enough to say that no power or potentate could have swayed in India more kindly, mercifully, and considerately than the British, and that none ever worked so universally for the benefit of its many races to the impoverishment of its own exchequer, and the sacrifice of the lives of so many noble,

MORAL DEGRADATION OF NATIVES. 321

zealous, and talented servants, whose careers have been little less than exile and patient martyrdom to the grand and worthy cause—moral and social elevation and liberty. Liberty and enlightenment, moral elevation and clean-heartedness, are quite antagonistic to the principles which have guided the rulers and ruled of this blood-stained land. They had not much to fear from what had been done, and was doing in a religious point of view, they are at present too well grounded in their own myths to yearn after a new and better and holier teaching; their *apathy,* understood in the broadest meaning of the word, cannot be conquered. More, the native, from the prince down to the household servant, however highly he may have been educated in our British schools, mixed in the best of English society, and shown a favourable superiority by these blessings, cannot forget his old ways, cannot conform to the moral restraint inculcated by us, and like the dog returns to his vomit. This is no exaggeration, but a truth painfully witnessed by us every day, and it has been so from time immemorial.

Whether this moral degradation depends upon the peculiarities of *race* is a question, and I must say I am inclined to believe much of it does. Recent inquiry into the cause of the universality of *perjury* by natives in our courts of law has pitiably demonstrated to us, and this, too, by their own leading men's acknowledgments, their total inability of adherence to truth for truth's sake. This is so common a thing in the East, that it may cause some surprise that it should be mentioned here, but in these days now we are doing much—perhaps too much—to put native officials into power to administer European justice, it may not be unworthy a remark. It is well known that a native never is at a loss for a lie, if he thinks that lie will please his master; and he is cunning in reading character.

At the period immediately prior to the mutiny of the Bengal army and the various contingent forces, there were several of these highly educated native princes sorely vexing under the restraint and unrighteousness of the British raj. They all had money; some were exceedingly rich and commensurately influential. Some, whose fathers had forfeited their countries by infamously treacherous conduct and villany in years gone by, concerted together for the seduction of the British forces in Bengal, and the expulsion of the British from the land; others who feared, perhaps, that a day of reckoning was nigh at hand for them, too readily joined, and by-and-bye there was a goodly conspiracy a-foot. There must be a king—a famous rallying point—and the old dotard of Delhi, with his young, ambitious, bad sons, and the famous city, became this, and the tools for clearer and more

STATE OF INDIA PRIOR TO THE MUTINY.

cunning heads; and women, deep intriguing women, were with them.

The native officers of the Bengal army knew their own power, and saw that there was, perhaps, a defective system carried on by our Government. The Bengal regiments refused to do what *they* did not like, or what *they* thought would not suit a certain caste. No one can say this did not betray a weakness on the part of the Bengal Government, to give it no harsher epithet.

All this was, doubtless, well weighed by the conspirators, so well, indeed, that they well nigh won the game. The awful result is too well known, but the great lesson it so woefully taught us is already beginning to be forgotten, and the cringing hypocrite again finds reliance and trust placed in him.

These cunning conspirators made a handle of Christianity. The blind, uneducated, fanatic sepoy believed a lie, and then the cunning hit upon the *grease*. Pigs' fat!! broken caste! that was enough. They passed the *cake* from regiment to regiment, from town to town, from village to village. It was cleverly done, and we all know the awful events which proclaimed sedition and conspiracy let loose over the whole land. I do not believe that they credited for an instant that we could withstand against such a combination; and I never did believe, nor do I see any reason to do so, that the fear of being made Christians was the cause of the mutiny.

The cunning, educated fiends who organized the whole had a grand stake to play, for they were disinherited, and they made use of every expedient to further their vain, ambitious ends, and Christianity was one, but not the main, lever by which they worked.

They had more captivating baits, larger pay, loot, anarchy, native rule, idleness, and their loose, slovenly, military system and swagger.

Such inducements as these were, in themselves, more than enough to tempt the infanticide Rajpoot, the bigoted Brahmin, the fanatic Musselman, and the luxury-loving fat-paunched ambitious Mahrattah, for they all joined together in the cause ; the cow-killer and the cow-worshipper, the pig-hater and the pig-eater, the crier of " Allah is God and Mahomet his Prophet," and the mumbler of the mysteries of Bram !

That the native had pretty strong faith in the cause he had espoused is evident, from the fact that mutiny went on in detail, and, indeed, such was his belief in the impregnability of great Delhi and the thousands arrayed there under the Mogul, that he continued to beat towards that city long after it had fallen into the hands of General Wilson. Nor was this all. Long after this city, Cawnpore, and

Lucknow, and other strongholds had been wrested from them, were they content to give in? No! with them it was still a hopeful cause so long as the cities of Central India were in their hands.

It often struck me that these men had a method of subsistence totally different to our ideas of how a large body of men should be fed; yet, in all the places we passed through after them, we found little or nothing. Again, although among their own people they constantly carried off girls and women from among them, and maltreated those to whom they belonged, yet did these same people supply them with food, and money, and news. The peasant, with the rebel sepoy, evidently dreaded and hated us. They were in and out, backwards and forwards in the many towns of Central India, and each town is in itself generally fortified in some way or other. Like rats before terriers, whenever our forces marched on a town or village the enemy had just gone, having emptied the flesh-pots and flour-bags, and people's purses, the same people always professing adherence and submission to the British, and always harbouring the rebel.

I frequently talked with natives about the present state of the country to elicit, if possible, a reason of their own for the rebellion. So far as I could understand from such as appeared to give the question any consideration, there had long been a distrust in the minds of the natives relative to their hereditary possessions from the more influential heads of their races to the pettiest zemindar of the land. Confiscation after confiscation had been made, which appeared to have thoroughly aroused their long dormant passions to a pitch hard to be restrained. Whatever plea we may have in extenuation of the act of wholesale annexation, it cannot be doubted, that while we went on despoiling royal houses, whose internal economy, domestic and politic, gave us such constant cause of irritation, and, indeed, were in many cases, according to European views, which teach us to regard the welfare of the *people* as paramount, fit objects of wrath, we took no care to strengthen our sprawling arms so as to be at any moment ready to hold with an iron grasp that which we had assumed with a feather.

Edicts after edicts had gone forth through the land, and thrones crumbled and princes became pensioners; some, indeed, had openly avowed their determination to live in comparative beggary rather than succumb to such an indignity as was offered to them by our Government; and this they persisted in, long after our civil and military servants had taken unto themselves the administration of the affairs of their states. The Ranee of Jhansi never would take the proffered pension.

These assumptions were so totally opposed to all

natives' ideas, who care nothing about the villany of their rulers' courts, the barrenness of their lands, the universal want of good roads through their territories, the injustice of subordinate officials, the rapacity of their *head-men*, and a score of other evils, that nothing less than deep-rooted hatred and a determination to exterminate their princes' oppressors, whose good *intentions* they *could* not understand, were engendered in their hearts.

Then there was their universal ignorance of British resources, geography, daily news, in a word, of everything concerning England, to strengthen them to run to deeper ruin. They saw the troops we marshalled to coerce them into subjection were their own brethren in everything save the sepoy's dress, and that the few European officers, civil and military, were everywhere, at any hour, an easy prey, whenever the word should go forth to rise and slay their enemies.

I remember asking one old man about the country and its owners, when he significantly said to me, " The jungles, sahib, the trees, the rivers, the wells, all the villages, and all holy cities belong to the Sircar; they have taken all — everything (*bhut-achcha*)—very good, what can we do ?"

I have no doubt it appeared quite clear to the heads of families, villages, towns, and states in the neighbourhood of such stations as we had already occupied, that the dreaded day of absorption was nigh at hand for all of them, for the mental eye of the native is exceedingly microscopic, and there was reason to magnify a dreaded evil when Oude and Nagpore and other instances were before them.

When the lamentable condition of their ignorance of everything, save their rice and pay, is taken into consideration, it cannot be wondered at if they rather approve of a lie, well magnified by each repetition, than a meagre, bare fact; and a well concocted lie, to the effect that all would be lost unless one final struggle for their ancient birthrights were made, would be enough to add to that which they already knew to be too true.

Real honesty, as understood by Englishmen, forms no part of a native's character. He is too cowardly to tell the truth, and too hypocritical and timid to resist his brother, if such has the shadow of a weapon at hand. I was often surprised at the child-like conduct of huge ugly-looking brutes in their quarrels with one another. To *hear* them, one would imagine torrents of blood and broken bones must result, but to see the way they scratch, and pull each other's hair, and bite, and then go off crying like children to complain to some one that they have had a beating, is ridiculous.

Education among them is generally of the most meagre description, and this, too, principally con-

LOW STATE OF EDUCATION. 329

fined to such as are the heads of their villages and towns, who accordingly lord it over the mass, and are looked upon as prodigies. Even when some few have extended their acquirements to the knowledge of several other languages, it appears to be productive of nothing beyond. Many, indeed, are conversant with four or five tongues; but this is not to be wondered at when the affinity of the languages and the constant inter-territorial communication are taken into consideration; and these many, though excellent masters of the English language likewise, cannot be called learned, for their learning leaves them pretty much as they would be without it. It does not expand their minds, it does not unfetter their prejudices; they are not free to act upon their extraneous attainments, but at all times must conform to the customs, however vile they may be —and many of them are certainly heinous—of the people to whom they belong, or *suffer* the martyrdom of excommunication, loss of *caste*, and all the social benefits of life. This is the *bugbear* of India. It destroys all the good that might otherwise accrue to those sensible of the benefits of English customs, and willing to conform to them.

But spite the opposition met with among their own people to the infringement on their time-honoured customs, the educated Brahmin knows little or nothing of geography or history, and never reads, as a rule, for the pleasure it brings. They have always an idea that one does so for the *money* it will make, and that that is the sole object of life. To do anything without getting rupees can never be understood, and to study the works of great men to feed the mind with their thoughts is to them marvellously absurd. They always shake their heads, seeming secretly to believe such an assertion a vague subterfuge.

As a mass, they appear to live in a mental cavern, and to be perfectly content with their primæval darkness. We may exclaim, " Let there be light !" and endeavour to penetrate their cavern with our torches, or reflect a little from without from the pure halo which surrounds us, but there are serpents and scorpions, and other horrors, and huge bats around and above, which cling to the dank unwholesome stones, and fight with the light we bear, till they have dashed it from us, or we are driven away by the venomous creatures in our path ; or cholera or deadly fever may sit at the gate, gathering their fated ones together, and whom they strike they slay, for their uncultivated minds are weaker than their bodies, and when these fall, the former cease to exist ; the town is taken, and the citadel is empty, and the fight is soon over.

I remember one day talking with one of these " well-educated Brahmins," who had received a fair training in English, about their dogged adherence to customs and things that should have passed away a thousand years ago. He was an intelligent fellow, and appeared instantly ready to combat every question put by referring to antiquity as the grand reason. What had suited so many millions for so many ages must be suitable to all eternity; whatever change might occur elsewhere, it signified little to them, for their books contained precepts and ordinances immutable. He had read the English Bible, and thought it " a very *interesting, clever* book," but nothing to be compared with their own more ancient records, and he could not understand why we should shuffle off a belief which had suited so many for this life, and told them so much about the next. To discard the religion of his fathers would be simply to evince a human weakness which he prided himself to be above; to change one's faith would be to raise a suspicion of instability in the newly-adopted one, and this was a danger not worth trying.

I was amused at his notion of the cause of earthquakes. He said they were informed and told to believe that there was a huge serpent coiled up in the bowels of the earth, and that when the prodigious creature required a little more breathing-room, or felt uneasy in his imbedded position, that he uncoiled his mighty body, shook himself, snorted, and reposed again in groans, and that the *earthquakes* assuredly followed these subterranean antics!

He also said that the world was doubtless far less Edenic now than it was when his ancient forefathers trod it; that "in those good old days there were good and holy men whose songs would cause the mountains to dissolve and rains to descend from heaven, and rivers to pour forth from barren places!" Happy times! and that "their wise good men could do so now—by what process he knew not—but that the people were not good enough for the working of such miracles; but that the sick and those possessed of the devil, the unfruitful, the lame, the blind, could all be healed now, as of old, by their good and holy men."

Their women cannot be permitted to read or write, or engage in anything elevating to the mind. They are the abject slaves of their husbands, to bear children while yet children themselves, and set his house in order. Can we wonder at the ignorance of these sons of such women, whose time is taken up with cants at the well in the morning, quarrelling and adorning themselves in jewels at home, or bedaubing their floors and walls with a solution of cow-dung and other abominations with their tiny hands prior to the evening gorge?

Then their *caste* precludes progress, social and

intellectual. Once a tailor, always a tailor ; once a carpenter, always a carpenter ; a cobbler, for ever a cobbler, from father to son to the end. Here the saying of Apelles of Cos is their immutable law, " Ne sutor ultra crepidam."

And thus striving to gain by enterprise out of their ordained walk of life never enters their minds ; and so *time* is nothing to them ; to-morrow will do as well as to-day, for at the end of the month he gets his price, and he and his all are contented. His mud-hut only requires a little cow-dung and whitewash occasionally ; his furniture consists of a few stones and earthen pots ; his bed is a mat, or now and then, his turban (an easy thing to take up and walk with); and his food, a little rice and spiced grease. They are all servants of servants ; independence of character they have none.

In such places as English rule and institutions prevail, the native appears only to have benefited in the amount of rupees he may obtain for his services, and these he diligently turns into silver or gold ornaments for his own wrists, and the noses, necks, ears, wrists, and ankles of his women ; added to this, experience declares that he has increased in *impudence* and drunkenness.

But drunkenness is an attainment they pretend not to possess, though they drink like fishes European drinks when they can obtain them, and at other times vile concoctions potent in poisonous inebriating qualities.

They know full well the great failing of the British soldiery, and where they could they always exposed their rude jars full of their deadly beverages to our troops. In more than one instance the officers of Sir H. Rose's force had to destroy gallons of vile trash called *toddy*, to prevent their men falling preys to the cunning natives.

In a conversation I had with a Brahmin in high position, I questioned him upon this topic, and said it was well known that rich and influential Brahmins drink the forbidden liquors even to excess. "Yes," he replied, "the high Brahmins in Calcutta and other large cities *can* do so, for who is there to censure *them;* gold covers a multitude of sins." This was the answer of Gunna-Shaster, the commissariat officer of his Highness the Maharajah Holkar.

Yet I have seen a Hindu positively dying from starvation (one of our many enemies) refuse the kindly offer of a little brandy and water to revive his exhausted frame. This, I fancy, was owing to its being tendered by the polluted being in the shape of an English officer.

Beggars, whose appearance looks very like people who have lived on their own fat for an indefinite period, will often come to one's tent-door slapping their bare shrivelled-up stomachs with their bony wrinkled hands, and pray for *food*. They don't want food, at least food from the hands of a vile *casteless* Briton ; for if you offer them some clean good bread, they will shrink away from you as one would from a leper; but they will greedily snatch at your copper coins! these, of course, are not polluted.

If you are parched, and ask for a drop of water, and have no cup of your own to drink from, their *brass pot* is too sacred a thing to be polluted by your lips, and so you must join your hands together, receive the water in them, and thus quench your thirst; yet have I seen, times out of number, these pure specimens of the genus homo—men, women, and children, all standing together up to their knees in a filthy tank or town-puddle washing their teeth, spitting into the water, washing their persons, their filthy rags, and their feet in the same, while pigs, dogs, and horses were wallowing in it, and polluting it, at the very moment women were bearing pots full of it away upon their heads for the culinary purposes of the day. A sweet wholesome decoction!! No wonder such seasoners as Harvey's sauce are at a discount among this cleanly race.

I know of few things more wearisome than keeping up a conversation upon any topic with these people. We are not blessed with the fitful freaks of a British climate. In India the weather is an eternal blue, glare, and frizzle, so this topic is not useful. There is always a fight somewhere, and fighting is almost like the weather, so constant and common a thing, that your friend in the turban thinks nothing of it—it is all *nuseeb*—luck. There is education, they don't care about that; your profession, your income, they know it to a farthing; but be you as poor as a church mouse, they never give you credit for poverty, firmly believing there is an inexhaustible treasury always open to you to any amount, and that my lord has nothing to do with his rupees but throw them away. A beggar looks upon a rupee no more gladly than a poor Englishman does upon a penny. Well, what can one talk about? Eating and drinking is out of the question; to speak of their prejudices and fanaticism is unprofitable, to say the least; husbandry and the industrial arts are nothing, the rice grows somehow and he eats it, and European articles of every kind are fast superseding native wares; and this is a pity, since the rubbish of British markets is displacing many of the really good and useful commodities made by the natives. A hawker's box or bundle is a really marvellous affair. He comes to one's tent, makes great salaam, squats on his haunches, and patiently exposes the wonders he carries about from the western shores to the City of

Palaces, so, finding no good topic can be discussed, one quietly turns round to the philosophic Hindu hawker and bids him *open!* to while away an hour in *observing* some new trait or peculiarity.

"What have you brought?" "I got everything, sahib, silk gowns, muslin dresses, socks, neckties, braces, blacking, cambric handkerchiefs, lucifer-matches, sardines, writing paper, eau-de-Cologne, black ink, dog chains, and hair-brushes; babies' socks and Epsom salts; essence of ginger and parasols; Windsor soap and curry-combs; plenty things got, sahib." "How much for that box of lucifers?" "Six annas (ninepence), sahib!" "How much for that bottle of blacking?"—"Two rupees, sahib" (only 4 shillings!) "How much for the phial bottle of essence of ginger?"—"Three rupees, sahib!" "Oh! that's too cheap!" "Stopper got, bottle, sahib!'—"Rowland's macassar! real—Europe—French—sahib! I swear." "Don't want, always use pigs-grease when bears can't catch!" "Wah—h! sahib very fine gentleman, think cousin to Governor-General!" says the cunning fellow; and so, looking at twopenny padlocks, shilling razors, rotten socks, Martin's blacking, and Congreve's infernals, all together not worth as many pence as these audacious hounds ask rupees, one whiles away an hour now and then, surrounded by wonder-gazing Hindus, each speculating on the amount of rupees sahib is likely to throw away. However, they *are* useful, very, sometimes, and, of course, one must expect to pay a little more seven or eight hundred miles away from Calcutta, Bombay, or Madras, for one's "Rowland's," one's "ginger." one's "babies' socks."

These men follow in the wake of an army, and make vast sums of money by the variety of trash they hawk about.

Not a little pleasure does it give one to witness the marked difference of the Parsees in their business habits and shops. The most like Europeans in independence, ability, enterprise, integrity, and mental worth, are these followers of Zoroaster, I have ever met with in India. If they are proud, they have a reason for it; if they are rich they owe it to no Hindu or Musselman; if they are better informed, as they all are, they owe it to themselves alone; if they lean more to the British than any other race in the land, it is because British justice and equable laws protect them from the rapine and persecution they have so often suffered under other powers. It has been said they refuse to use firearms, and in any way to have anything to do with this *elemental* emblem of the Deity—fire. As a rule, there can be no doubt that they strictly adhere to their tenets; but there are no laws which do not admit of exceptions, and in the case of the last mutiny, the Parsees found that they might bear

INTEGRITY OF PARSEES.

arms against the treacherous Hindu, and shoot down the murderer as a dog. They suffered equally with the Europeans at the hands of the mutineers, and in many cases worse, but they are a peaceful people, and bore their distresses manfully while we punished the aggressors. Through these merchants we obtained all that was necessary for the march from Bombay to Gwalior, and in a regular manner. Necessarily the price of articles increased the farther we journeyed, and it was not so much at Cursetjee or Jamsetjee that we grumbled as at Messrs. Allsopp and Co. and Bass and Co., or their bottlers, for infamously defrauding us of our *just measure*. A quart bottle of beer in India is not a *quart*, it is *an imperial pint and four ounces by measure*, or a little more or less, as the bottom of the bottle is poked up higher or lower.

Now, when it is remembered that we paid from *fifteen* to *twenty-six rupees* (30 to 56 shillings) per dozen for our beer, it must be confessed that it was hard to be robbed of one's beer at such a price ! for instead of getting a dozen *quarts* we only had a dozen imperial *pints*, and about a third of a pint ! !

If Messrs. Brewers, Bottlers, and Co. only felt an Indian hot season, and the want of a *quart* of beer for their hard-earned pence, they would surely *increase* the size of their bottles as much above the just quart as they are now above the *pint!!*

The towns and villages we passed through are eminently characteristic of the people. Usually they have not the remotest pretence to regularity, and their hovels are clustered together just as though they had tumbled from the clouds—some on mounds, some in hollows, some on the top of older ones. This looks very odd at first sight, but it is easily accounted for. The filthy, lazy hound is too idle to walk a hundred or fifty yards from his door to carry away his dirt and household rubbish. There are no municipal associations in Hindu towns, and so he deposits this at his door, or more generally at his neighbour's, and around his house from day to day and year to year, for the crows, pigs, and pariah dogs to carry away. His wattle and dab hut, valued originally at about eight shillings, by-and-bye begins to crumble away, and at last tumbles in a body upon the heap. The proprietor either goes to a new locality, or re-erects another hut upon the heap made by his rubbish and ruins, and so from year to year the village rises and rises upon these accumulated dung-hills, and gives the peculiar appearance so frequently observed.

However beautiful the pasturage may be around towns and villages, the people always drive their cattle into their towns and huts at night, and back again into the grazing land in the morning. Owing to the dry sapless nature of the herbage in general, the milk and butter are wretched productions. The milk they take at night is usually boiled to keep it till the morning, then they pour it into *brass pots*, and carry it about for sale with their dirty black fingers usually soaking in it. The butter looks, and frequently tastes, like sickly melting spermaceti ointment. One can scarcely wonder that *pork* and *pigs* should be the forbidden food of the East. We all know that the cleanest pig of the most scrupulously clean English farmer is, at best, but a dirty, grubbing brute ; but in India, where they run loose about the streets and slums of the towns, voraciously seizing and feeding upon the vilest excrements and other bestialities, it may be imagined what food their flesh would be ! They are almost all black, and shaped more like hyenas than anything else. To call a man a *pig* is considered very vile abuse, and usually provocative of great anger. But not one whit viler than the pigs are the village *dogs*. They skulk about the gullies and heaps of dung all day, with their mouths always wide open, and grin, and snarl, and howl all night. They feed upon every kind of offal ; I have seen them tearing one of their own dead species to pieces, and voraciously feeding upon dead human bodies. They frequently go mad, they belong to no one and are rarely killed, consequently they swarm in each village and town. The mild Hindu is certainly a lover of cleanliness !

When people live as these live, can we wonder that any more vigorous race should have conquered them and tortured them into better ways, for I verily believe they will do nothing for their own good save by coercion from without ! The Musselman despises them, and he is not a very electric being, save when lit up for the hour by fanaticism and love of feud. The women, generally speaking, are tolerably good looking when young, some are almost beautiful, but they marry so young and live in such vicious habits that they soon age, and then are little less than hideous hags. Intermixture of the European and Hindu races is a total failure. In most cases the offspring becomes blacker than the mother, inherits all the failings of the native, and the vices of the European without his energy. They are frequently pitiable specimens of moral and physical degeneration.

As a rule, the native women run away and hide themselves at the sight of Englishmen, but they do not veil, and many a well-got-up Rebecca may be seen with her pitcher at the well in the morning time, canting and laughing, while some huge Brahmin, totally naked save a tiny rag, is scrubbing his carcase close by her. The East induces a totally different code of morals for its people to what we have been accustomed to in Europe.

Almost all of them, men, women, and children, chew betel-nut, lime, and a pepper leaf. They don't know why they do it—it is custom, and as I was told, when mixed with cloves, mace, cardamoms, and coriander seeds, "becomes enchanting." The custom might have originated in some wise advice, for the compound is astringent, antacid, and carminative, and possibly a good thing in a country where diarrhœa and cholera are so frequent; but the habit is a very disgusting one, and the use of the compound discolours and destroys the teeth, while it gives to the tongue a "dragon's-blood" hue, which is very revolting to witness, particularly in an otherwise passable young lady. The more stir and bustle there is going on, the faster they chew and eject saliva. I shall never forget the truly awful amount of chewing I witnessed among his Highness Maharajah Holkar's attendants, when we visited his durbar at his palace in Indore. It was almost dangerous to pass through these *betel-enchanted* beings to the presence of their prince.

As Jezebel of old painted her eyes to add to their dazzling brilliance, so do the Jezebels of India to this very day. Antimony and fine charcoal from a little box is carefully painted on the edges of the eyelids. It may add to their beauty in their lord's eyes, and they also say it strengthens the sight; but this I question, as the shrivelled old women, whose sight is fast declining, do not appear to patronize the paint. Perhaps, they have seen enough.

Race, doubtless, has much to do with the colour of man's skin, but there can be no doubt that the sun has a marvellous influence upon the texture and colour of his tissues. The farther one travels from the line, so far as my experience enables me to judge, the lighter colour the skin assumes in India. I have seen Mahrattahs nearly as fair as English, quite as fair as Italians. I have seen Musselmen in Southern India as dark as Cingalese, and in Cawnpore as fair as ourselves. I have seen a Musselman tolerably fair in the Deccan, and after eighteen months marching in the sun almost as dark as an Ethiopean. I have seen an English officer, rosy and fair from Great Britain, nearly copper-coloured at the end of our campaign.

I was always struck at the peculiar childishness of the amusements of these people. As they are vacant in mind, so are their amusements rendered. Tom-toms, squeaking pipes, and dancing girls, snake charmers, and jugglers, are their standing amusements. And old men and young, equally credulous, form willing audiences, but never so willing as when there is a sahib who is anxious to spend a rupee or two for the tamashah. Indian jugglery is very clever, but not to be compared with our British wizards' feats. The most extraordinary thing I ever saw in my life was a trick of suspending all apparent vitality in a little boy, and causing him to sit in a constrained posture upon the top of a walking-stick some three feet high without support. And there he sat motionless in the air for some time, until he was taken down and laid upon the earth! He was stiff and cold,—eyelids firmly closed and motionless, stomach shrunken in like death, and chest motionless. His jaw was fixed, and the fingers and thumbs doubled in as in epilepsy. By-and-bye the man breathed into his nostrils and lips, touched his eyes with his thumbs, made passes over his face and chest, slapped his abdomen, and chafed his legs and feet a good deal; and by degrees, the muscles of the chest and abdomen began to move slowly, then the abdomen swelled and collapsed, the chest heaved, and a deep sigh escaped from the child. "Ah-h-h," said the father, and again passed his magic hand over the face and chest, and chafed the feet. The eyes opened—an awful stare—now the mouth, and then the father flexed the joints, and by-and-bye the lad rose up and made a profound salaam. He seemed much exhausted and pale, and the mother very anxious for him. I never saw anything so like a miracle in my life. There was no chloroform, there were no assistants, the stick he sat on was a common thick walking-stick, the catalepsy was not feigned, it was real and awful, for I carefully examined the child. The father said, "He had died, sahib, and I caused life to come again." Had Mesmer ever been in India?

Perhaps one of the most curious of Hindu sights is the witnessing of the celebration of their festivities. Great preparations are made for them by old and young of both sexes. Money is subscribed by all in greater or lesser sums, according to their social positions.

All things being fully prepared by those delegated to take the prominent parts in the celebration, the tom-toms and pipes commence to call the various grades to each particular locality decorated for the festivity.

About 9 o'clock at night fires are kindled, torches lighted, little lamps trimmed, and their tawdry temples set into order and bonfire-like brilliance.

The poorer class have but a sorry display. Their show consists of a few leaves and tinselled paper, inside which a fainting light struggles for existence in the bottom of a bit of cocoa-nut shell. Some two or three score of natives assemble round this spot, and commence their hideous orgies, which are to last day and night for days together. About three yards from the door of this fragile show stands a pyramidal bundle of sticks, cotton, and cocoa-nut leaves. This dirty mass of vegetables represents the god they are about to sing of, pray to, invoke, and ultimately burn.

When a motley assembly has arrived, three or four of the most demoniac specimens of antediluvian ignorance appear round this pile, followed up by some dozen others not quite so madly attired. They then commence their songs, dancing round the pile, while they emulate Apollo with short sticks and shells, against which they constantly clink a rude brass chain. The dance quickens, their gestures become more savage, their clinking louder and louder, while one of the privileged quietly walks among the people looking on, and suddenly smothers some unfortunate wretch's face with a handful of red dust—dragon's blood—which gets into his eyes and mouth, and which he bears and quietly walks away to rub off.

The multitude are all hubbub, vacantly staring, laughing, or fighting. Then comes a break into the savage scene of dancing. A gaudy coloured paper box-like temple, of some size, is borne upon the shoulders of four men, preceded by tom-toms, sticks, and what they call songs. I remember seeing one of these paper lantern-looking things carried to the scene of dancing, and with great care lifted to the ground. While the fanatics were bowing and grimacing before it, some wag of their own people quietly dropped a stone through the roof. Oh! the rage, the deadly passion displayed by their priests! One rushed about frantically, swearing he would kill somebody or something, while the mob bahbahed him and dissuaded him. He tore and foamed, stammered with rage, and shook his head until I really expected it to drop off. I interrogated him, and wished to know what he would do if he caught the perpetrator of so blasphemous an act, and he savagely said, "I would take his life from his throat —yes!" By-and-bye, peace being restored to the troubled waters of their hearts, they muttered something, and cried out in English, "Quick march!" Off went the tom-toms, and sticks, and shells, with the fractured paper temple in their rear.

Wandering from this sight to another, I was greatly struck by the wide difference exhibited in all the details of the getting up part of this second tamashah. This I found to be a show of the havildars—native serjeants—and their friends.

In the centre of a large area was erected a kind of temple of some considerable size, large enough to admit of people walking in and out of it. It had six pillars gaudily painted and tinselled, and the back of the temple was all pure white silver paper. The lamps outside were so arranged as to throw a brilliant light upon the silver-looking scene within, which in its turn reflected out from the temple.

Upon the pillars outside ballet-girls were painted, one playing a fiddle, another salaaming a monstrous production of the imagination, while another was flying upon the back of a *fish*. At a short distance from this temple lamps were placed about four feet apart, and on either side the multitude squatted or stood, while in the centre of this assembly, and opposite the temple, were the dressed-up individuals who were to sing and perform.

One handsome young havildar was dressed up as Huri-Vishnu-Chandroodoo, another as his wife, another as his daughter, and a fourth as pantaloon. The latter important personage created much merriment; his face was foolishly besmeared; he wore an artificial white beard à la Socrate, and a paper fool's-cap, an old red jacket, and black trowsers; he carried in one hand a slender reed, in the other a goatskin full of cotton, with which he frequently belaboured the youth who intruded within the magic circle.

Huri-Vishnu was a most important personage, brilliantly arrayed in gold and silver tinselled-work about the head, shoulders, and waist; from his helmet to his epaulettes, which were prodigious, fell a most graceful garland of flowers on either side, and from these others streamed down to about his ankles. Around his neck hung a chain and other wreaths, which mingled with the folds of his dress in a very picturesque manner. In one hand he held an arrow, in the other a bow, and looked to me very like pictures of ancient Egyptian kings. His wife—Madame Huri-Vishnu, if you please— was an equally well got-up recruit, as was also the daughter, of smaller size. Chaplets and crowns, necklaces and furbelows, made their personations excellent, very far removed from the masculine gender.

All being ready—the clown having cleared the stage—the multitude having taken to their haunches —the play commenced. A prompter, painfully visible, read aloud from a book songs of war, peace, and love, and the transformed went through them admirably. The women—*i. e.*, the men—were very graceful, and, to complete their disguise, their *nose-rings* and *toe-rings* were not the least conspicuous parts of their dress. They sang and danced, and sang while the crowd laughed and smoked their hubble-bubbles, and murmuringly praised them.

This continued till dawn. Many were the piles that blazed that night in honour of Vishnu; loud, and long, and awful was the tom-toming, and distressingly shrill the strains of the pipe of India's Pan.

I may as well mention in this place a little interesting incident, which I noticed in one of my evening rides, characteristic of the religious state of

SACRIFICES.

thousands of Hindus. One evening on my return home, quietly indulging in the cool refreshing air, and the soft beauties of the setting sun, I saw in the distance the faint flickering of a fire. The moon was rising bright and beautiful, and, as I felt nowise inclined to hurry, I turned my horse's head towards the fire. When I arrived at the spot the following scene presented itself. Five men, three women, and four children were busily engaged in the preparation of a burnt-sacrifice to God. They had chosen a flat piece of the plain for their work, and here they had brought together their various offerings.

On a small area of ground—about five feet square—they had scraped up the soil about three inches high so as to form a small square inclosure, which was again divided in like manner by two other little ridges of earth. Into each of these divisions were placed, facing the moon, bits of cocoa-nut shells in which a little cotton-wick was burning oil. Between these little lamps were pieces of cocoa-nut and boiled rice upon leaves, upon other little leaves pieces of sugar, and here and there plantains and tiny wreaths of varied coloured flowers. Behind this primitive fane an old man and a little boy held up a sheet. On the other side of the sheet were three other members of this sacrificial family, preparing various things for the consummation. By-and-bye they bound a goat, sprinkled it with water, and prepared to slay it. The priest then took off his turban, and with a rusty bill-shaped knife, by one blow, severed the goat's head from the body. The bleeding head was taken by the woman, and placed upon the ground opposite the moon. She then sprinkled it with water, and while the eyelids opened and closed involuntarily, she smiled, muttered some few more words, sprinkled it again with water, and closed the eyelids with her fingers.

The body of the goat was left where it fell bleeding.

A male fowl was then brought and sprinkled by the woman. This the priest put between his legs, and quietly cut off the head. He flung the body away, and gave the head to the woman, who placed it beside the head of the goat with care, and honoured it with no less sprinkling, muttering, and smiles.

The boys then proceeded to blow up the fire with their mouths, and the people to prepare to eat. At this stage they offered me some cocoa-nut milk, rice, and sugar. I ate and drank a little with them; this seemed to please them amazingly. I was now told that they were sacrificing to Vishnu in heaven for the benefits vouchsafed to them in restoring a sick brother to health.

The fires burnt brilliantly, and while the flesh was being prepared for consumption, they sang some little hymn, and said a few prayers, all the while bowing and salaaming towards the moon.

The smell of the cooking was very savoury, the flesh from the pot might have been good, but I now left them to their rice, flesh, and their God, with a salaam, and rode home. As I rode away I could not help thinking of the Jews, their flesh-pots, their sacrifices, and their progress from polytheism to the one grand magnificent idea of the Deity.

No one can form an idea of the physical beauty and grandeur of Indian scenery whose experience is limited to the arid districts of its coasts. But we cannot amplify upon such a topic. Once removed from the scorching, dazzling, arid climate of the sea-boards, and over the ranges of the mountains which divide Central from Southern India, a totally different climate is entered, and every feature of the country is altered. Here, indeed, is a land suited to European colonization and enterprise, at least a thousandfold better than the torrid, swampy, pestiferous deltas they appear to have tried and failed in. Every kind of vegetable required by man and beast flourishes; the plains are like extensive parks; the jungles, very often, like mighty forests; the rivers, to which our rivers of England are but rills, are beautiful and burdened with wealth, with gems and precious metals, choice marbles and other stones; the hills are clothed with stately trees, sweet smelling shrubs, and plants rich in perfume and medicinal virtues; the cultivated plains abound in the sugar-cane, the opium poppy, wheat, maize, and multitudes of other valuable cereals used by man and beast; there are long groves of tamarind trees, mango trees, peepul trees, gigantic banyan trees, and wood-apple trees, all yielding grateful shade to the weary traveller in the mid-day hours, and some delicious fruits for his daily repast; jungle shrubs and cultivated plants give up their brilliant permanent dyes for the cotton which is so soon to be woven from their neighbouring plants; iron-ore of the most superior quality abounds in many districts, but is only worked by the natives in a rude way. Carbonate of soda and common salt are obtained and sold for distant states. I can never forget the *common salt* we, for the time being, made use of while the battle of Koonch was being fought. It was as white as snow, and in crystalline masses, as large as the finest crystals of the iodide of potassium! This salt was being transported from one state to another when we fell in with it opposite Koonch.

With such rivers and tanks, and hills and verdure, such richness of nature poured out so lavishly for the scanty care the swarthy sons of India bestow upon her, one is perpetually constrained to exclaim, " What a lovely country !" and, " What would it not produce were Englishmen blessed with such a charge !" Then there are the never-ceasing wonders of God's heavens to delight and astonish one ; such warm and wondrous colouring with sunrise, a volume of glories in every beam of light ! Angry frowns, streams of blood, and cold steel-like flashings of light, herald his coming through a thousand cloudy gates to reign supreme, and to pass away in fields of golden rosy æther to other lands and colder skies. One dip below the horizon, one moment more, and then we turn to cold deep bluey starlight nights ; all that was brilliant and eastern is gone, and we are surrounded by stars like magic. This is the condition of this part of India for upwards of seven months, cool, enjoyable, invigorating, and healthy ; then gradually comes on the heat day by day, and for *four* months it pours down with intense and truly terrible powers, the rivulets dry, the rivers become but rivulets, wells dry up by the road sides, and the trees turn from green to yellow, and brown, and white, and ultimately lose all their leaves, as they do in the keenest winds of our northern blasts and snows. No contrast can possibly be more astonishing. A month or two back you were eating ices in your tent and dressed in warm woollen clothing, or sitting over a good cheerful fire at night in your room, now you are panting for very breath, crying for water to quench a burning thirst, enveloping your head in wet towels, hunting for the least morsel of shade to creep into or cover the throbbing head, ill at ease with everything and with yourself, feverish, nervous, irritable, exhausted and refreshed by turns, dreaming of the day when the end of your trials will arrive, longing for cold, for a plunge into an ice-bath; in a word, living with vitality strung up to its highest pitch, breathing an air hotter than the current of the blood, thermometer 130°, twenty hours out of the twenty-four, and constantly looking upon a glaring blinding light, little less than that produced by phosphorus burnt in oxygen gas!

In such a climate, then, constantly enduring all the evils of the heat, our troops were daily engaged. It cannot be wondered at that scores fell ill from sheer exhaustion, others from nervous excitement, others from blood disorders and affections of the abdominal organs, others from *heat, asphyxia, coup-de-soleil*, and that some positively lost their reason! On retrospection it seems little less than positive miracle that any European should have gone through it without for ever shattering the goodly frame-work which holds his indomitable spirit. Such, however, is his constitution that there appears no cold too great, no heat too intense for the peculiarly elastic elements of his race.

The rebels did all they could to destroy us, for a hot weather campaign to *them* is an awful thing. The way in which our troops endured their constant harassing in the heat must have amazed the sun-baked Hindu no little.

It is quite evident that the resources of this country, instead of being developed and improved, have been permitted to lie as they did a thousand years ago, and decay; that such of the native arts and manufactures as used to raise for India a name and wonder all over the western world are nearly extinguished in the present day; once great and renowned cities are mere heaps of ruins—dens for hyenas and jackals! its colleges are no more—the wise men of the East live only in fable and histories of the past; its temples and wondrous caves of Adjuntah, Ellora, and other places are crumbling fast to dust, and by-and-bye there will scarcely be a trace of them left; its tanks and caravanserais are going or gone to rapid ruin; its canals for irrigation are filled up and forgotten; whole districts have been deserted by their inhabitants, and the jungle and wild beasts have succeeded them, and deadly malaria closed them. Where native princes once dwelt, and native opulence and prosperity reigned around them for miles, there are ruined palaces, beautiful in their decay—deserted or fast shrinking towns, comparative poverty, roads overgrown with scrub and jungle, and very often total desolation and ruin, in the midst of natural wealth,—a plague spot on the cheek of beauty; ruin, ruin, poverty, and natural wealth everywhere, as though a leper had touched the land, and it were hastening to decay. A question constantly asked of oneself is—"Whence arises all this?" and the conclusion one arrives at is, that *something sinfully wrong must have caused such a terrible result, and that something equally bad continues to perpetuate so great a calamity!* Whether this ruin has been the natural result of a vicious feudalism, or misgovernment on our parts of territories and their cities, absorbed by British power, is for others to decide.

No one, who has eyes and ears to use, can doubt for a moment that we have almost totally neglected the resources of such a mighty country, while we have introduced the trash of our manufacturing towns into every cranny of the land.

It appears as though we had endeavoured to destroy every inherent useful production of an eastern nation for the introduction of western merchandise. And what *must* be the end of such short-sightedness if such an erroneous line of policy be pursued?

It matters little to us now how this people were ruled by their own princes; we have taken upon ourselves the onerous charge, and it is our duty not only to push forward British goods among them, but also to save from destruction their ancient arts and sciences, and to develope them to the fullest extent, and to resuscitate their deadened energies to what they must have been under the enlightened rule of a prince like Aurungzebe.

When one looks upon their ruined temples and works of statuary—some of which will not blush by comparison with those of Greece—one almost mourns to see what degenerative time will work. Everything Grecian is, of course, classic,—their temples, their statuary, their poetic myths, and obscene tales of the loves of gods, goddesses, and men; their bared legs and arms and breasts; their seamless robe; their very gods' names have become mere household words with us,—we swear by them. Well, we are near neighbours, and so, perhaps, it is as well to tutor the minds of our youth with a little Homeric heathenism as well as Christianity. Now, these semi-nude, belligerent, shameless philosophers, poets, dancers, statesmen, and peasantry, appear to me to have had almost everything in common with the Hindu of to-day; the latter has a little more sun, but he has the seamless robe; he girds his loins for his journey, he wears his jewelled sandal, he bares his leg; he treats his better-half the same,—she is sprinkled with jewels, bares her body to a fabulous extent, is his household slave, dances to the pipe and tabour, and chinks the castanet, while she evolutes in all the grace of Grecian "graces," to the songs of war, and love, and sorrow about defunct deities, heroes, faëries, angels, and princes! Yet this is not classic—it is *barbarous,* because, perhaps, it *exists.*

We have done a good deal in India; we have made a few good bridges over a few rivers; we have built travellers' bungalows for officers of the army along our trunk roads; we have built large standing camps very frequently in most uninhabitable localities, and have deserted them, when the church-yards were filled, or the whim of a governor thought fit; we have splendid Government offices, and a few good modern forts in positions in which Europeans drop down, sometimes lifeless—struck by the sun, while on guard duty under ample shade; we have large permanent hospitals with none of the modern improvements of English hospitals; we have dammed mighty rivers, irrigated thousands of square acres, filled the natives' purses, spent tens of thousands of rupees in trying to navigate rivers in whose bosoms millions of tons of sand constantly collect, as constantly to form impassable barriers; we have, indeed, girded the land with iron-wire for our telegraphs—which all Europeans appreciate, and natives consider the *devil;* we have extended our territory east, west, north, and south—are truly very mighty—and are very poor instead of being rich; we have well saturated the thirsty soil with British blood in many glorious battles, and doubtless shall do so again; we have tried to do good through many scorching years of trial—we have not been appreciated—our western habits and customs *will* not accord with those of the Hindu—and we have had wholesale mutiny and butchery to crown our efforts.

Other notes, which I feel would only run out my narrative to a tedious length, I must omit, and suffice myself by concluding with a description of a dâk, as a mode of travelling totally different to that by which one dashes from the north-west provinces along that splendid Grand Trunk Road to the City of Palaces.

Most people travel to and from the north-west provinces by what is. called "horse dâk." This kind of dâking is all very well, but as every part of India is not blessed with a Grand Trunk Road, and as dâk-gharies are not to be had for love or money elsewhere, it may not be uninteresting to recount in what manner an officer is enabled to prosecute his journeys.

Save the opportunities he may have of going by sea from port to port, he has generally to travel hundreds of miles at a stretch by a palki-dâk.

When one is comfortably located in a station, and expects to remain some time, perhaps, he suddenly sees his name in the Gazette, ordering him to march forthwith to join a corps proceeding on foreign service. This is very annoying, but he must go, so he packs up his kit, sells off what would be a trouble to him on his march, always at a loss; procures bullock carts for his necessaries at an awfully high rate of charge, and prepares to march, a solitary traveller on horseback, or to dâk it. If he dâks it by palki, he has to inform the magistrate of the station of his intention, who writes off to the authorities of the various stages to have bearers posted in readiness when he shall have arrived at each bungalow *en route*. The day arrives for his departure; he packs his tea-kettle, pots, &c. upon his palki, stows away heaps of necessaries inside, and arranges his bed and pillows; he then packs his clothes in one "cavady" box, his boiled chicken and tongue, sardines, bread and beer in another, and in the intensest misery feels himself ready to start to some unknown region, and ultimately for foreign service. His "cavady" boxes are strung from a bamboo, and hoisted upon the shoulder of a coolie; his bearers are ready, and taking his weight to an ounce as they swarm round him ready to tear him away, and at last, all being in readiness, he stoops and backs steadily through the little doorway of his palki, descends gingerly a few inches, draws in his head and shoulders, and then with a sigh flings in his legs. There's a groan outside, and he feels himself hoisted upon the shoulders of six men. A shout! and off they go at a quick jog-trot, six other men running by his side, and a seventh with a flambeau and leathern oil-bottle.

Well, he is off, and gives himself up to the gentle care of fourteen natives, who speak a strange tongue, and look at him as a living El-Dorado.

By-and-bye the shades of night fall, the palki stops, he looks out, and finds his bearers chattering about oil. He purchases oil, his torch is lighted, and off they go again. By-and-bye it is nine o'clock, he looks again out of his palki, this time he finds himself well off the high road meandering in a swamp. First the bearers are up to their knees in mud, then in water, now splashing through a rice-field, then galloping along a bit of hard earth for fifty yards; slow again, the fellows are now *finding* a way. All is darkness around save the glare of the torch immediately preceding. This is a time for calm reflection! A sudden flash from the darkness above reveals his utter loneliness. Rumble, rumble from the dark clouds; onward he goes, a pitiable wanderer. Suddenly his first stage is over, he pays his bearers, gives them an *inam* (present), buys fresh oil, fees the Government servant (*this is always done*), and starts afresh. He is luckier this time, the road is good, the sky clear and bright with planetary beauty; ten thousand shrill, chirruping crickets, bull-frogs croaking like croupy dogs, "Serve you right, serve you right," and fire-flies flitting past him, perhaps, make amends for his loneliness. Morning comes apace, and oh! what a sunrise! No wonder that the watchful shepherd of the East bows in worship to the radiant god of light. Earth lifts up her face to his smile, and luxuriates in the dewy softness of the hour; woods echo with the wild dove's song, and an universal chorus of joyful sounds welcome the coming day.

And again the palki stops, this time at one of the Indian wayside hotels—the "travellers' bungalow." One might fancy a travellers' bungalow a nice comfortable kind of country inn, wherein all the necessaries of life may be procured, but it is nothing of the kind. Why do we pack up chicken and tongue, sardines, and the tea-kettle? No, here he is in a barn, and the printed rules relating to this said barn hang upon the wall, showing who may lodge therein, and who may not.

He carries his own larder, and in the said bungalow *may* get a table whereon to spread his viands.

When he has refreshed his external man with a bath, and his internal economy with what he hath, he makes friends with Morpheus, and refreshes his soul till the meridian heat is past; then he repacks his provender and sallies forth for another midnight race across country. Having run two days, he, perhaps, nears a large village in the evening just as it is beginning to rain. He has the prospect of a delicious run before him. The oil-man supplies the oil, he buys a little milk, and waits a short time to stretch his legs, and breathe in the perpendicular position.

It rains very hard, a distant rumble is heard, the bearers look at the sky, and the peon tells him he had better be off. This looks ominous, but he buckles to, lights a cheroot, and secretes himself in his palki. It grows dark, the torch-bearer makes a blaze, the bearers raise him upon their shoulders, and he is off into the jungles. Soon he finds himself in the midst of dense forest-land dark as Erebus; the clouds open and vicious forks of lightning dance above and around him, as though they only waited for an opportunity to pierce him with a vivid prong, and carry his soul into ghost-land; a loud wind rushes past him, it smells of earth, and puts out the torch, and down comes the heavy merciless rain! The bearers stop and place him under a tree, and crouch, and fold themselves up into almost nothing.

Howl, rush, whine goes the wind, and the storm flies past, and onward he goes again. Suddenly they slacken their pace; he asks wherefore, and is told a little river must be crossed. The bearers take off their clothes, and in they bear him; but it runs very fast and deepens, nay, he thinks it must run through his palki, and wash him out, but at this instant he feels himself raised in society, looks out, and finds himself above the heads of the bearers, who are now under him and up to their breasts in water. Quietly, steady, the river is forded, and again he sinks to the pole, and is off at a quick trot. At length he takes a nap; fifteen sweet minutes of still forgetfulness have scarcely fled, when he finds a couple of black faces peering down upon him, and these tell him that there is another *very big river to cross!* Very well, it must be crossed; "Can't do it, sahib," is the reply. He gets out of his palki to reconnoitre, but this time finds it really no joke. Pitch dark all around, and a mighty rapid before him, with its soft muddy banks quietly dropping in and quickly widening the stream. To see to the opposite side is impossible. Here he is, in the midst of Indian luxury! some two hundred miles from his destination, and he knows not how nigh unto death.

Enveloped in darkness, on the bank of a rapid river, in the hands of fourteen coolies, at the witching hour of night! Half in and half out of his palki, quietly consoling himself with the knowledge that things might have been worse, while his bearers are eyeing him like cannibals and yelling like fiends, he hears a small voice from the opposite bank, and in time his torch-light reveals three fellows up to their chins in the midst of the rapid, pushing a bamboo raft across. Such a frail looking thing! However, he supposes all to be right, withdraws into his box, is then placed upon the raft, and trusts in Providence.

The bearers all get into the water, some to push, some to pull, some to hold up the raft, and away he goes upon the stream, swelling, rushing, bubbling, and whirling around and beneath him, expecting every instant to see the coolies carried away, and his palki, raft and all, go swinging down the stream to destruction.

However, they know their work, and have a keen sense of the value of rupees, which he does not forget to scatter when across. Once again on terra firma, up he goes, and the bearers commence their songs as they rush through the long avenues of banyan trees to another bungalow. These songs are very funny. The leader starts with an inarticulate " hum," another says "ah!" a third " he," a fourth "ho," and these quicker and quicker, till at length he hears something like an aspirated "up and down," by another "mind your eye;" then " de-de," in louder tenor, " heigha," " I'm going to 'Merica ;" then " oh ! Tommy," " oh ! my God," " heigha," and a "*hee*" like a screech-owl. Then occasionally he fancies they are saying they've got a " hairy-baboo " inside, and " cocoa-nut—ha !" and " throw him out, there ;" and these extraordinary exclamations continue to pour upon his ear, echoing through and through the dense foliage all the time till, with a rush and a " ha-ha," they deposit him at each bungalow. In his journey, perhaps he may meet with an engineer in the public works department, who has been two years in the jungle, and months without having seen an European face, who has had jungle fever thrice or four times, sundry strokes of the sun, and frequent attacks of dysentery. But his dâk is not yet over. Another set of bearers run him from point to point across a pathless swamp, now bearing him shoulder high through deep sedgy water, now ploughing their way through mud up to their knees, and having for their only guide the stars, till at last cloud on cloud collects, and they are again lost in mire at 1 A.M. Then they wander, and stop, and howl, and wander, and the bull frogs croak till the ear is deafened, and the fire flies swarm in myriads. At length, rosy morn again points out the path, and they are off; and, oh! what sights of wild fowl! Tens of thousands of all kinds—pelican, stork, geese, duck, quail, teal, and snipe in clouds. By-and-bye he leaves the swamps, gains the road again, and perhaps finishes his run about mid-day, feverish, excited, pale, wretched, and worn-out, and by-and-bye to start on the longer journey of field service.

THE END.

www.ingramcontent.com/pod-product-compliance
Lightning Source LLC
Chambersburg PA
CBHW031131160426
43193CB00008B/104